The King and You

BY *Bob Mumford*

Living Happily Ever After
The Purpose of Temptation
The King and You

THE KING AND YOU

Bob Mumford

FLEMING H. REVELL COMPANY

Old Tappan, New Jersey

Library of Congress Cataloging in Publication Data

Mumford, Bob.
    The King and you.

    1. Kingdom of God. 2. Christian life—1960–
I. Title.
BT94.M8   248'.4   74-10065
ISBN 0-8007-0672-2

CONTENTS

PREFACE

As author, I wish to acknowledge my allegiance to the King. Seeing His right to rulership in my life has led to a continuing relationship with Him, out of which has emerged the contents of this book. My desire to present the King to you through these pages is best expressed in some of the closing verses of the Book of Acts.

The Apostle Paul is a prisoner of the Roman government and it is recorded that he:

> . . . expounded and testified the kingdom of God, persuading them concerning Jesus, both out of the law of Moses, and out of the prophets . . . .
>
> v. 23

The teaching of Paul received two divergent responses. These will be repeated in the reading of *The King and You.*

> . . . and some believed the things which were spoken, and some believed not.
>
> v. 24

This did not hinder Paul's efforts and The Acts of the Apostles closes with this triumphant statement:

> Paul . . . received all who came unto him, preaching the kingdom of God, and teaching those things which concern the Lord Jesus Christ, with all confidence . . . .
>
> vs. 30, 31

It is with this same confidence that I continue this same message. As always, the issue boils down to a crucial twosome: the *King and you.*

As you read, and find yourself faced with choices, I join the audience described in Romans 8:19:

> The whole creation is on tiptoe to see the wonderful sight of the sons of God coming into their own.
>
> PHILLIPS

And may I acknowledge, as well, the untiring and dedicated editorial assistance of one of the King's subjects, Janet Baum.

BOB MUMFORD

◈◈

FOREWORD

◈◈

As the title implies, this is a book about two people—the KING and you, the individual reader.

THE KING *is* Jesus Christ! His throne rights were proclaimed hundreds of years before His birth. His rights to rulership were asserted by Jesus, Himself, throughout His three years of public ministry. At His Crucifixion, the title placed over His cross read:

JESUS OF NAZARETH—KING OF THE JEWS.

While these words were placed by the authorities in derision, they declared His rightful title—**KING!** He arose triumphant from the grave three days later and stated unequivocally, "All power is given unto me in heaven and in earth" (Matthew 28:18). His Kingdom has moved relentlessly forward on that premise for twenty centuries.

You? Are you interested in knowing about the Kingdom over which Jesus Christ rules, as well as what it holds for you? If so, you will find here:

> The Constitution of the Kingdom
> Concepts of Kingdom Living
> The Fifteen Bylaws of the Kingdom
> Your Own Personal Passport to Freedom

Freedom is the most sought-after commodity in every generation. As taught by Jesus, freedom is the King's guarantee to you:

> Ye shall know the truth and the truth shall make you free.
> John 8:32

Bob Mumford, apprehended by the King while serving in the U.S. Navy, incorporates in this book Kingdom truths as he has found them valid and operative through twenty years of pastoring, counseling, teaching, as well as personal experience. *The King and You* is practical, prophetic, and profitable reading!

THE PUBLISHERS

9

PART ONE

THE KING
AND
HIS KINGDOM

1 INTRODUCING—THE KING!

Who is this King whose rulership affects the life of every man, woman, and child born upon the earth? Where is His Kingdom—that sphere of His rulership?

Who is this King whose Kingdom you cannot even see until you have acknowledged His throne rights—and whose Kingdom you cannot enter until you express a desire to abide by Kingdom laws?

Who is this King whose rule you can reject—whose Kingdom is only over that territory where the King is present?

This King is Jesus—the Son of God!

He is the One who was present when God said, "Let us make man in our image . . . and let them have dominion over . . . the earth" (Genesis 1:26).

He is the One whose birth upon this earth, was proclaimed with the words, "For unto you is born this day . . . Christ the Lord" (Luke 2:11). Angel-heralded and star-directed men worshiped at His crib.

He is the One who said, "I will build my church; and the gates of hell shall not prevail against it [—My Kingdom!]" (Matthew 16:18).

He is the One of whom it is written, ". . . the kingdoms of this world are become the kingdoms of our Lord, and of his Christ; and he shall reign for ever and ever" (Revelation 11:15).

He is the One who said to twelve men, "Come, follow me." After some three years of intensive training, this nucleus of Kingdom citizens had enlarged to one hundred and twenty persons. These were commissioned to take news of this Kingdom to the entire world of their day—with the promise that their King would always be with them.

These Kingdom citizens, along with the men and women who

willingly took out citizenship papers in the newly established King-dom after hearing the Good News, are those who proclaimed to their generation, "Christ is Lord! Jesus is King!" These words caused many of them to feel the hot breath of lions upon their faces—lions unleashed to tear them asunder. They are among those who saw the blaze of consuming flames—flames ignited to make of them human torches. In time, these Kingdom citizens silenced the cry, "Caesar is King!" by maintaining the peace of their King within and the witness of His Lordship on their lips.

Many years later, this same King inspired a master musician to com-pose words and music proclaiming Him "King of Kings and Lord of Lords." Handel's *Messiah* so stirred one earthly monarch, King George II of England, that he stood to his feet as he listened to this proclamation of Jesus' Kingship.

Today men still willingly lay their all at Jesus' feet. They still join in singing of His Kingship and Kingdom. They continue to tell His story—still "forsake all and follow Him." (*See* Matthew 19:27.) They look forward to His return. "The King Is Coming" is sung in gatherings around our known world; the Good News of His Coming is printed in almost every known language. Men still face death for His sake—death to self, for that is a prerequisite for true Kingdom living.

This, then, is the King!

Now, what about you? Do you know Him? Do you acknowledge Him Lord of your life? How familiar are you with His Kingdom opera-tion? Are you acquainted with the Constitution and Bylaws by which He rules?

These are eternal and life-changing questions we are asking.

2 INTRODUCING THE KINGDOM

Why do we attach such importance to acknowledging King Jesus? Because God, the Father does. Listen:

John 3:16 For God so loved the world, that he gave his only begotten Son, that whosoever believeth in him should not perish, but have everlasting life.

Acts 2:36 Therefore . . . know assuredly, that God hath made that same Jesus . . . both Lord and Christ.

How can we so confidently declare God's Kingdom and the King? Because of the rights of creatorship:

Genesis 1:1 In the beginning God created the heaven and the earth.

Genesis 1:27, 28 So God created man in his own image . . . and God said unto them, Be fruitful, and multiply, and replenish the earth, and subdue it . . . .

The Kingdom of God's creating was before time, and will remain after it—time as we mortals measure it. *But for you, the Kingdom of God is here and now! How you evaluate its claims and accept its teachings determines your here and hereafter.*

In introducing the Kingdom, let us capsule some basics:

God's initial intention in creating the heaven and earth was to establish a place where man—His crowning creation—could live and move and have his being. Man, created in God's image, *had the potential of holiness. He was endowed with ability to have authority* over all other creation. God desired fellowship with man; and He desired that (through this fellowship) His love might flow to all the creation placed under man's authority.

What happened to that divine intention? Most of us are familiar with the disobedience of Adam as he took of the fruit of the tree of the knowledge of good and evil—thus breaking fellowship with his Maker. By exerting his will, a gift from God (for fellowship can only be maintained on a voluntary basis), Adam found himself in an ego box of his own making. Disobedience had made him a little god to whose rule he was now bound.

The result? God continued to have fellowship with those men who chose to acknowledge His right to rulership in their lives and to obey His commands. Enoch—Noah—Abraham—Isaac—Jacob—Joseph —Moses—Joshua—there were always some who realized the holiness of their God. This brought a resulting wholeness in their own lives. These could be entrusted with the authority God desired man to exercise. He could fellowship with them—permit His love to flow through them, nourishing and leading the men of their day. But the majority of men? This is a record of their condition: "In those days there was no king in Israel: every man did that which was right in his own eyes" (Judges 21:25).

Yes, God's rulership can be rejected by men. Hear God's reply as He talks with the Prophet Samuel after the Israelites came to the prophet requesting an earthly king such as their neighbors had: "And the Lord said unto Samuel, Hearken unto the voice of the people . . . for they have not rejected thee, but they have rejected me, that I should not reign over them" (1 Samuel 8:8).

Most of the kings of this nation of Israel, which had been founded by God to carry forward His ever-present desire to have a people for Himself, chose (as had Adam) to follow their own leadership rather than that of their God. One notable exception was King David, of whom it was said that he was a man after God's own heart. This was true because David, through all his failure and struggle, permitted God to establish His rule in his heart.

From the house of David, God, some centuries later, invaded time and space once more. Jesus of Nazareth was born in Bethlehem of Judea. From this beachhead, God continued to present His love and concern for man.

During His public ministry, Jesus told all who would listen that

His Father was still in the business of maintaining in His creation that *holiness and authority* which He had intended from the very beginning. However, He made it clear that this high privilege was only available to those who acknowledged God's Son as Saviour and Lord of their lives. Hear His words to Nicodemus, a ruler of the Jews: ". . . Except a man be born again, he cannot see the kingdom of God" (John 3:3).

Jesus taught very plainly and carefully the meaning of the Kingdom of God and how its citizenship could be obtained and maintained. He pulled no punches—He accommodated His message to no censorship, except that of His Father. Men found many of His principles difficult to accept, preferring their own interpretations or the interpretations of tradition. This condition still prevails today.

It is the purpose of this book to bring to *you,* the reader, the claims of the King and His Kingdom. We will follow the teachings of Jesus as recorded in Matthew, chapters 5, 6, and 7—that great portion of Scripture referred to as "The Sermon on the Mount."

And there followed him great multitudes of people. . . . And seeing the multitudes, he went up into a mountain; and when he was set, his disciples came unto him: And he opened his mouth, and taught them. . . .

Matthew 4:25, 5:1, 2

Jesus dealt with everyday issues as He presented eternal truths. Isn't that what we all want? You will find yourself walking through every chapter along with the disciples, for men are made of the same stuff today as they were in A.D. 30.

Each listener on that mountainside was presented with choices. Each reader of this book will likewise have placed before him the responsibility for decisions. You can say, "Conquer me, King Jesus —establish Your rule in my heart!"

The King and you—it's strictly between the two of you.

◆◆

3   THE CONSTITUTION OF THE KINGDOM

◆◆

Most of us manage to become familiar with the constitution of any earthly corporation of which we are a part. It *is* important to know the ways in which a business is organized, as well as acquainting ourselves with its system of laws and principles of operation.

As a citizen of the United States of America, I can easily quote the Preamble of our nation's constitution:

> *We, the People of the United States, in order to form a more perfect union, establish justice, insure domestic tranquility, provide for the common defence, promote the general welfare, and secure the blessings of liberty to ourselves and our posterity, do ordain and establish this Constitution for the United States of America.*

Do you think God would be any less specific in affording to citizens of His Kingdom information on how His business is organized, its system of laws and how they operate? Of course not.

All the information an individual can possibly need regarding the Kingdom of God has been gathered and preserved for us. This legacy is the Bible.

Some questions may immediately come to your mind: What is the Kingdom? Where is it? When is it, and why? From the Bible, God's Word, we find the answers.

WHAT?   *The Kingdom of God is a condition—the rule of the King in the lives of His willing subjects.*

Luke 12:32   So don't be afraid, little flock. For it gives your Father great happiness to give you the Kingdom (LB).

Colossians 1:13   For he has rescued us out of the darkness and gloom of Satan's kingdom and brought us into the kingdom of his dear Son (LB).

18

WHERE?   *The Kingdom is within the individual believer's heart. This is where God wants to reign—even as He does in heaven.*

Matthew 6:10   We ask that your kingdom will come now. May your will be done here on earth, just as it is in heaven (LB).

2 Corinthians 3:17   The Lord is the Spirit who gives them life, and where he is there is freedom [from trying to be saved by keeping the laws of God] (LB).

WHEN?   *The rule of the King is constant and continual. It is a lifetime itinerary upon which we are launched when we accept His rulership while the King changes our character.*

2 Corinthians 3:18   But we Christians have no veil over our faces; we can be mirrors that brightly reflect the glory of the Lord. And as the Spirit of the Lord works within us, we become more and more like him (LB).

WHY?   *To free us to become participating citizens of the Kingdom and ambassadors for the Kingdom. It is the desire of the King that we become acquainted with every aspect of His business—that we may fellowship with Him, and then carry the Good News into foreign territory—the world!*

Matthew 28:18–20   He told his disciples, "I have been given all authority in heaven and earth. Therefore go and make disciples in all the nations, baptizing them into the name of the Father and of the Son and of the Holy Spirit, and then teach these new disciples to obey all the commands I have given you; and be sure of this— that I am with you always, even to the end of the world" (LB).

Now for the Preamble of the Kingdom Constitution:

Romans 14:17   For the kingdom of God is not meat and drink; but righteousness, and peace, and joy in the Holy Ghost.

The three functional outworkings of the Kingdom are the three most scarce commodities on the marketplace of daily living. Why is this so? Endless numbers of words, untold wealth, myriads of councils of men have been employed in search of apprehending these three foundations for man's welfare: right living—peace—happiness. No lasting answers have emerged from all of man's efforts.

However, *in the Body of the Constitution of the Kingdom of God we have the proclamation of the Way to righteousness, peace, and joy.*

ARTICLE I   "O Israel, listen: Jehovah is our God, Jehovah alone. You must love him with *all* your heart, soul, and might. And you must think constantly about these commandments I am giving you today" (Deuteronomy 6:4–6 LB).

ARTICLE II   "And now, Israel, what does the Lord your God require of you except to listen carefully to all he says to you, and to obey for your own good the commandments I am giving you today, and to love him, and to worship him with all your hearts and souls?" (Deuteronomy 10:12, 13 LB).

ARTICLE III   Jesus replied, " 'Love the Lord your God with all your heart, soul, and mind.' This is the first and greatest commandment. The second most important is similar: 'Love your neighbor as much as you love yourself.' All the other commandments and all the demands of the prophets stem from these two laws and are fulfilled if you obey them. Keep only these and you will find that you are obeying all the others" (Matthew 22:37–40 LB).

These statements, which form the *Body of the Constitution* are basic, irrevocable, and binding! Can righteousness, peace, and joy emerge from such a straight and narrow concept? Yes, they *can* and *do*.

As we investigate the *Concepts of the Kingdom of God,* we shall see for ourselves just how these principles produce the results guaranteed in the Preamble of the Kingdom Constitution. Through limiting ourselves to the prescribed lines laid down by God, we come into true freedom which alone affords righteousness, peace, and joy.

4 KINGDOM CONCEPTS

As a foundation for understanding the concepts of the Kingdom, we use a very familiar teaching of Jesus in order to make some important distinctions:

> Then said Jesus to those Jews which believed on him, If ye continue in my word, then are ye my disciples indeed; And ye shall know the truth and the truth shall make you free.
>
> John 8:31, 32

Notice that Jesus was talking to those who believed. He was explaining that if they continued as His disciples, they would reach the objective He had in mind for them—freedom! The way by which they would arrive at this given objective was through knowing the truth. We shall discern that *Kingdom Concepts* are Jesus' idea of "the truth."

Nicodemus, a ruler of the Jews, came to Jesus and asked about believing. John 3:1–21 gives a very detailed account of what is involved in becoming a believer. We might liken the conversation between the two to an interview between a prospective investor and the corporation president. Jesus was present when the Kingdom Charter was drawn up. He signed the document with His life's blood. He is Joint Heir of the controlling stock. By believing in Him, one becomes a stockholder in the Kingdom—the greatest business ever launched.

When we accept His offer of eternal life, we enter into a new relationship which affects every area of our lives—both here and hereafter. We are "born again" into the Kingdom—even as we were born into our earthly existence. We receive a new nature—just as we received a nature at the time of our physical birth. We must take into account that as we were born a mere infant with years of learning and growing out ahead of us, there is *more* to the spiritual life than being "born." *Here is where the "continuing" comes in.*

The word Jesus used when He said, "If ye continue," is the same word He used in John 15:4 and 7: "abide in me" and "my words abide in you." Do you see that the new birth provides a once-for-all transaction, imparting to us a new nature—*but there is a continuing process* necessary in order for us to arrive at the goal of spiritual freedom? Just as continuing is vital after physical birth, so it is after spiritual birth. Many believers are still floundering in the state of infancy when ample provision is made for maturity and usefulness in the Kingdom of God.

Let us draw another parallel between the physical and spiritual. There is much struggle and stress for the infant as he learns how to adjust to his new environment. This is true for the new Christian. Learning how to walk, talk, and conduct ourselves is part of the journey in both the physical and spiritual aspects of life.

There is an element of reasoning involved in Jesus' statement that as *continuers* we would come to "know the truth." Each of us must examine for himself the truths of the Word of God and, with the help of the Holy Spirit, make certain personal choices. It is through grasping the truths laid out before us in His Word, and by choosing to make them a part of our daily living, *that we come into freedom.*

What is *your* concept of freedom as incorporated into the Kingdom of God? What is *His* concept of this freedom? Do they agree, or are you operating under vague, or even faulty, conceptions of this valuable commodity Jesus offered His followers?

FREEDOM OR BONDAGE

We pick up the conversation between Jesus and the Jewish believers as recorded in John 8:33–36. He had told them that if they continued as His disciples, they would know the truth and the truth would make them free. Are you surprised at their reply?

They answered him, We be Abraham's seed, and were never in bondage to any man: how sayest thou, Ye shall be made free?

Note that even in their proud assertion as to their freedom they were open to the Teacher's explanation of being free. Are we? Here is Jesus' response:

Verily, verily, I say unto you, whosoever committeth sin is the servant of sin . . . If the Son, therefore, shall make you free, ye shall be free indeed.

One of the most difficult of all spiritual problems is to help people who do not *know* that they need help. This is what I may term *unconscious bondage*. Weird and wonderful aberrations have continued for so long that we consider them normal, or at least part of our personality makeup. For instance, the fear of man is a bondage which the Scriptures isolate and define very clearly. Proverbs 29:25 says, "Fear of man is a dangerous trap . . ." (LB). We call it being bashful, timid, or even "diplomatic." Hence the term *unconscious bondage*. Jesus is presenting to His listeners and to you the way to true freedom—knowing the truth about the Son and the Kingdom which He came to establish. He says that if they *continue* on with Him, He will lead them out into a place called freedom. And He will do it by manifesting to them every area in their lives where they *are* in bondage.

Are you following the reasoning of Jesus? Whosoever commits sin is the servant of sin—and being a servant is being in bondage to a master. Is sin a hard taskmaster? Can a Christian be in bondage to anger? pride? sexual irregularities? even religion? *Yes,* says the King, to these questions. The Jews may have been unconscious of their bondage—and you may be unconscious of yours. But Jesus desires to reveal the areas of bondage to you, offer the means for breaking bonds, and bring you into freedom.

Consistent teaching on this matter is found in Romans 6:12–17. Paul is writing to Christians and is talking about being in bondage to sin. Read it in its entirety. To help us tie together sin—bondage—obedience—freedom, we use verses 12, 16 and 17:

12   Let not sin therefore reign in your mortal body, that ye should
     obey it in the lusts thereof.

16   Know ye not, that to whom ye yield yourselves servants to obey;
     his servants ye are to whom ye obey: whether of sin unto death,
     or of obedience unto righteousness?

17   But God be thanked, that ye were servants of sin, but ye have
     obeyed from the heart that form of doctrine which was delivered
     you.

The Apostle Paul reiterates Jesus' teaching that *whosoever sins is
in bondage.* God wants to set us free! This is something that He is
after in the life of every believer. And a person cannot be set free if
he does not know he is in bondage, can he? One can think he is free
just because he has been released from some of the *externals* of former bindings, such as cigarettes, alcohol, or drugs. It is cause for rejoicing to be set free from four packs a day and two quarts a week.
Overt sin can be calculated that way. The King, however, is after the
internals, as well. And this is why many believers *choose not to continue.*

Some believers prefer to pretend they are free. They may talk as
if they were free—impressing others as to their freedom. Only *you*
and God know if you are really free. *You* know, when you go down
the street, what your eyes do when the girls go by. Only *you* know
what happens when you are on a tight schedule and hit every red
light along the way to your destination. *You* know what makes your
own personal thermostat reach "blow" level. How free are you when
a situation demands that you make a justifiable complaint? Is being
a "people-pleaser" being in bondage?

Suppose you sit down in a restaurant next to a police officer; or
during your coffee break the new secretary in the same department
where you work walks in. God says, "Witness." Something inside you
tightens up. Thoughts that you might be considered a religious fanatic
—or be invading another's privacy—or too inquisitive—are these

valid reasons for not obeying when the Lord speaks? Is it possible *you* could be in bondage in this area?

It is the Lord's obligation to show us when and where we are in bondage. He doesn't do it to condemn us, but to show us realms where we are unknowingly stunting our spiritual growth—for unconscious bondage results in this. God may show us these areas by simply giving us a job bigger than we are. Usually it doesn't take very long for us to wake up to the fact that we could use His help. *You cannot be free if you don't know you are in bondage!*

DESIRE AND ABILITY

This brings us to another concept where we need to make some basic distinctions: *desire and ability.*

When God gave us our new nature (upon accepting His Son as our Saviour), He placed within us a *desire* to please Him. Jesus said upon the same occasion we have been discussing (when He was talking to the Jewish believers about freedom), ". . . for I do always those things that please him" (John 8:29). He was referring to His Father. This is another of the objectives He has in mind for us as we *continue* with Him—that we might have the *ability* to do only those things that please the Father. This will free us from all bondage!

You see, the desire and ability to do those things that are pleasing to God are two entirely different things! When, as a young man in a sailor uniform, I knelt at the altar of a church in Atlantic City, New Jersey, there was born in me a *desire* to please God. But to fulfill that desire was something else again! What about our other strong desires that conflict with this newly born desire? Is it possible to be in bondage to "self"? What about the ideas—opinions—desires of others— especially of those whom we admire or love? We simply cannot please God when we are hedged in by the desires to please self or others.

Let's get something straight. I am a believer. I have received a new nature, which is the nature of Christ. This new nature is the source from which my new *desire* springs. But as I continue in His Word, He begins to deal with my character, which—in turn—affords the *ability* I now lack to fulfill my new desire. *Nature is given; character is developed.* There is no way that anyone can impart to another the gift of character—*no way!* Character is developed in the believer by continuing in His Word—discovering God's will and then doing those things we discover will please Him. As Christian character is developed, my *desire* to do God's will is turned to the *ability* to do God's will; and we then understand the difference.

What about God's will? In answering our opening questions about the What and Where of the Kingdom of God, we said that the *Kingdom is a condition in the heart of the believer where the will of God is done, even as it is in heaven.* Jesus taught His disciples to pray, "Thy will be done in earth, as it is in heaven" (Matthew 6:10).

We need to understand that there are two different words used in the Greek for our English word *will,* as it is used throughout Scripture. One is *boulema,* the other is *thelema. Boulema* means the eternal counsels of God which are unfolding through the ages—His purpose —His determination. It is going to be done whether you and I like it or not. God's intention will come to pass. However, *thelema,* which means God's wish or desire, most often depends upon the response of each individual for fulfillment.

Referring again to Jesus' words in Matthew 6:10, "Thy kingdom come, thy will be done in earth as it is in heaven," do you see this prayer brings the wish or desire of God into an earthly setting? Without getting theological or complicated, could you understand when I say God's will (His wish, desire) is *not* being done on earth as it is in heaven? This has nothing to do with the eternal counsels of the Almighty, but rather His intimate intervention in the affairs of our lives.

It is *not* the will (wish, desire) of God that divorce, family problems, poverty, sickness, continue in this world unchallenged. God sent His King, in the power of the Kingdom, to change and adjust the situation to conform to this desire. Examine for a moment the demonized man who could neither see nor speak. Surely this is not the wish of our God!

Jesus—King Jesus, if you will—intervenes in the situation to bring God's will and desire to pass. Taking authority over the evil spirit and ejecting him, the King gives us this glorious piece of the good news of the Kingdom: "But if I am casting out demons by the Spirit of God, then the Kingdom of God has arrived among you" (Matthew 12:28 LB).

When Jesus spoke about, "I always do those things that please my Father," He was referring to the Father's wish or desire. We know that Jesus was also fulfilling the eternal counsels of God by His very life in the flesh—His death upon the cross—and His Resurrection. But we are thinking here of the everyday conduct of Jesus during His thirty-three years on earth. Is it possible to be so closely attuned to the Father's wishes that we can detect them? Yes, it is, and this is one of the Father's desires for us.

Doesn't the thought of rejoicing the heart of God by pleasing Him through your actions excite you? It does me. Then, why don't we? Why can't we say, as Jesus said, "I always do those things that please the Father"? *The ability factor has to be taken into consideration— that's why!*

THREE HINDRANCES

Why can't I "always do those things that please the Father"? Here I am with a burning *desire* to know the will of God and do it. My new nature has brought with it this desire. My *ability* to carry this desire over into actual conduct is where I have the trouble.

I have seen my younger son illustrate the difference between *desire* and *ability* when seeking to learn to tie his own shoes. No one had more *desire* to accomplish this task than he. However many times I explained and showed him how, he still could not—*inability!*

In his case, the nerve system was not developed and the coordination necessary to have the *ability* was not present.

In our case, the hindrance between a fervent *desire* to do the will of God and the *ability* to do it resides in three distinct areas. Here they are:

    (1) Rebellion—"I won't!"

    (2) Resentment—"Why does this happen to me!"

    (3) Independence—"I'd rather do it myself, God."

Do any of these responses sound familiar to you?

First—Rebellion If you will recall, there were some references in the Constitution of the Kingdom about commandments and obedience. The rebel will rise up and show his ugly face when we are brought up against a situation where our own will is in opposition to the revealed will of God. Strange how we can twist and turn and try to misinterpret "commands" when they don't meet with our desires. Deep within us we know when we try to avoid doing God's will. And He knows it, too, and will do something about it, you can be certain!

Next—Resentment This is more subtle than rebellion. We can move in obedience and yet have such seething resentment within us that it may be even more repugnant to God than actual disobedience. "Why should God treat me like this?" we may ask. We are not only doubting God's goodness and wisdom, but actually may harden our hearts to His commands. Too often we put up a facade of obedience and *harbor* a spirit of rebellion.

Finally—Independence Here is yet another step in the wrong direction. When are we ever going to learn that we cannot do anything of ourselves or for our own glorification? We are part of a cooperative effort; we move according to prescribed rules and regulations. This attitude of independence manifests itself when we say, "Teach me twice, Lord, and I will take it from there." You don't learn to pray for the sick—cast out demons—even pray or study—*on your own.*

You learn to be dependent Your own ways may work for a while, but when the Lord finds you getting to the point where you are ex-

hibiting a method and trying to tell God how to do it—watch out!
He will precipitate a situation where your own way just won't meet
His requirements. Then it becomes a choice of rebellion—resent-
ment—or return to the source of your dependence!

*These three "character flaws" must be brought out into the open,
faced, and dealt with before God can bring us into a Kingdom relationship.* These three infect, attack, complicate, and thwart my *ability*
to carry out my *desire* to please the Father.

Looking at the way these three hindrances were handled in the life
of Jesus in relation to His Father, we see the following.

Rebellion   "The Lord God hath opened mine ear, and I was not
rebellious, neither turned away back. I gave my back to the smiters,
and my cheeks to them that plucked off the hair: I hid not my face
from shame and spitting." Isaiah (50:5, 6) was writing about Jesus.
Did this prophecy prove fact in every detail? Yes. Also, recall the
incident told in Luke 9:51, ". . . when the time was come . . .
he stedfastly set his face to go to Jerusalem . . ." in obedience.

Resentment   "The cup which my father gave me, shall I not drink
all of it?" Again—obedience. Questioning? Yes, but not with any
doubting of God's goodness or wisdom. And no question of any
other action than moving according to the known will of the
Father. (*See* John 18:11.) There was complete absence of resentment due to *what* God, the Father, was requiring of Him in the
Garden.

Independence   "I can of mine own self do nothing . . . I seek not
mine own will but the will of the Father which hath sent me." Here
in John 5:30, Jesus displays complete dependence.

How did Jesus overcome these hindrances to the doing of His Father's will? Often, we misunderstand the reason why we are required
to obey. Listen to the writer of Hebrews: "And even though Jesus was

God's Son, he had to learn from experience what it was like to obey, when obeying meant suffering" (Hebrews 5:8 LB).

How is God going to help us overcome hindrances? We need purging from these strange diseases that eat us up on the inside (spiritually) just as cancer can eat us up physically. God intends to do a work in our hearts that will enable Him to establish His Kingdom in us. He has His Ways and Means Committee. *It is possible* to enter into such a relationship with God that we can walk with Him without rebellion, resentment, or independence to hinder.

In Acts 14:22, we find this phase of Kingdom operation affecting the lives of the early church members. Paul and Barnabas are ministering in Lystra, Iconium, and Antioch. These people were born again, baptized in water, and filled with the Holy Spirit. They were leaders in the Christian community of their day. But they needed something else and Paul is preparing them for "working on."

Confirming the souls of the disciples [believers] and exhorting them to continue in the faith, and that we must through much tribulation [pressure, problems, lessons] enter into the kingdom of God.

Did you notice the words, "exhorting them to continue" and "enter into the Kingdom of God"? And, also, "through much tribulation"? Do you still want to continue?

If you continue, God is going to work on you, changing your character so that you can carry out your *desire* to do His will. When desire becomes ability to obey, the Kingdom of God becomes reality. Do you recall these words in the Constitution, ". . . listen carefully to all he says to you, and to obey for your own good the commandments I am giving you today . . ."? This is from ARTICLE II, in case you had forgotten.

At times we hesitate to throw ourselves open to the workings of God for fear He will ask us to do something we don't want to do. That is a very real possibility. But as we do it, we find it is for our good. *We also find rebellion, resentment, and independence being replaced by righteousness, peace, and joy!*

ALIGNMENT

This one rather innocent-sounding word covers a lifelong process. As a *Kingdom Concept* it is related to the others we have considered: Freedom or Bondage? Desire and Ability. Three Hindrances. Through proper alignment, we are brought into the realization of true freedom. We learn how to turn our desires into ability. We find our character conforming to the teachings of Jesus. And the hindrances along the way become stepping-stones into the Kingdom.

We are going to use a series of diagrams to help us visualize the meaning and intent of *alignment*. First, we picture the *will of God*.

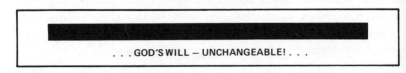

. . . GOD'S WILL — UNCHANGEABLE! . . .

God's will is straight, inflexible, and unchanging. It does not bend or vary for anyone. It is an iron bar and forms the *standard* by which all actions will be measured. There is neither variableness nor shadow of turning. It remains the same for every man, regardless of race—color—station in life—intellectual or physical abilities. God does not bow, yield, or play politics. You cannot bribe, threaten, beg off, or deceive Him. You just can't!

Next, we take a look at the will of Jesus while He was here on the earth during those years of public ministry. He stated, "I do always those things that please the Father." His will and the Father's were one and the same.

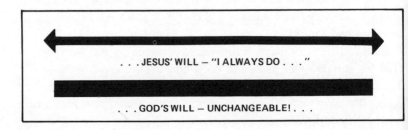

. . . JESUS' WILL — "I ALWAYS DO . . ."

. . . GOD'S WILL — UNCHANGEABLE! . . .

This ability to always do the will of the Father was a *learned accomplishment* in Jesus' life, just as it must be in our lives. We mentioned that, "and even though Jesus was God's Son, he had to learn from experience what it was like to obey, when obeying meant suffering" (Hebrews 5:8 LB).

Putting aside one's will for that of another's will can cause suffering. But Jesus' will was perfectly aligned with God's will in all instances—regardless of personal inconvenience, preference, pain, or outcome. That is the reason why our second diagram looks like two railroad tracks. Wherever His Father's will went, Jesus went. This is alignment—the created will in perfect alignment with the uncreated will of our Eternal God!

Now we add a third *will* to our diagram. This is where chaos and confusion come into the picture. It is the will of man. The man who is owner of this will is a believer. He has a *desire* to do the will of God—to make his will "line up" to God's will—*but!* What about that *but? The believer must become a continuer.* That desire must move over into ability. That new nature must mature into conduct. Here's how man's spiritual EKG looks in comparison with the railroad tracks of the wills of the Father and the Son.

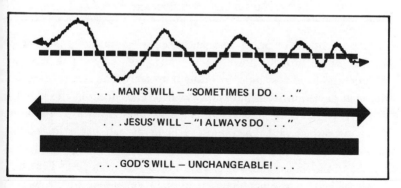

. . . MAN'S WILL — "SOMETIMES I DO . . ."

. . . JESUS' WILL — "I ALWAYS DO . . ."

. . . GOD'S WILL — UNCHANGEABLE! . . .

You may be asking, "What does all this aligning business have to do with the Kingdom of God?" We said in our *What* of the Kingdom of God that it is a condition where God's will is done on earth as it is in heaven. That EKG of man's will doesn't bear much resemblance to the straight and unbending lines of the wills of the Father and Son, does it? Is there any possibility of bringing that erratic will into line with the even heartbeat of God? Yes. *The Bylaws of the Kingdom are designed just for this specific purpose.* This is the essence of the message of the Kingdom of God.

The message of Isaiah as quoted by Luke: " 'Prepare a road for the Lord to travel on! Widen the pathway before him! Level the mountains! Fill up the valleys! Straighten the curves! Smooth out the ruts! And then all mankind shall see the Savior sent from God.' " This is the way Luke 3:4–6 (LB) describes the process we are seeking to impart.

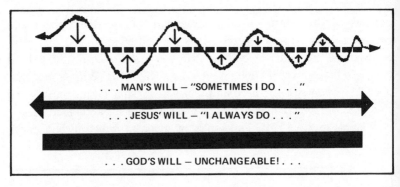

. . . MAN'S WILL – "SOMETIMES I DO . . ."

. . . JESUS' WILL – "I ALWAYS DO . . ."

. . . GOD'S WILL – UNCHANGEABLE! . . .

The mountains of pride, arrogance, self-will, rebellion, and resentment must be brought down (↓); while the valleys of depression, despair, and loneliness must be brought up (↑). The curves of deflection and deviation from the known will of God must be straightened (←→). The ruts of past habit, pattern, and "my ways" of doing things smoothed out! Then those around us can begin to see the Saviour—in us—demonstrated by a life which is changed and conformed to the image and will of God's Son, our Lord Jesus Christ.

We will use one other diagram to show something of the way in which God works out this purpose. Here is depicted the "before and after" of the alignment necessary on the inside in order to bring about alignment on the outside—which expresses itself in our conduct.

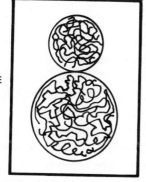

**NATURE
DESIRE**

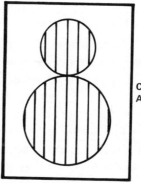

**CHARACTER
ABILITY**

Once the believer catches the challenge of the possibility of bringing his will into line with that of the King, he can say to God, "Lord, I want to do Your will. Help me!"

To this plea, the Lord may respond, "You do?" *He wants to be certain that you know what you are asking for!* Once you express this desire, you are eligible to become a *continuer*. God now begins to conform your will to His will. It involves some tightening of loose screws, some joining of nuts and bolts, untangling of wires, and general overhaul to bring alignment out of the conglomerate most of us would see on the inside should we expose ourselves to God's X-ray equipment.

We might as well face the fact that it isn't going to be easy and it may not always be pleasant. Are you willing to spend some time with the "tribulations" in order to come into alignment?

Do you think you could get tired while the Lord is dealing with you? Yes, but He provides for every eventuality along the way. A friend of mine had a dream which depicted the procedure like this.

The first scene was one of a beautifully calm river wending its way invitingly through the countryside. Many people were enjoying its pleasures. Then rocks began to appear along the banks. Soon the scene changed and the riverbed narrowed as it came to a crevice in the rocks. The waters became turbulent, with swirling rapids and undercurrents. Some distance farther, the river once again came out into an inlet and resumed calmness and quietness. But only for a short while. Again came the restriction of narrowing and turbulence. So the river went on and on to its destination.

These changes in the course of the river represent God's procedure during the times of alignment. It is a matter of individual choice where we will place ourselves in its flow. Some people will choose to spend their lives in the calms and shallows, while others are willing to risk the dangers of the changing currents. There will come times of resting in the larger, quieter expanses during which we will ready ourselves for the challenge of the quickening pace and currents that will eventually lead once again into restfulness. So the procedure moves ever forward until the final goal is reached—*alignment to the will of God.*

Are you willing to turn yourself over to the Master Mechanic in order to come into the "righteousness, peace, and joy" of the Kingdom? If so, we will move into our next area of operation. I promise you: *These Kingdom Concepts will revolutionize your life.*

WHY DO WE HAVE RULES?

Now we come to one of the least popular of the *Kingdom Concepts*— but one of the most vital. We might as well begin our investigation for an answer to the question, "Why do we have rules?" by acknowledging that everything from seedtime and harvest (As a man sows, so shall he reap.) to Johnny's Cub Scout Troop (A boy shall be eight years of age to qualify for membership.) has rules. They are a part of life. No corporation could operate with any degree of success without rules. You may counter, "Then what's all this talk about freedom? I thought freedom meant no rules. Didn't Jesus say the truth was going to make us free?"

Yes, you are right—He said just that: ". . . If ye continue in my word, then are ye my disciples indeed; And ye shall know the truth, and the truth shall make you free" (John 8:31–32. That is where the rules come in. *They are part of "the truth" He was talking about.*

They are designed to make us free. Stick with me and we will see how it works.

Let's start with the end result and work backwards. Would you like to be so completely free that you wouldn't have to *think about rules?* And this would apply in every area of your life relationships: home—family—business—recreation—total!

In chapter 5 of Galatians, Paul uses some of the same words we have been considering: freedom—bondage—law (or rule). We take only three verses to present his concept of freedom:

1 Stand fast therefore in the liberty wherewith Christ hath made us free, and be not entangled again with the yoke of bondage.

22 But the fruit of the Spirit is love, joy, peace, longsuffering, gentleness, goodness, faith,

23 Meekness, temperance: against such there is no law.

Notice, too, the closing words of verse 21, "the kingdom of God." Paul is talking about *Kingdom Concepts,* one of which is the possibility of freedom from bondage through a heart condition where no rules are needed.

God's primary objective is to align our wills to His will. When this undertaking is completed, we can move through life as Jesus moved throughout His earthly life—in complete freedom. We can meet every situation with the assurance that our actions and reactions are lined up—straightened out on the inside, as well as running parallel with God's will and Jesus' will on our spiritual EKG which we pictured earlier. Envision the righteousness, peace, and joy which would result from such assurance! This is truly Kingdom living.

As you have probably recognized by now, this is not an instantaneous transformation. Straightening out the snarls is a lifetime journey, becoming more satisfying every step of the way. Each step brings its own portion of freedom.

Haven't you, at one time or another, found yourself involved in a problem of such magnitude that when you finally stepped out of the snarls into the fresh air of God "straightening," you knew you were different from when you stepped into the tangle? Did you realize this was part of God's alignment in your life? Once we gain a victory over bondage in even the smallest segment of our lives, we are that much farther down the road to the freedom both Jesus and Paul were teaching about.

In introducing you to the individual's journey into freedom, we mentioned three hindrances which interfered with arrival at the desired destination. They were: *rebellion, resentment, and independence.* Where do these fit into this rule business?

We find them right at the entrance into Kingdom relationships. Perhaps we are not at all aware of their presence in our pathway until our eyes become opened to the possibility of freedom. Remember the stout claim of the believing Jews: "We were never in bondage!" But when Jesus began unfolding the *Bylaws of the Kingdom,* which are the rules, their blinded eyes gradually opened—focusing and adjusting to the new light which revealed the extent of their individual bondages. The rules are intended to have this effect. Again, we are reminded of that one clause in the Constitution: "to obey for your own good."

Now God is not surprised when rebellion, resentment, or independence manifest themselves as a person comes up against one of His rules. We are the ones who are surprised! God knows our "downsitting and uprising" (*see* Psalms 139:2) and brings us into situations that will reveal these responses to us. This is absolutely necessary for our coming into freedom. The desire within us to please God by doing His will may be very strong. But when He presents us with an opportunity to translate that desire into actuality, that is something else again!

This takes me back to the days when I was dean of a Bible college. In answer to the request for application from a prospective student, there would be mailed to him certain forms to fill out. One of the questions on the application form was, "Will you cheerfully abide by all the rules of this Bible college?" When the answer came back with a big bold *yes!,* I knew the reply was coming from a heart filled with *desire* to keep the rules. *But the ability to keep the rules* was going to be measured by the rules we were going to place on the aspiring entrant. The struggle to obey was very real in the lives of these young people. When they succeeded, it was a source of joy to those of us on the faculty; and when they failed, we knew the pain of failure along with them.

Do you see that when God puts a rule in our paths we have before us a choice. We can either:

(1) Rebel—"I won't"—or submit and obey the rule.
(2) Resent the rule—"Why does it have to be like this, anyhow?"—or permit God to purge from us such a reaction.
(3) Independently set up our own ways for complying, "I'd rather do it my own way, God"—or acknowledge our inability and do it His way.

You see, God doesn't change His rules for anyone—we are the ones who must change. If we refuse to change the first time around, He has a strange way of letting us know about it a little farther down the road. We may think we have gotten away with something—then along comes the same situation. We never graduate from the first grade into the second grade until the lessons of the first are satisfactorily learned. How many of us have failed the first grade three or four times (besides me—that is!)?

HOW DO WE RUN?

Now that we have settled the question of "Why Rules?"—we come to another extremely important question: How are we going to conduct ourselves in carrying out compliance with the rules?

Below is depicted a race track and two runners—you and the other fellow! Let's say that you are Runner Number 1 and you go plodding along, keeping within the prescribed course—abiding by all Kingdom rules and regulations. You think you are doing fairly well until you get to looking ahead and thinking how long and tedious the running is going to be until you make it to the finish line.

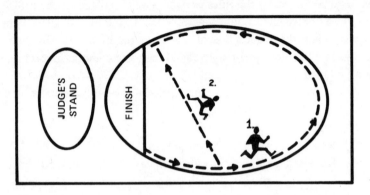

Along comes Runner Number 2. He, also, begins to wonder if he is ever going to make that finish line—and if it is going to be worth his time and effort. Suddenly he comes up with the idea: Why not cut across the track and saunter over the finish line just as if he had not taken a "shortcut"? All right, why not? Does this ever happen?

Yes, all too often. Sometimes it seems to Runner Number 1 that Runner Number 2 is getting away with his infringement of the rules. The field referee may be busy watching another runner. But do you see that Judge's Stand overlooking the entire field? That Judge—the One who made the rules and laid out the track—occupies that stand. There is never any possibility of His being "otherwise occupied" or of His winking at the trickery employed by Runner Number 2. What is the result of the latter's hopeful strategy? *Disqualification from the race.* Listen to the Apostle Paul and some "race talk."

In a race, everyone runs but only one person gets first prize. So run your race to win. To win the contest you must deny yourselves many things that would keep you from doing your best. An athlete goes to all this trouble just to win a blue ribbon or a silver cup, but we do it for a heavenly reward that never disappears. So I run straight to the goal with purpose in every step.

I fight to win. I'm not just shadowboxing or playing around. Like an athlete I punish my body, treating it roughly, training it to do what it should, not what it wants to. Otherwise I fear that after enlisting others for the race, I myself might be declared unfit and ordered to stand aside.

1 Corinthians 9:24–27 LB

Please note two things before we make a practical application of Paul's advice.

(1) The Greek word used in saying, "ordered to stand aside," is *"disqualify."* Paul seriously considers the possibility of "running" in such a way as to be disqualified and not being eligible for the reward the Judge has waiting for runners who finish according to the rules.

(2) Paul was not afraid of losing his gift of salvation. He knew his standing with the Judge was secure and established. It was being *disqualified* for the crown—his reward for a specific assignment in the Kingdom business—*that* was his concern.

Now to bring the illustration a little closer home. Say we start out on a course designed to bring about harmony in the home—a proper use of finances—or rearing our children. We have been made aware of the rules for running the race that will bring us to our desired goal. However, we decide it is going to take too long, and take too much effort, to do it "that way." So we take it upon ourselves to cut across the field. What happens when we come up to the finish line? We see the Judge shaking His head, indicating He has seen where we by-passed some necessary discipline or expected change in attitude. He cannot allow the rebellion, resentment, or independent action which may have triggered our attempt to set up our own rules.

Just as a judge of any type contest makes it very plain to all entrants exactly what the rules entail, God will make it plain to us where we have misunderstood, misjudged, or infringed upon His laws. Does He give us opportunity to start over again and make use of the experience of failure? Yes, the race goes on and the runner can make a fresh start. *Can you see how rules are designed to bring about a change in our conduct?*

As we move toward a developing understanding of the need for rules, and the necessary discipline for keeping them, we are going to hear Jesus saying to us, as He was saying to the *early continuers,* "If you are going to be My disciples, you have to abide by the rules."

This is Kingdom relationship!

NEED AND PLACEMENT

Speaking of Kingdom relationship, there are several other *Kingdom Concepts* we must become familiar with before we are ready to get down to studying the actual Bylaws (or rules) of the Kingdom. This particular one, *Need and Placement,* has to do with our part in bringing the Kingdom to our world.

Over and over again all of us have prayed, "Thy kingdom come, thy will be done on earth, as it is in heaven." But do we ever accept any part in bringing the Kingdom to earth? Do we even consider ourselves a part of the answer to that prayer?

For many years, salvation—in its "born-again" aspect—has been stressed as the main objective of the Gospel thrust. This overshadowed the necessity for new believers being brought to a realization that there is *more* than the initial believing—that they *must* become continuers if they are to enjoy Kingdom citizenship as the New Testament intended. Likewise, these new believers, with their new natures and desires, have probably been pressed into some area of service in the church. They were made to feel this was "the thing to do" regardless of when or where or how.

We do not in any way minimize the importance of either evangelizing (seeking to save the lost) or of service. But the Kingdom cannot come on earth as it is in heaven until we acknowledge the importance of advancing in our understanding of God's desire and will for developing the work and workers.

First, it is God's will that every *believer* advance to the role of a *continuer.* This is necessary for his own growth and for the growth of the Kingdom. Does a newly born child need careful teaching and encouragement to motivate him to continue as he meets new opportunities? Every parent knows the hours and agonies involved in teaching a child to walk—talk—establish good eating habits, and so forth. It is equally important that believers be motivated to move on to new frontiers. They must learn to look upon their world with the eyes of Jesus. Matthew tells us how Jesus viewed His world and His responsibility:

> And Jesus went about all the cities and villages, teaching in their synagogues, and preaching the gospel of the kingdom, and healing every sickness and every disease among the people. But when he saw the multitudes, he was moved with compassion on them, because they fainted and were scattered abroad, as sheep having no shepherd. Then saith he unto his disciples, The harvest truly is plentious, but the labourers are few; Pray ye, therefore, the Lord of the harvest, that he will send forth labourers into his harvest.
>
> Matthew 9:35–38

The phrases, *"seeing the multitudes . . . moved with compassion,"* must become a part of our heartbeat if we wish to look upon the world through the eyes of Jesus. What do we see when we get in a crowd—read the newspaper—watch television coverage of world events? Are we aware of those who may be perishing for lack of teaching—the mentally tortured—the physically disabled, as well as the spiritually handicapped? There is so much need and so many calls for help today that unless we seek to respond from Jesus' perspective, we will be forced to close our eyes to the multitudes and our ears to their cries. The scene can appear hopeless.

But right here is where Kingdom Concepts enable us to see and respond correctly. *God is establishing a Kingdom.* Every member of that Kingdom is needed to take his part in the operation of the corporation. As the Kingdom is established *within us,* we move with compassion to find the place where we can best serve. As we become aligned to do His will and learn to keep the rules of the race, *the needs of the multitude can be met!*

However, we must realize that the task must be done "according to the Father's will." Do you know that as much damage is done in the Kingdom of God by people who try to help God out, as by people who fail to do anything at all about needs? Does this statement puzzle you? Again we must look at it from Jesus' point of view and we find Him saying in Matthew 7:21–23:

> Not every one that saith unto me, Lord, Lord, shall enter the kingdom of heaven [or kingdom of God]; but he that doeth the will of my Father which is in heaven. Many will say to me in that day, Lord, have we not prophesied in thy name? and in thy name have cast out devils? and in thy name done many wonderful works? And then will I profess unto them, I never knew you: depart from me, ye that work iniquity.

Here we see works (or service) done in the name of Jesus—yet the workers are disqualified. Their works are not acceptable—even though done for others. The last word, *iniquity,* is better translated "without rules." The works were done in disobedience. The runners were disqualified. Why? They may have seen a need and immediately taken off to meet the need in their own way. God did not send them. He didn't ask them to do it. God *did* honor their efforts insofar as accomplishing the meeting of needs; but He could not put His stamp of approval on works done in violation of the rules He had set up.

The ultimate goal is relationship—not ministry. What did Jesus say was His goal? "I do always those things that please Him."

So, first of all, we must see the needs and then we must find where God intends that we fit into the picture for meeting the needs. This is a basic problem. We have become so ministry-oriented that we fail to understand that the desired goal is relationship to the Father. *Knowing and doing His will (wish or desire) is the ultimate criterion.* As we come into this proper relationship (and coming into it is part of the alignment process), we learn *placement*. Placement may be a new concept to you. *It means that I learn to function in the realm or area to which God calls me. This demands obedience.*

How did Jesus come into that kind of relationship to the Father which resulted in His always doing the right thing? Just as you and I must come into it. He learned to function in obedience to the Father's will by obeying! Taking just one incident from many examples, we see Jesus (having met the physical needs of a great crowd of followers) leaving them and going into a quiet place to pray.

> And when he had sent them away, he departed into a mountain to pray.
>
> Mark 6:46

Since Jesus said He always did the things that pleased the Father, we can take it for granted that the Father said, "Son, it is time for you to leave these people and spend some time in prayer."

It may not have been easy for Jesus to turn aside from the demands of the crowd with all kinds of opportunities to heal sicknesses, deliver those who were demonized, or open blind eyes. His heart of compassion may have told Him that if He stayed, He would be able to accomplish many good works. But, in obedience, He left. If you are moving in compassion, it is sometimes difficult to turn aside from meeting needs—even at His command. But it is more important to be obedient than it is to minister when the Father lets His will be known to you.

We have watched runners in today's race become disqualified because of not running according to the rules. We have heard what Jesus had to say to workers who moved in ministry "on their own." Now let us share a startling story on placement which is recorded in 2 Chronicles 26:1–21. This time it is a king—and you would think a king could set his own rules, wouldn't you?

Uzziah became King of Israel at age sixteen and reigned fifty-two years. We are told that "he did right in the sight of the Lord." God prospered him in war, in building programs, in agricultural undertakings—so much so that, "his name spread far abroad; for he was marvellously helped, till he was strong" (v. 15). Then verse 16 gives this sad commentary: "But when he was strong, his heart was lifted up to his destruction: for he transgressed against the Lord his God . . . ."

As long as Uzziah was dependent upon God, he prospered. But when he struck out on his own (independence), he met his downfall. The king decided to go into the temple and burn incense. What was wrong with that? He was king! Couldn't he do what he wanted? No. God had called him to be king—not to the priesthood, whose function it was to burn incense. In fact, Azariah, the chief priest, and eighty other priests "withstood Uzziah the king, and said unto him, 'It appertaineth not unto thee . . .' " (v. 18). What they were saying was, "This is not what God called you to do."

It appears that Uzziah was not only rebellious, but resentful as well! He became angry and took the censer in his hand to go ahead in his self-willed action—only to find his forehead leprous! As a result, he was "cut off from the house of the Lord" (v. 21) and his son reigned in his stead.

Uzziah lived out his days alone—a leper. Do you think that along with the rejection as king and the temporal losses related to kingly living, he also suffered eternal separation from his God? No. That is not the result of disobedience when God's children act independently or in rebellion. They are disapproved, but not disowned.

What happened to Uzziah was this: his ministry and his relationship to the Lord were broken when he stepped out of his calling. We might say this was a character flaw in the king who started out so brilliantly and obediently.

Rules are instituted to reveal these flaws and give us the opportunity to bring ourselves into a right relationship with the Father. And right relationship involves:

(1) Seeing needs through the eyes of Jesus.

(2) Seeking His will for our placement in meeting those needs.

DISCIPLESHIP AND MINISTRY

These two words, *Discipleship* and *Ministry,* are an integral part of the right relationship to our heavenly Father which we are endeavoring to incorporate into our daily living. In considering them, we want to see how they apply to us in relation to *Kingdom Concepts.*

We have been using Jesus and His earthly ministry as an example to follow. Noting that Jesus could say, "I always do those things that please the Father," we set this as our pattern for proper relationship. In viewing the needs of His day, we saw that He was "moved with compassion" as he realized the magnitude of the task of meeting needs. He must have known that, *by Himself,* He could never meet all of the demands. So what did He do? He drew aside His *disciples* and began to teach them—so that they could move into *ministry* with Him and for Him.

One of the things that God is saying to the church today is this: The needs of the world will never be met by professional ministers alone. There is a necessity for every *disciple* to move into *ministry.*

This means you, as well as me. God's plan is for "body" ministry. Every member of the body of Christ should be in a ministering capacity to some degree.

Will every member of the body be willing to accept such a responsibility? Will every member place himself in God's hands for preparation for ministry? Sorry to say so—but no. Not everyone will meet the challenge. Jesus presented this challenge to men of His day in these words: ". . . If any man will come after me, let him deny himself, and take up his cross, and follow me" (Matthew 16:24).

Some men did just that. And some did not. So it is today. Some will be challenged to be *continuers;* some prefer to remain merely *believers.* Both will eventually go to heaven. However, the continuer goes on into full discipleship; while the other is content to take out his "life insurance" and enjoy the fringe benefits without ever knowing the excitement of becoming involved in active ministry with Jesus Christ.

After Jesus drew His disciples aside for the teaching session as recorded in Matthew 5, 6, and 7, we might paraphrase His opening words (5:2) as, "Men, I am going to straighten you out so you can straighten others out." These men were soon going to be left with the Kingdom business in their hands. Jesus knew they could not "give out" what they did not yet possess. Do you see why it is vital that we be taught before we move into the ministry of teaching? In fact, all ministry demands preparation, for we teach by our actions, not just by words.

Here is what I am trying to convey. God is establishing His Kingdom *in you* because He wants to bring His Kingdom *through you*. As the Kingdom is realized *in* us, it can come *from* us. The men whom Jesus was teaching were just beginning to embrace His way of life—we might call them *new converts*. Today's new converts—the believers—also need a period of searching and straightening. Jesus wants us to come under the reign of God. To help us, He is going to give us some rules.

The question may come up: "Bob Mumford, are you trying to put us under law? I thought that was an Old Testament concept—that the New Testament stressed freedom." Let me say first, that the Old Testament concept was this: The individual took God's law upon himself in an endeavor to keep it. The New Testament concept of the Kingdom of God is not a set of laws or a place, but it is a condition *where God's will is being done in the individual as it is in heaven*. But rules are necessary to bring about the desired condition.

Jesus makes it very plain throughout all of His teachings that *discipleship* and *ministry* involve *participation and obedience*. In Matthew 11:29, 30, He presents the relationship as a *yoke*. Those who heard Him were familiar with the restrictions of a yoke.

Take my yoke upon you and learn of me . . . for my yoke is
easy and my burden is light.

You have to get into yoke before you can learn the things required for ministry. His yoke is easy but it is a yoke nonetheless. For
in ministry, we are going to be teaching. Listen to this further development given in Matthew 5:17–19:

Think not that I am come to destroy the law, or the prophets:
I am not come to destroy, but to fulfil . . . . Whosoever therefore shall break one of these least commandments, and shall
teach men so, he shall be called the least in the kingdom of
heaven: but whosoever shall do and teach them, the same shall
be called great in the kingdom of heaven.

Matthew is referring to the same Kingdom of God of which we
are speaking. Isn't it interesting to note that we are told that he who
breaks one of the laws of the Kingdom shall "be called the least in
the kingdom." You notice that this does not cause him to forfeit his
position as a citizen of the Kingdom; but he does not inherit what
belongs to him because (1) he doesn't *understand* (ignorance); or
(2) he doesn't *choose* to keep the rules (disobedience).

It is interesting, too, to note the words, "shall do and teach." It
evidently isn't enough to know the rules—the disciple must *do* and
teach. And teaching does not necessarily mean verbalizing rules,
but *what you are teaching others to do about the rules by the way
you are doing!* An age-old saying goes, "Your actions speak so loud
I can't hear what you say."

What was God's biggest problem with the people of Israel during
their declining years as a nation? It was *saying* one thing and *doing*
another. The warnings of the prophets—God's messages to the
people—stressed the fact that although they were observing all kinds
of holy days and meticulously keeping religious rituals, their living
and teachings were unacceptable to Him. Isaiah 58:1–7 covers this
condition. Note that the people were fasting and observing ordinances,

but their motives were not right. They were not "loosing bands of wickedness . . . dealing bread to the hungry . . . clothing the naked." (*See* 58:6, 7.)

We, too, are living in a day when there is an abundance of so-called religion, but a lack of performance. This condition is representative of a strange disease that sets in among God's people of every age and it is called "dichotomy." This means there is a split, or variance, between what we teach and what we do. Jesus was aware of this problem in His generation and made the following statements of warning.

. . . Woe unto you also, ye lawyers! for ye lade men with burdens grievous to be borne, and ye yourselves touch not the burden with one of your fingers.

Luke 11:46

For I say unto you, That except your righteousness shall exceed the righteousness of the scribes and Pharisees, ye shall in no case enter into the kingdom of heaven.

Matthew 5:20

Do you detect dichotomy in these two statements? First, "Pharisees, you load men with burdens, yet you do not bother to take any of these same burdens upon yourselves." Secondly, "People, unless your righteousness exceeds that of these men, you cannot enter into Kingdom living."

For a very simple illustration of dichotomy, let me relate something that happened early in my ministry. I was in a meeting with a pastor who was preaching to his people about the tremendous move of God in their midst. He challenged them to be a part of the sweep of the Spirit—even to the point of fasting (abstaining from food) to maintain a high level of participation. When he asked for all who would join him in such a fast, about two-thirds of those present raised their hands—including me. When the meeting was over, the pastor came down from the pulpit and the first thing he said was, "Come on, Bob, let's go get something to eat." And a big cheeseburger was first on the menu! This is "teaching and doing" all out of perspective.

Which brings us to examine two aspects of the word *righteousness* as presented in the Word of God.

RIGHTEOUSNESS—IMPUTED/IMPARTED

When an individual comes to Jesus Christ as a believer what happens is this: We say, "Lord Jesus, I believe. I repent from my sins and I want You to be my Saviour." To which Jesus replies, "My child, I see your faith and I have a gift for you—a robe of righteousness." *This is imputed righteousness.*

To the problematic Corinthian church, Paul writes:

> But it is from Him that you have your life in Christ Jesus, Whom God made our Wisdom from God [that is, revealed to us a knowledge of the divine plan of salvation previously hidden, manifesting itself as] our Righteousness *and thus* making us upright and putting us in right standing with God; and our Consecration—making us pure and holy; and our Redemption—providing our ransom from eternal penalty for sin.
>
> 1 Corinthians 1:30 (AMPLIFIED)

Paul says, as well, to the Ephesians, "Because of his kindness you have been saved through trusting Christ. And even trusting is not of yourselves; it too is a gift from God" (2:8 LB). The robe of righteousness is a gift—it is white and made of fine linen—but inside that robe! You guessed it—there is a mess that needs straightening out! God wraps us in the gift of righteousness so that we ever remain acceptable to Him. Imputed means to be made righteous by the act of another—our Lord Jesus Christ.

Now comes imparted righteousness. Again we find Paul writing to the Ephesians:

For we are his workmanship created in Christ Jesus unto good
works, which God hath before ordained that we should walk
in them.

                                                              2:10

What are the good works which God ordained—that walk upon
which we should embark? *Works of obedience.* Remember—we are
not saved *by* works, but we are saved *unto* good works ordained of
God. This is His purpose in salvation. We are created for works of
obedience—keeping the rules—that by them we shall be examples of
righteousness—*His* imparted righteousness. *When He imputes righteousness, He gives us the desire to obey and please Him. As He
imparts righteousness, He enables us to do works that are acceptable
to Him.* He does this by His Word and His Spirit.

In Revelation 19:7, 8, imparted righteousness is described. The
Amplified Bible reads:

> . . . for the marriage of the Lamb [at last] has come and His
> bride has prepared herself. [Ps. 118:24.] She has been permitted
> to dress in fine (radiant) linen—dazzling and white, for the fine
> linen is (signifies, represents) the righteousness—the upright,
> just and godly living [deeds and conduct] and right standing with
> God—of the saints (God's holy people).

The word *righteousness* as used here, is not the gift of righteousness, but it is deeds of right living, just acts, and conduct. The
preparation of the bride is done by good works—not the kind which
is the gift of righteousness—*imputed* righteousness.

Can you see that one kind of righteousness is a gift—the other is
worked in you? He imputes the one *to you* that He might impart
the other *within you.* The latter impartation is taking on the nature
of Jesus Christ. Paul refers to this work as "being conformed to the
image of God's Son." (*See* Romans 8:29.) I have referred to this
same process as the straightening out of the individual's will—alignment!

Returning to Matthew 5:20 where Jesus told the disciples their righteousness must exceed that of the scribes and Pharisees or they could not enjoy Kingdom living, we ask ourselves about the "doings" of the leaders to whom He was referring. These men were the acknowledged teachers of that day. They liked their phylacteries and scrolls and the chief places in the synagogues. They liked to be called upon for counsel. What hindered them from serving effectively? The breakdown between their teaching and their doing. This sounds very much like the trouble Isaiah was talking about in his denunciation of the leaders of those earlier centuries—outward show and inward depravity.

Can this situation exist today? Just because we know the contents of the Bible and teach its precepts, having an outward display of religion, *this does not qualify us for the Father's approval.* He wants to work something on the inside—even as He did in Isaiah's day, and at the time Jesus was teaching.

Jesus said that it was the Father's purpose to fulfill the Law and the Prophets *in* Him—and then *through* Him, using those believers who became continuers as the channel for accomplishing that objective.

God is going to bring forth a people in whom the Kingdom has been formed. Did these teachings raise questions among the men hearing them for the first time? Yes, the scribes and Pharisees, as well as many of the common people, bombarded Him with queries. Here we have one such question, along with Jesus' answer:

And one of the scribes came, and having heard them reasoning together, and perceiving that he had answered them well, asked him, Which is the first commandment of all? Jesus answered him, The first of all the commandments is, Hear, O Israel; the Lord our God is one Lord: And thou shalt love the Lord thy God with all thy heart, and with all thy soul, and with all thy mind, and with all thy strength: this is the first commandment.

And the second is like, namely this, Thou shalt love thy neighbour as thyself. There is none other commandment greater than

these. And the scribe said unto him, Well, Master, thou hast said
the truth: for there is one God; and there is none other but he:
And to love him with all the heart, and with all the understanding, and with all the soul, and with all the strength, and to
love his neighbour as himself, is more than all the whole burnt
offerings and sacrifices. And when Jesus saw that he answered
discreetly, he said unto him, Thou art not far from the kingdom
of God . . . .

> Mark 12:28–34

Do you see *knowing* and *doing* involved here? Just because the
scribe knew the workings of the Kingdom Constitution this did not
make him eligible for *entering* the Kingdom. Jesus told him he "was
not far from the kingdom of God." There's more to it than a knowledge of the way it operates. That further step of putting into action
the knowledge you have is mandatory.

Paul amplified on this teaching some years later when he wrote
to the believers in Rome the following:

Owe no man any thing, but to love one another: for he that
loveth another hath fulfilled the law. For this, Thou shalt not
commit adultery, Thou shalt not kill, Thou shalt not steal, Thou
shalt not bear false witness, Thou shalt not covet; and if there
be any other commandment, it is briefly comprehended in this
saying, namely, Thou shalt love thy neighbour as thyself. Love
worketh no ill to his neighbour: therefore love is the fulfilling
of the law.

> Romans 13:8–10

Is light beginning to dawn? Jesus came to fulfill the law. Love is
the way to fulfilling. The natural outworkings of loving the Lord
with all one's heart, soul, mind, and strength is loving one's neighbor.
*The trouble is that God's command to love is not taken seriously
enough to effect changes in relationships to one's neighbor*—then
or now!

Today there is much talk about "love"—but is it mostly talk? It has to involve walk—those "thou shalt nots" we like to dismiss from our minds and hearts. Not committing adultery—killing—stealing—envying. That's where the rub comes in. You cannot love without correction and change. Here is the where and why of Kingdom rules: *They measure our love right down to the quarter inch.*

We all know that we must discipline our children or face the eventuality of having a child on our hands we are unable to handle! It is the same with God and His children. In order to fit us for entrance into His Kingdom (and this is different from being born into His family), He must invade the areas of our lives where the *saying* and *doing* are not in agreement.

God must show us that we cannot trust our own feelings. Today I may feel like a saint—and tomorrow I may feel like I ain't! In other words, *I know but I don't always do.* Imparted righteousness is needed to translate knowing into doing.

We are now prepared to see how Jesus, as Teacher, went about laying the groundwork for incorporating these Kingdom Concepts into His Kingdom Bylaws. He had no visual aids upon which to rely, other than the daily living of His pupils—the soil, the birds, the marketplace. He had no reams of mimeographed notes for them to refer to. His words had to carry their own impact. His audience was not a hand-picked group of executives—but men and women who had the desire to hear more and know more of what He had to offer—Himself!

5 INTRODUCING THE TEACHER

Never in the history of mankind have all men recognized or acknowledged Jesus as being the Son of God. But most have recognized and accepted Him as one of the greatest teachers ever to leave a deposit of basic human-relation principles upon which civilization could build. One such deposit is often referred to as the Sermon on the Mount.

However much one may adulate and propose the Sermon on the Mount as being a wonderful literary masterpiece, I see it as the divine command from a Holy God, given to us through His eternal but virgin-born Son. If there is any portion of God's Word that demands supernatural insight and assistance to read, understand, and obey, it is chapters 5, 6, and 7 of Matthew, which we use in our study on the subject of the *Kingdom of God.*

Jesus' entire three years of public ministry were used as a "classroom." He consistently taught through life situations, whether it was while walking along in a wheat field or sitting by the seaside. Seldom do we have any recorded activity of the Teacher that did not carry with it a *principle* for us to follow.

Jesus was always interested in the "whole" man as He saw the needs around Him. There were physical healings—deliverances from mental and religious bondages—and forgivenesses for sin. In His compassion, He sees the same needs as He looks upon our world today. That is why He desires to establish His Kingdom Concepts within our being. He wants to bring us into freedom whereby we can establish a responsible and fruitful relationship to Him as Lord of our lives. Only then can He move us out into ministry to meet the needs of others who desperately need to hear the Gospel of the Kingdom of God.

As we launch out into the teachings, which we shall study, we first look at the Teacher and His pupils. For a setting we pick up the picture from Matthew 4:23–25.

> And Jesus went about all Galilee, teaching in their synagogues, and preaching the gospel of the kingdom, and healing . . . all manner of disease among the people. And his fame went throughout all Syria: and they brought unto him all sick people that were taken with divers diseases and torments, and those which were possessed with devils, and those which were lunatick, and those that had the palsy; and he healed them. And there followed him great multitudes of people from Galilee, and from Decapolis, and from Jerusalem, and from Judea, and from beyond Jordan.

Here are some facts I see; you may see more. The more God extends our appreciation of the Teacher, the more we can gain from His teachings. Jesus was a man on the move. He went where the people were. He taught in the synagogues, the teaching centers of His day. He walked the dusty roads—sat along the roadside—He moved in and out of the temple in Jerusalem.

His message was the same one we are sharing—"the Gospel of the Kingdom." He had built up quite a reputation for Himself—He was famous—He had a great following—not just country folk, but the city population was represented, too. Were someone of His magnitude and following on a teaching tour today, we can imagine reporters would be in the crowd. Television cameras would be clicking. His healings would be flashed via satellite around the world. News articles and interviews would be on the agenda.

As it was, I am sure the camel caravans carried word-of-mouth reports of the Miracle Worker. At the city gates His words were being repeated. Women drawing water at the community wells were probably passing along what their husbands had come home telling them about this new and dynamic force they had encountered. Were not men leaving their homes and businesses to become a part of the Kingdom move? Women, too, were a part of the new movement, ministering to the physical needs of the itinerant group. Yes, Jesus had a very real effect upon the lives of the people with whom He associated.

What did Jesus see in all of this? How did it affect Him? The words most often used to describe His response are the ones we have already shared: "He was moved with compassion." This includes more than pity or sorrow. It might be expressed as, *your hurt in my heart*. Compassion is a creative force. Nowhere do we get the impression that He was overwhelmed with the immensity of the needs; but everywhere do we sense the driving purpose He had for meeting the needs. *He moved steadily forward to lay a foundation for the work through the preparation of workers.*

At this particular time Jesus had just called some of the twelve men chosen to form the nucleus from which would emerge those who would be called upon to carry out the work when He had completed His task upon the earth. So we find them—Teacher and learners:

> And seeing the multitudes, he went up into a mountain: and when he was set, his disciples came unto him: And he opened his mouth, and taught them, saying . . . .
>
> Matthew 5:1, 2

What strategy did Jesus use in laying the foundation for the work and workers? These men believed in Him. As yet, however, they had little vision of the enormity of the task or the means for accomplishing it. The Teacher began where His pupils were, using their present knowledge upon which to build His new concepts. Scattered throughout the lesson, we hear these words: "Ye have heard that it was said . . . but I say . . . I am come not to destroy but to fulfill." (*See* Matthew 4:17.)

The Teacher might have begun with these words from the Book of Proverbs, which formed a part of the common teaching in the synagogues, "Where there is no vision, the people perish . . ."

(29:18). Peter, John, Andrew and the others were familiar with this statement. Yet their vision was limited to their nation's expectation of a messiah who would restore the Kingdom of Israel to world power.

They saw people perishing daily, both for lack of teaching and attention to their physical needs. They may have been desperately wanting to do something about this but had no knowledge of how to go about it. Perhaps, they sensed in Jesus, and His evident compassion and ability to meet needs, *the answer!* Was this what made them willing to leave all—deny self—and follow!

What was it Jesus knew must be laid upon that foundation for the recognition of *Him* as the answer? What must be changed? Jesus was teaching to the "new nature" these men had received by believing in Him. Before He moved into the actual teachings (which we have chosen to refer to as The Bylaws of the Kingdom of God), Jesus dealt with:

(1) the *character* of those who would qualify for Kingdom service and ministry;

(2) the *conduct* which would be expected from those carrying on this work;

(3) the *influence* these Kingdom emissaries would have as they moved into their own particular sphere of ministry.

Why are *you* interested in the teachings on the Kingdom of God? Do you see needs—do you have a desire to meet them—do you feel Jesus offers the only answer—both to the problems in your individual life, as well as those so evident in our society? If so, Jesus' teachings will prove as penetrating and purposeful in your life as they were in A.D. 30!

JESUS TEACHES ON CHARACTER

And he opened his mouth, and taught them, saying:

3 Blessed are the poor in spirit: for theirs is the kingdom of heaven.
4 Blessed are they that mourn: for they shall be comforted.

6 Blessed are they which do hunger and thirst after righteousness: for they shall be filled.

8 Blessed are the pure in heart: for they shall see God.

Matthew 5

One of the first questions raised may have been, "What do You mean by *blessed?*" Well, what *did* He mean? Literally translated, He was saying, "To be envied are . . . ." Apparently, a surface understanding here will not suffice. What makes these conditions—poor in spirit, mourning, hungering and thirsting for right living; or having a heart condition which might be considered pure—something to be desired? Why should others envy those having this quality of life? In explanation, the Teacher might have replied.

"Men, there is more to this Kingdom business than meets the eye. I believe you have already caught some of the implications or you wouldn't be here. If you can come to a clear understanding of what we are sharing today, you will have in your possession a *quality of life* that is truly to be desired by others. You will be blessed and envied."

Poor in spirit? This has to do with self-evaluation. If a person is so self-confident and self-assured that he doesn't believe he has any needs, how are you going to help him? If he feels he can get through life without God and the Bible—that all this "faith talk" is just a crutch—how can he receive teaching?

Then there is a diametrically different-type person—the one who is "religiously rich" in his own estimation. "I have God—the Bible— a nice church with stained-glass windows and a pipe organ—who needs anything else?" Do you see self-satisfaction here, too? The truly "poor in spirit" will realize there are many riches he hasn't yet touched. There is a longing for more of God and His Kingdom.

Mourn? This leaves a questionable taste in the mouth. A *mourner* —to be envied? Yes, when one has the quality of life that can *repent* in God's presence, *that one receives comfort from God that truly blesses.*

The modern concept of life is demonstrated by a recent saying: "Love means never having to say you're sorry." This shows how totally different is Christ's approach to life than that of the modern philosopher or scriptwriter who avoids "mourning" like the plague.

King David, who transgressed morally, lied, and then plotted the death of one of his own men, understood what it meant to be *blessed* by the ability to mourn. Mourning has to do with the ability to repent, be forgiven, and enjoy the resultant change in action and attitude. King David says with deep expression, "Blessed—happy, fortunate [to be envied]—is he who has forgiveness of his transgression continually exercised upon him, whose sin is covered" (Psalms 32:1 AMPLIFIED).

The more I have counseled and become acquainted with the deeper problems of life, the more certain I become that repentance (or the ability to mourn) is a gift from God. Some people have wanted to feel sorry and change their action or attitude, and have not been able. Blessed is he who can say with a conviction and meaning, "I'm sorry for the way I have acted."

Hunger and thirst? This is a sign of health! Usually when one is physically ill, appetite is lacking. Upon return to normal, the request may come, "Please fix me two eggs." Welcome request! Yes, one who hungers after more of the Word of God—who thirsts for His Spirit— *he is to be envied—for he shall be filled.* God will see to it that his longings are satisfied.

Right now there is a definite cry of hunger coming from the body of Christ (His church). There is an expressed need for teaching. This is a healthy sign. The body of Christ is in the process of recovering from a two-thousand-year illness! God is honoring that cry.

Pure in heart? This does not have to do with a heart without sin —though there will be a turning from all known sin. The deeper meaning is "one without guile." Jesus described one of His disciples, Nathanael, as being a man without guile. (*See* John 1:47.)

Guile is deceit—pretense. It is easy to "play games" in an attempt to enter the Kingdom. But God distinguishes the real from the sham.

A facade of "wouldest—shouldest—canst" will not impress the Father. He wants us to come and talk to Him according to the intents of our hearts—not according to ritual or prescribed traditions of men. If there is a question or doubt—get it out into the open. Then He can reveal Himself to you and meet your needs. *You will see God and be blessed.*

Have you seen that these four characteristics represent a vertical relationship—oneself upward toward God? The ability to properly evaluate one's needs—to repent—to hunger and thirst for the spirituals—and to stand free of pretense before God—here are the attitudes that will bring joy and satisfaction, and cause a desire in the hearts of others to have this same relationship.

JESUS TEACHES ON CONDUCT

And he opened his mouth, and taught them, saying:

5   Blessed are the meek: for they shall inherit the earth.
7   Blessed are the merciful: for they shall obtain mercy.
9   Blessed are the peacemakers: for they shall be called the children of God.

                                                        Matthew 5

Moving from a vertical relationship (that of man toward God) we now find instruction in the horizontal relationships of man toward his fellow man. Here the characteristics discussed develop out of a right attitude toward God, which results in *Kingdom conduct* in daily living. How well acquainted are we with the type of conduct expected from citizens of God's Kingdom?

Meek? Like the word *mourn,* this word has seldom been accurately depicted in our society. There is no "doormat" or "milk-toast" inference here. In fact, Jesus is teaching just the opposite!

Moses was described as a man of meekness. He typified strength and leadership. He stood head and shoulders above the millions who looked to him for their very existence. Yet, under undue pressure from the Israelites during their desert trek, Moses blew his meekness. Yes, meekness is hard to come by—and even harder to maintain.

Jesus, also referred to as a meek man, told His listeners that those who cultivate this standard of conduct would *inherit the earth.* In what way? Meekness results in teachableness—ability to receive help —poise under pressure—confidence in God's ability to meet every emergency. That man will control himself and be in command in every circumstance of life. What an inheritance!

Merciful? Here is expressed conduct that is more easily understood by practical applications than words. One such application, from my own personal experience, is the practice I have adopted of always stopping when traveling if I see a woman stranded with car trouble. Do you know why? My wife may find herself in the same predicament some day. Running out of gas—a dead battery—these are emergencies which God can meet "mercifully" by sending just the right person to the rescue.

Mercy is not always easy to come by, either. Often Christians are very harsh and judgmental when another Christian falls into sin. One friend told me how God had dealt with him and brought a lesson in this area of his life.

This man had severely berated a fellow worker following the disclosure of adultery in his life. "You've disgraced God! You've ruined your testimony!" That night the "self-appointed" judge had a dream.

He found himself dangling over a bottomless pit, and as he started falling into it, the Lord quietly began removing the robe of righteousness with which the man was clothed. In utter dismay, my friend began pleading, "God have mercy on me." To which the Lord replied, "You haven't shown mercy to your brother. Why should I have mercy on you?"

However, the robe of righteousness was restored as my friend continued, "God, if You will give me Your mercy, I will have mercy on my brother."

Blessed are the merciful—*for they shall obtain mercy*. We all need mercy—and we all need to be merciful. Have you ever heard some people complain that no one seems to show them any mercy? Perhaps a check on their dispensing of that commodity known as mercy might be in order.

Peacemakers? The ability to bring a "quieting influence" to others is, in essence, the result of this manner of conducting oneself. It isn't necessarily a matter of words, though these may be involved at times. It is rather, when you walk into a situation where the sparks are flying and tempers are short—does the situation get better or worse?

At the airport in Dallas, Texas, there is a statue of a Texas Ranger, with the words ONE RIOT, ONE RANGER. It commemorates this event. In response to an urgent plea, "Send us some men," one man appeared on the scene. The reason for the call for help had been a big riot; yet when this one ranger appeared (with two big .45s on his side), peace was restored. One man walking into the middle of a riot can have that effect—if the man comes rightly prepared and armed.

As an active participant in the Kingdom, you can walk into a situation and God's peace can flow through you—peace can be restored. What a blessing in our society of turmoil and confusion! There is also the promise that you will be recognized as "a son of God," for the peace you bring will carry with it divine overtones.

Meekness—Mercy—Peacemaking—is this conduct evident in our society on any large scale? Are *you* willing to continue on with Jesus and develop this type conduct so that you will be able to display His characteristics and conduct to others?

Characteristics result in conduct.

Conduct results in influence.

Jesus builds slowly but surely toward the moment when He will present the Bylaws of the Kingdom. He said He had not come to destroy but to fulfill. A spirit of expectancy must have gripped the listening men as Jesus unfolded the adventures ahead for all who travel in His company.

JESUS TEACHES ON INFLUENCE

And he opened his mouth, and taught them, saying:

13 Ye are the salt of the earth: but if the salt have lost his savour, wherewith shall it be salted? it is thenceforth good for nothing, but to be cast out, and to be trodden under foot of men.
14 Ye are the light of the world. A city that is set on a hill cannot be hid.
15 Neither do men light a candle, and put it under a bushel, but on a candlestick; and it giveth light unto all that are in the house.
16 Let your light so shine before men, that they may see your good works, and glorify your Father which is in heaven.

Matthew 5

Salt? What more common illustration could the Teacher have chosen to underscore the importance of influence? Every one of His listeners could identify with this method of seasoning and preserving foodstuffs. Salt cannot afford to lose its "saltiness." Neither can words afford to lose the backing of action. We return to the importance of matching conduct and teaching. If words alone could solve problems, the Kingdom could have come long ago. God's prophets pounded again and again at the dichotomy evident in their time. Jesus constantly warned against this condition. If words and actions do not equate, then that man and his influence are "good for nothing." Not a very desirable epitaph, is it?

I mentioned earlier about my encounter with Christ in an Atlantic City church while on leave from the navy. Upon returning to my ship, I tried to take my usual place among my shipmates of three-years' service together. But when I would walk up to a little group engaged in the usual "ship talk," sudden silence fell. The laughing and the jokes stopped. What had happened? *A pinch of salt had found its way into a bed of corruption.* Even though I did not move into the group with any thought of preaching a sermon, the salt began taking effect. Before it had been drinking—fighting—carousing. Now?

Strangely enough, New Testaments appeared—Bible study became an accepted part of our leisure time—sailors seeking spiritual help often came to my room at 2:30 A.M.—reminding me of Nicodemus who came to the Teacher by night to ask questions.

Once the Kingdom of God has been established in a person, it can flow through that person, and wherever he walks—there is influence! Salt is working. What are people looking *at?* What are they looking *for?* You are not required to produce a lot of words. Someone is watching you at your desk typing. Someone is looking to see what kind of a job you are doing as you lubricate his car. In the home— with children and guests—the milkman and the paperhanger—these are places where salt can have its effect.

Light? Just as salt was an absolute necessity for preserving and seasoning food, so was the candle in furnishing light in that day. Jesus always spoke simply and directly, and related His teachings to subjects His hearers could understand.

In our twentieth-century world, nighttime is almost as well lighted as the daytime in a large percentage of the populated areas. Our homes, roadways, every center of activity has the benefit of illumination. But once the sun went down and twilight deepened, the first-century world was blanketed in darkness. One candle or one light of any kind attracted the attention of anyone within seeing distance. *Lights are made to be seen.*

Along with a light affording the means of illumination, there also comes an opportunity to acknowledge the source of the light. Jesus says our good works are the means by which we can glorify the Giver of light—our Father in heaven. When men receive benefit from our "good works," this is our opening to turn the eyes of the recipient to God.

False humility is a stench to God. If you have a chance to do good and someone comes to thank you, don't shrink from accepting appreciation. Accept it and acknowledge the source of your ability for meeting that need. If God has afforded a means of your exerting your influence—take the glory expressed and send it back to God. The one who received help may be trying to get across to you that he recognized a quality in your life that is not your own; and yet he does not know how to formulate his feelings. Watch for opportunities to point people to the One who can save—heal—deliver.

You are salt. You are light. You are influence. That is why we all need to walk with an openness and freedom before the Lord. People are looking at us and to us. God is calling a people who will walk with their heads in the clouds and their feet on the ground. This results in a "stretching" experience. It is offered by the Teacher to each one who hears His words and puts them into action.

6 SUMMARY

Before we join Jesus and His disciples in the teaching session on the Bylaws of the Kingdom, as given in Matthew chapters 5, 6, and 7, we need to summarize the *Kingdom Concepts* we have shared.

FREEDOM OR BONDAGE We cannot achieve true freedom until we are aware of the unconscious areas of bondage in our lives. Jesus has promised that if we continue in His teachings, He will manifest these areas to us. Pretense here will never serve any good purpose. *God knows. And He will let us know—for the asking!*

DESIRE AND ABILITY The new desire with which we are endowed when we accept Christ as Saviour demands expression. This desire is to please God. However, the ability to fulfill that desire is not endowed. It must be cultivated and developed. *The new nature must grow into new character, from which right conduct results.* God stands waiting and wanting to help us do this. Desire changed to ability results in obedience and maturity.

THREE HINDRANCES God is aware of the hurdles to be overcome—even though we may not. He places us in situations where any *rebellion, resentment, or independence* that may be interfering with Kingdom progress are surfaced. We may be completely surprised to find these reactions within us. Here we face choice. Will we place ourselves in God's hands for purging and preparation for internal release which results in complete freedom in that area?

ALIGNMENT This is God's way to accomplish the purging and preparation for complete freedom. By aligning our wills with His will, these hindrances may be turned into stepping-stones toward our goal of conforming to the image of the Lord Jesus Christ.

RULES—WHY AND HOW   Rules are designed to permit us to measure our progress while being aligned. In effect, Jesus says, "If you are going to move with Me into a Kingdom relationship, you have to keep the rules." These rules do not change for anyone; and no one is permitted shortcuts!

NEED AND PLACEMENT   We must see the needs around us through the eyes of Jesus. He was "moved with compassion." Then we will seek His will for using us in meeting these needs. Each of us must determine the where and how of service for himself. God has a specific place for each of us; and serving within that framework demands obedience.

DISCIPLESHIP AND MINISTRY   Continuing discipleship demands discipline. This is what Jesus meant when He spoke of believers becoming *continuers*. Discipleship necessitates getting into the yoke with Jesus in order to minister effectively.

RIGHTEOUSNESS: IMPUTED/IMPARTED   Both of these aspects of righteousness are our rightful inheritance.

Imputed righteousness is a gift given to us when we acknowledge Him as Saviour. This enables Him to impart the righteousness that will result in our being conformed to His image. Since Jesus' life consisted of "deeds of right living, just acts, and conduct," these will be a part of our lives, also. His love will be manifested *to us* and *through us* to others.

Do you feel prepared to meet the King in His role of itinerant Teacher from the hills of Galilee? No one can sit under His teaching and remain the same. Individual response is automatic at even the mention of His name—**Jesus!**

PART TWO

BYLAWS
OF
THE KINGDOM

INTRODUCTION

Our study on the Kingdom of God is addressed to *believers* in Jesus Christ as Son of God and Saviour of man. The purpose of the study is to bring believers into the freedom God intended that men should know through accepting His Son, and then becoming acquainted with Jesus' teaching and example.

Jesus spoke to *believers* of His day, presenting to them the choice of moving from the status of believers to that of *continuers*. John 8:31, 32 states the choice:

> Then said Jesus to those Jews which believed on him, If ye continue in my word, then are ye my disciples indeed: And ye shall know the truth and the truth shall make you free.

Since these words are directed to *believers,* we know Jesus is teaching to the new nature of man. This nature is imparted to man when he repents of his sins, turns to God for forgiveness through the death of Jesus on the cross, and receives new life, made possible by the Resurrection of Jesus.

If you are a *believer* in Jesus Christ, you are automatically qualified to enroll in a course of discipleship. It is for anyone—ages seven, seventeen, or seventy—educated or uneducated—rich or poor—it is open to everyone!

Jesus said, "If any man will come after me . . . if ye continue in my words . . . ." *If!* It is a matter of choice, just as it was a matter of choice when you became a believer. Then you made the choice between spiritual life and spiritual death. Now you face the choice between spiritual growth and spiritual stagnation. It is not a matter of losing one's salvation, it is rather a matter of learning from Jesus the hows, whys and the why nots of the Kingdom. Some will be more successful than others—not because one has more opportunity than the other, but because one has greater desire to *know and do* the will of the Father. Those who desire to do so will move from desire to ability—from nature to character, adding to his imputed righteousness the imparted righteousness available to him.

Yes, you can stay just like you are—*a believer* and a child of God —but not interested in growing into the intended maturity of a freed citizen of the Kingdom of God.

In three of the Gospels, Matthew, Luke, and Mark, Jesus tells us what receiving the teachings of the Kingdom is like. We refer to this as the Parable of the Sower. We are going to draw upon all three accounts to get a composite picture of this teaching. References are: Matthew 13:1–23, Mark 4:1–20, Luke 8:4–15.

Both Mark and Luke refer to the teaching as relating to the Kingdom of God; Matthew uses the phrase the "Kingdom of heaven" (v. 11). We know Matthew uses this expression because he was writing to the Jews and they did not use the word *God* for fear of taking it in vain, thus breaking one of their commandments.

All three writers state that the teaching was given to the multitudes; and that it was later—upon request—interpreted to the smaller group of the disciples.

> And he said unto them, Unto you it is given to know the mystery of the kingdom of God . . . .
>
> Mark 4:11

To us, also, it is given to *understand the mystery of the Kingdom.* The seed sown then, Jesus said, was the Word. So, it is today. This particular study is "sowing the Word." *What is going to be the result of the sowing—your reading of this book?*

Hear how Jesus explained what was going to happen to the seed He was sowing. He presented four possibilities.

(1) Satan comes and takes away the words.

> When any one heareth the word of the kingdom, and understandeth it not, then cometh the wicked one, and catcheth away that which was sown in his heart . . . .
>
> Matthew 13:19

(2) *Word received with gladness, but shallowness prevents rooting and growth.*

. . . when tribulation or persecution ariseth because of the word, by and by he is offended.

V. 21

(3) *The Word is rendered unfruitful because of the cares of the world, the deceitfulness of riches, pleasures of this world.*

. . . are choked with cares . . . and bring no fruit to perfection.

Luke 8:14

(4) *Bring forth fruit—30 percent, 40 percent, 60 percent, even 100 percent!*

But that on the good ground are they, which in an honest and good heart, having heard the word, keep it, and bring forth fruit with patience.

V. 15

Have you been considering your own reception as you see the four possibilities to understanding the Word? Determination to know God means harassment from the Enemy. Satan is eager to interfere. Lack of being established in the basics of our faith is a barrier. Tribulation, temptation, persecution will have to be overcome. The cares of the world, its riches, pleasures, and pulls will need to be taken into account.

Then there is the fourth possibility—that of fruit-bearing. The word can speak to an honest and open heart to the extent that it is received, understood, and kept.

Besides acknowledging how the understanding of the Kingdom of God would be received, Jesus made it clear that *the Kingdom of God is present tense.* He repeatedly said, "The Kingdom of God is . . . ." In its spiritual form, the Kingdom is come on earth. True, it is not yet on earth as it is in heaven. But, applying the Kingdom Concepts and the Bylaws will bring fulfillment to the prayer, ". . . thy kingdom come, thy will be done on earth as it is in heaven."

In some translations the Kingdom of God is called the *Reign of God*. Do you see that the Kingdom is the reign of God in the hearts of men? The Reign of God is now—twentieth century. *It is here where you live.*

As we leave the realm of believers and become continuers, we shall review the Constitution and investigate the purpose of the Bylaws.

The Kingdom of God is a government. All governments are duly constituted. Here is the Preamble to the Kingdom Constitution and Articles I, II, and III:

> For the kingdom of God is not meat and drink; but righteousness, and peace, and joy in the Holy Ghost.
>
> Romans 14:17

ARTICLE I Hear, O Israel: the Lord our God is one Lord: And thou shalt love the Lord thy God with all thine heart, and with all thy soul, and with all thy might (Deuteronomy 6:4, 5).

ARTICLE II And now, Israel, what doth the Lord thy God require of thee, but to fear the Lord thy God, to walk in all his ways, and to love him, and to serve the Lord thy God with all thy heart and with all thy soul, To keep the commandments of the Lord, and his statutes, which I command thee this day, for thy good? (Deuteronomy 10:12, 13).

ARTICLE III Jesus said . . . Thou shalt love the Lord thy God with all thy heart, and with all thy soul, and with all thy mind. This is the first and great commandment. And the second is like unto it, Thou shalt love thy neighbour as thyself. On these two commandments hang all the law . . . (Matthew 22:37–40).

The first thing we need to settle is *what the Kingdom of God is not*. In Romans 14:17, Paul used the expression, "meat and drink," to rule out completely the restrictions of outward actions. All of the "Thou shalt nots" will never make one free. It is a matter of inner attitude. Righteousness, peace, and joy are inner qualities, not outward restrictions. They result in outward conduct, but the conduct springs from inward change.

An example of this is the way in which leaves fall off a tree. When autumn comes, the sap is withdrawn from the tree; then the leaves begin falling off automatically.

So it is when the Kingdom of God is established in one's life. As rebellion, resentment, and independence are dried up in response to Kingdom truths, the "thou shalt nots" begin dropping off like falling leaves. You do not need to pick off the leaves—nature takes care of the process.

The second thing we need to settle is *Why Bylaws and How Do They Operate.*

In every corporation, governmental or business, the *bylaws are given to interpret the constitution.* We need to know if we are living up to the intent and demands of the constitution. One dictionary defines bylaws as "subordinate laws for the government of members or stockholders."

So, subordinate to the law of loving God and our neighbors as ourselves, come these fifteen bylaws to measure our conduct. They spell out what is expected of us as citizens so that there can be no doubt in measuring our love and loyalty. They delineate how we are to conduct Kingdom business.

How do they operate? It is the purpose of the Bylaws to produce within us an understanding of the Word, receiving it into our lives, and putting the teachings into practice. Just as the seed found lodgment in good soil and was carefully cultivated in order to bring forth fruit, so must we respond to these teachings. The percentage of the yield is up to each of us.

As we come up against a particular law, our response will reveal if there is need for alignment to the will of the Father in that area. Take time to review the teachings on Alignment—that process of bringing our wills to a matching line with the inflexible unchanging wills of the Father and Son.

If we find a discrepancy in matching our wills with His, we must admit the deviation and seek His remedy for setting us straight. This is not natural or easy; but it is absolutely necessary. We may discover, much to our surprise one or more of these hindrances as detailed in Chapter 4.

(1) rebellion—"I won't!"
(2) resentment—"Why does this happen to me?"
(3) independence—"I'd rather do it myself, God."

Again, I emphasize that these three character flaws must be brought out into the open and dealt with before we can move into Kingdom relationship and know the freedom that is our rightful inheritance. The Bylaws are given to do just this—reveal areas of need for alignment. By honestly facing our problems and asking Him to help, rebellion can be broken—resentments can be purged—and independence can be overcome. We can step out of God's dealings a whole man! It is easy to deceive ourselves, but the Bylaws provide a measuring stick for our responses. This eliminates our thinking we are doing better than we really are!

Necessary to accomplishing an adequate appraisal of our reactions to the Bylaws, are the attitudes Jesus put before His hearers when He was laying the foundation for His teaching on the Bylaws. He was teaching on character and He listed four conditions of the inner man which would cause him to be envied.

Can you see their value even more clearly now than ever before?

To be envied are the poor in spirit (those who properly evaluate themselves).

To be envied are they that mourn (those who can repent in God's presence).

To be envied are they which do hunger and thirst after righteousness (those who have an appetite for the spiritual).

To be envied are the pure in heart (those who are without deceit and pretense).

These characteristics are essential to interpreting the Kingdom By-laws effectively.

I THE LAW OF ANGER

And he opened his mouth, and taught them, saying:

21 Ye have heard that it was said by them of old time, Thou shalt
not kill; and whosoever shall kill shall be in danger of the judgment:

22 But I say unto you, That whosoever is angry with his brother
without a cause shall be in danger of the judgment: and whosoever shall say to his brother, Raca, shall be in danger of the
council: but whosoever shall say, Thou fool, shall be in danger
of hell fire.

23 Therefore if thou bring thy gift to the altar, and there remem-
berest that thy brother hath ought against thee;

24 Leave there thy gift before the altar, and go thy way; first be
reconciled to thy brother, and then come and offer thy gift.

25 Agree with thine adversary quickly, whiles thou art in the way
with him; lest at any time the adversary deliver thee to the judge,
and the judge deliver thee to the officer, and thou shalt be cast
into prison.

26 Verily I say unto thee, Thou shalt by no means come out thence,
till thou hast paid the uttermost farthing.

Matthew 5

We are stepping into Kingdom territory. Are your eyes focused on
the freedom waiting for you out there on the horizon? It is there for
the claiming. Let us walk and work toward it through these teachings.

The first *commandment* Jesus brings to the attention of His hearers
is: *Thou shalt not kill.* This law is sixth in the Decalogue or Ten
Commandments which formed a part of the Jewish law. These commandments were given by God to Moses at the time of the formation
of the Israelites into a nation. Commandments are specific instructions and the people of Jesus' day knew exactly what was involved in

Thou shalt not kill. A literal translation of the Hebrew is, *Thou shalt do no murder.* This was a person-to-person relationship. It had nothing to do with war or punishment for conviction of crimes. Warfare was a necessary part of their existence. So was punishment for sins against society, which was meted by stoning.

Do you see where problems have arisen down through the centuries by interpreting this commandment, "Thou shalt not kill"? Of course, it is the desire of God that wars shall cease—that men shall live in peace. Also, if this commandment would be universally observed, capital punishment would not be necessary. This is the ideal expressed in the prayer, "Thy kingdom come, thy will be done on earth as it is in heaven." As individuals, we are part of the coming of the Kingdom.

Just to be certain that we see the distinction between killing and murder, let us build a hypothetical case. The scene is frontline battle —the enemy is approaching. My buddy and I are facing attack; yet a far more foreboding enemy is at work in our hearts, for we have had a serious quarrel. While involved in the combat, my inner enemy stirs up the anger within me and I turn to my buddy, pull out my .45 and shoot him down. Then I am forced to turn upon the incoming forces and use that same gun for an entirely different purpose. The intent is very different in the first instance. Motivated by anger, hate, or revenge, such action stands condemned before God.

The second fact that we need to establish is that Jesus made it clear that He was giving His hearers new rules for His Kingdom. Each time He referred to a command of the past, He began with, "Ye have heard . . ." (*see* Matthew 5:21). Then He quickly announced, "But I say . . ." (*see* v. 22). He was not just adding to the former commandments, he was instituting new rules that were structured to bring about changes in man's understanding of the *intent* of God's original commands. He was not *destroying*—He was fulfilling. Jesus was showing them the way into a freedom where there would be no need for a law saying, "Thou shalt do no murder."

Wouldn't this be an advance for mankind? All the psychologists, sociologists, and educators have not been able to accomplish this.

No research has ever come up with an equation to change the sinful nature which erupts and results in murder. Yet, here is Jesus telling us how this state of being can become a reality. Let's follow His reasoning.

"You have heard it was said . . . you shall do no murder, or you shall be in danger of judgment." Being apprehended in the act of murder, being convicted and facing the consequences for breaking the laws of society is a very real danger. So is facing the judgment of God upon one's action and the condition of heart that triggered the act.

". . . but I say . . . whosoever is angry with his brother without a cause . . . ." We need to stop here and note that Jesus is discussing anger *without a cause*. This implies there are times when anger is a justifiable response. Anger is not sin. But it is not necessary to allow anger—whether justified or not—to result in sin. Paul, who was a continuer in the Kingdom, wrote these words: "Be ye angry and sin not: let not the sun go down upon your wrath: Neither give place to the devil" (Ephesians 4:26, 27). By handling anger immediately and not allowing the devil to take control of our responses, we can learn to handle explosive situations in accord with Jesus' teachings. How does He recommend we go about this?

In verse 22, we see the progression of anger. The Bylaws were instituted for our good. They protect us by exposing our reactions. The road to safety lies in realizing *what* arouses anger within us, as well as realizing *how* it grows once ignited. Is it self-justification— prejudice—pride—an interference with some ambition or pleasure? All of these come under the heading "without cause." *We* may consider them cause, but God wants to show us to ourselves—*as He sees us*. He judges our motives. There is danger in judgment, for then we face the responsibility of dealing with the *cause*.

From our first response of anger, we move into *phase two*. Anger comes alive and we lash out with *"Raca!"* This is an expression of derision: "You idiot!" This response places one in danger of the council—being called before a governing body for discipline.

Then comes phase three. One is moving toward murder—anger builds and takes on even more scathing verbalization, "Thou fool!" Revenge is rising: "You dog—you rat . . . ." Not only do our mouths get out of control, but our thoughts run riot and our bodies respond. We use expressions like "seeing red," . . . "my blood boiled," . . . "I blew my top."

Revenge is the hub around which endless stories are written and plays enacted. Cowboys and Indians—criminals and law enforcement officers—the hero and the villain of the love stories. Real-life dramas touching millions of lives fill our news headlines and flash from the television screens. Some people live in this type of atmosphere so much of the time that it becomes an accepted way of life. It saturates business transactions, sports events, love affairs, family relationships. Anger and revenge—if given a beginning—build and eventually produce a hell on earth.

Jesus warned that he who lets his anger run wild is in danger of hell. He is pressing these responses out into the realm of extreme peril. Here we are apt to find ourselves saying things and doing things we never intended should happen. Fires that destroy are kindled by the seed of anger. Jesus says, in effect, "If you will let Me, I will deal with that anger in your heart until you are freed from it."

In the Old Testament commands, the problem was in the act. In the New Testament, the Teacher brings the act right where it belongs: to the origin of the act—in the heart. This is where the clean-up is needed. One has to be free from anger *in his spirit;* against this freedom there is no need for the law "Thou shalt do no murder."

Such freedom comes when we learn how to deal with anger. Verses 23 through 26 give us Jesus' formula. He begins with "therefore," and we always need to see why what follows is "there for."

In this case, Jesus moves the scene to the temple. A worshiper has come to offer his gift to God at the altar. Here there is brought to his remembrance an incident of anger—one which he may have thought no one was aware of but himself. Have you ever found yourself in this situation? What better place for God to speak? The Holy Spirit is the One who nudges us into remembering that angry thought

or act. Perhaps this is the only time we have become quiet enough
to hear His promptings.

Here I am in church worshiping, and thoughts of harsh judgment
or verbal lashings I have been guilty of rise up before me. I can now
do one of two things. I can do as Jesus is recommending (v. 24),
leave the temple, seek out my offended, or offending, brother, and
say to him, "I'm sorry this happened. Please forgive me for my part
in the incident." Or I can turn my back on the suggestion and say,
"That's the devil—condemnation—I'm under the blood—there is
therefore now no condemnation." Which decision will I make?

Jesus continues His teaching by telling the result of the second
choice—not following the counsel to leave our gift at the altar and
be reconciled to our brother. Notice, we are to agree with our adversary—that one with whom we are having trouble—quickly, while
he is willing to negotiate peace. The consequence facing us may be
that the adversary will deliver us to the judge—the judge deliver us
to the officer—and we will find ourselves in prison.

This sequence of events was the way in which justice was handled
at that time. There were no long delays in hearings—possibilities of
bail or appeals to higher courts. The ordinary course of action was
swift and certain. Once in prison, freedom was not gained until the
last dime of the fine or final day of the sentence was paid.

I believe the judge in the court scene is the Lord Jesus Himself.
He knows the hearts of men—He is the Judge before whom all believers stand. The officer, as Jesus was depicting the scene, is the
Holy Spirit—He who is appointed to convict men and bring them
into truth. The Judge turns us over to the Officer, who will then see
to it that we are "shut up"—imprisoned—until we have paid the
price for release. Did you know some people never get out of this
"spiritual jail"?

What does it mean to be "shut up"? Don't forget the Judge and
the Officer are on twenty-four-hour-a-day duty—every day of the
week. Do you recall the race course we diagrammed—and the shortcut Runner Number 2 tried to get away with? The disapproval which
resulted when the Judge saw the infringement is part of the "shut-

ting up" process. Also, our diagram on Alignment shows what needs to take place during our imprisonment. Some bolts may need tightening—some kinks taken out of the wires. The flow of fellowship and ministry may be withheld until we "have paid the last farthing." We must come to the place where we can see anger for what it is and what it does to us, and others. Even more important, we must come to see the cause—that seed which germinated and bore the fruit of our actions. We may end up "shut up" from ourselves, our associates, and our God. Let me illustrate from life.

An evangelist was in a certain city for a two-week meeting. He was asked by a friend to visit a woman in the hospital. She was dying with cancer. On the first visit, the patient was expecting the minister to pray for her. However, he felt the restraining of the Lord, "Don't pray for her." He was obedient and said to the woman, "I'm sorry I cannot pray for you." She responded somewhat disdainfully.

Upon being asked to return, the evangelist did so. Again the Lord warned him not to pray for the woman. This time he asked her, "How are you related to your pastor?"

This question brought about a torrent of pent-up anger. "Don't talk to me about him. I hate him! You don't know what he did to me. Don't ask me to forgive him!" It was later learned that for some fifteen years the woman had been harboring and nursing hate mixed with anger. She didn't want to give up her feelings, either.

Further urging from family and friends resulted in still another visit to the hospital. This time the patient was hanging onto life by .a bare thread. Reaching for the hand of the evangelist, she whispered, "Call my pastor." The pastor came; forgiveness was effected; there was joy and reunion. There was also healing as a result of that breaking and forgiveness. Do you catch the meaning of "shutting up until the last farthing has been paid"?

I, too, know what it means to be "shut up." If things are not right between my wife and me, I am in jail. Once I left town for a series of meetings when some matters were not straightened out between us. On the plane, the Judge and the Officer took over and went to work on me. I knew I had to fulfill my preaching engagement and could not possibly do that while in jail. As soon as we landed, I went to the hotel and got on the phone. When the connection was made, the first thing Judy said was, "I was waiting for your call." We both knew! The moment I agreed that I had been wrong, I was set free. The Kingdom of God is righteousness, peace, and joy. Once you are aware of the blessings these afford, you will do everything possible to insure their presence in your life.

Can you see where such awareness can have advantages? Do you see why one has to take care of the seed of anger so that it doesn't get a chance to grow? This kind of teaching can keep one from backsliding. If I take the attitude, "I don't need to take that from anybody!" when offended, the Judge says to the Officer, "Did you hear that?" The Officer replies, "I surely did." And then they both get on my case—and I land in a spiritual jail.

But if I respond with, "I'll leave my gift here at the altar and search out my brother and tell him I'm sorry," what is that doing for me? First, it is freeing me from judgment. It is also permitting resentments to be purged—if these are causing trouble. If it is rebellion, I find it broken; or if an independent spirit is the root cause, it is destroyed by a move toward reconciliation.

I may not want to say, "Brother, I need you," but I honestly do need my brother. I need him to help me deal with stumbling blocks to my spiritual progress. When I deal with anger in phase one, or even in phase two, I find I am free from the progression of anger and the painful consequences.

What if I am perpetually angry without a cause? I must admit that I am a hothead and cannot control my temper and realize something is wrong on the inside. The rule, "whosoever is angry . . ." is manifesting the fact that here is a character flaw that needs attention. No rationalizing ("It runs in the family . . . I'm not nearly as hotheaded as Uncle Bill or Deacon Brown."). I must say, *"There is something wrong with me. God, I need Your help."* The Law of Anger exposes my weakness.

In the world, anger may be taken as normal. We have all come up against vitriolic responses from motorists when caught in a traffic

snarl—and venomous comments while waiting in line for service—
and four-letter words flying around loose in order to unload anger.
We are even told by some psychologists it is good to explode and
get rid of pent-up resentments. It is true that we must rid ourselves
of these feelings, but Jesus gave us the better way. Root up the seed
before it has a chance to germinate.

Let's review Jesus' formula. First, there was the warning. *Beware!*
If you are angry with your brother without a cause, you are in danger.
You will find yourself in a series of progressive actions, each one
more dangerous than the former. You will find yourself doing and
saying things you had not intended. Therefore: When the Holy Spirit
reminds you of your ungodly conduct, leave your gift at the altar
and go at once and seek forgiveness. If the breach is allowed to
widen and deepen, the Judge and Officer will see to it that you are
shut up to the flow of spiritual blessings. And you won't be freed
until you see it His way, and do something about it.

Some people have been in jail ten—twenty—thirty years. Anger
is a spiritual cancer. It grows and it feeds on itself, and anything else
that comes into its path. This proves an expensive feast. The Kingdom
of God is righteousness, peace, and joy. You cannot know this kind
of living and at the same time hate your mother-in-law, your parents,
your employer, your enemies, or even that cantankerous neighbor.
Don't trade your inheritance rights for hatred, envy, or any other
reaction that will result in anger. You can go through an entire lifetime imprisoned by these thieves. It isn't always easy to forgive, but it
is *possible* and *profitable*.

Jesus' formula is the only way out of the prison house which anger builds around the one who indulges himself in this response. No matter how many psychologists' couches are pressed into service— regardless of how many pills, shots, and rest cures are prescribed— there is only one permanent cure: "I'm sorry."

The Law of Anger is designed to expose any weakness in this area. The object in exposing it is so that *we will know it!* Then we face the choice of following the advice of the King whose Kingdom we seek, or continuing in rebellion, resentment, or independence.

God is interested in the whole man. His command is to love Him with our whole heart, soul, and strength. We cannot know or trust our own hearts, souls, or strength until each has been brought into line with the will of God. God will not be satisfied until all the kinks are ironed out of our vacillating wills. He wants us brought into perfect alignment.

This is freedom as Jesus lived it. It is ours for the taking.

II THE LAW OF PURITY

And he opened his mouth and taught them, saying:

27 Ye have heard that it was said by them of old time, Thou shalt not commit adultery.

28 But I say unto you, That whosoever looketh on a woman to lust after her hath committed adultery with her already in his heart.

29 And if thy right eye offend thee, pluck it out, and cast it from thee: for it is profitable for thee that one of thy members should perish, and not that thy whole body should be cast into hell.

30 And if thy right hand offend thee, cut it off, and cast it from thee: for it is profitable for thee that one of thy members should perish and not that thy whole body should be cast into hell.

Matthew 5

No one can accuse Jesus of attempting to evade the issues of the day—His day, ours, or any in-between. *The Second Bylaw* He tackled was the seventh of the Ten Commandments: "Thou shalt not commit adultery." Probably no two areas of man's basic responses have inflicted more damage on society than murder and adultery. Jesus took His battle for the whole man right onto the battlefield of life as it really is.

Besides the intense practicality of His teachings, there was the equally intense personal application. "But I say unto you, *whosoever!*" Just as God's will is the unbreakable, unshakable iron bar by which we shall all be judged, so is the comprehensiveness of that word *whosoever*. It includes rich and poor—intelligentsia and uneducated—king and slave—male and female—everyone. *Whosoever* covers it all—young and old—married and unmarried—no exceptions! "Thou shalt not commit adultery."

Commandments are specific instructions. Jesus reiterated the fact that He knew that they knew the command about which He wished to speak to them: "Ye have heard . . . ." And to be certain that His hearers would not have their guards up against new teaching, He had previously warned them that He had not come to destroy their laws, but to fulfill them. How carefully he laid the groundwork. Then He went to work!

We are going to try to catch the implications of His interpretation of this most closely guarded of all social breaches. Even with our present blatant acceptance of sexual freedom, individuals and families shield themselves, and build facades against openly advertising involvement in this area. Parents, children, business reputations, possible social stigma—all these and many other considerations contribute to this attempt to cover up—hide—excuse sexual irregularities.

The two words used throughout Scripture to deal with sexual sins are *adultery* and *fornication*. Each has its own particular meaning, plus being comprehensive terms. *Adultery* usually refers to improper relations with a man or woman who is presently married. *Fornication* covers the same sexual relations outside the married state. However, these two terms are also used as all-inclusive expressions of wrong and perverted sexual relationships.

Jesus used the broader meaning of both words as He went to the root of the problem—which is where the trouble starts—the heart. Listen to this piercing statement from Him, as recorded in Luke 6:45: ". . . an evil man out of the evil treasure of his heart bringeth forth that which is evil."

The first item we might as well settle is that sex, in itself, is *not* evil. It is a God-given gift—stimulating—energizing—and one of the most joyful and satisfying relationships of life. That is how God intended it. It is not only His provision for procreation of the human race, but it is the basis of the family relationship, which itself is God-ordained. God instituted marriage and within its bonds, where sexual relationships are the normal outlet for the sexual drive, men and women find oneness and completeness. This is seen from the very beginning: "Therefore shall a man leave his father and mother, and shall cleave unto his wife: and they shall be one flesh" (Genesis 2:24).

The home is the basic structure of society. That is why Satan delights in undermining marriage relationships and causing havoc with thought patterns and emotional responses from earliest childhood right on through youth into adulthood. He carries on a relentless battle to destroy the freedom and enjoyment of sex which Jesus makes clear is God's will. Jesus also, places this freedom within the realm of possibility.

We mentioned earlier the Parable of the Sower, in which the Word of God was likened to a seed. We reviewed various possibilities that interfered with germination of the seed. One of these was, "the fowls of the air came and devoured it up" (Mark 4:4). In explaining the meaning of this portion of the parable, Jesus told the disciples, ". . . the devil taketh away the word . . . lest they believe . . ." (Luke 8:12). Now I had always pictured the fowls of the air as big black crows; but I have come to see it isn't necessarily the crows that steal the seed—sometimes it is canaries.

Canaries are small and attractive birds. They seem harmless and sing beautifully. None of the rush of dark wings or harsh caws of the crows—but the same insatiable appetite and same indiscriminate search for food, regardless of the source. We have all seen male and female canaries at work destroying the seed before it has a chance to take root and bear fruit. Many wonderful and powerful ministries have been destroyed by an illicit affair with some beautiful or handsome canary!

We are living in a day when the morality of our whole society says, "There is nothing wrong with sex as long as there are two consenting adults." Youth today is legally declared an adult long before his moral fibers have had opportunity to be strengthened to the point of judging cause and effect. Our television screens bombard adult, youth, and child alike with music set to the tempo of stirring the emotions—inflammatory words pour out suggestions—advertising blurbs link sex appeal to toothpaste, hair spray and breakfast foods. Nothing is too trivial or too sacred for Satan's attacks.

Really, the sexual appetite doesn't need all of this exposure, for in itself it is one of the most powerful human forces known to psychology, physiology, or sociology. But with the floods of pornography, x-rated movies and the wide-open outlets on our street corners, what chance does the young person have for forming a basis for sound moral judgments? The twisted, perverted sexual relationships that are flaunted before us make the presentation of Jesus' evaluation and recommendation for proper handling of sex an absolute must in the lives of believers and continuers.

When we, as individuals, become increasingly aware of this "must," we can boldly and confidently claim Jesus' teachings to meet our needs, as well as proclaim them to our contemporaries.

A letter from a teacher came across my desk recently. In desperation, she had written: "Bob, I teach fourth graders and what I see almost overwhelms me—third and fourth graders attempt to copulate in the school yard." Seeing is believing—even though it seems unbelievable to those of us who were pulling pigtails at that age. What conceptions of sex and marriage can children be expected to form out of a background that would result in the above kind of behavior?

Sexual magnetism has a tremendous drawing power—leashed and unleashed alike. Most of us have seen a little gadget that affords momentary amusement, as well as an excellent illustration of this magnetism we are probing. There are two little scottie dogs—black and white—and you get them on a smooth surface and toy around with them. First thing you know, they are automatically spinning around and drawn to each other—just like that!

That is often the way it happens with male and female. There have been times in counseling when a woman will say to me, "Mr. Mumford, I just don't understand why men are always chasing me." I do—and so do most of you reading this book. Sex is something like electricity—there is a positive and a negative charge. Any man or woman who is putting out a positive charge is open for trouble; not only open—but asking for it!

It isn't just the woman who gives off the positive charge, of course. However, there is a strange way women have of saying *no* when they mean *yes.* Also, there is a way of saying, "I'm on the make," without saying anything! There are mannerisms—ways of dress and ways of walk and talk that communicate availability and desire to the opposite sex. Have you ever heard this remark? "Why, I didn't say a word to him and he came right up to me and started getting fresh."

I know why—and you do, too. In such situations, I want to shout: "Listen, if you know and care anything about the Kingdom of God, turn off the electric! Shut it down before you get yourself in trouble!" This is true of the male, as well, of course.

In our day, it isn't just the man who is the aggressor, it is frightening but fact. But as aggressor, the male has ways of getting across his intentions and desires, too. There are both high and low sales pitches. Some come on with smooth, flattering words, and kindly invitations to continue advances. Others can figuratively undress a female with their eyes. The sexual current can light up in any given situation—church choir to barroom. It can, also, be recognized and warded off, just as turning off a light switch breaks the connection. Be alert and aware of the dangers. The magnetism given off opens one for continual sexual temptations. *We are responsible for controlling the outlet, as well as preventing wrong connections.* When Jesus' teachings are understood and accepted, the source is under control and the electric is no longer given off on your part; plus the fact that a strong radar system can be installed to detect signals— and repel them.

One such temptation and response is recorded by Harald Bredesen in his autobiography entitled *Yes, Lord.* The author frankly treats a life situation which depicts, not only how two adults can find themselves in an explosive situation, but how the fuse can be removed and damage avoided. He tells of an evening on the beach when everything conspired to envelop two know-betters in a compromising act. Suddenly the woman sat up and prayed, "For what we are about to do, forgive us, Lord."

Harald writes that when he saw how ludicrous Satan's temptation was, he burst out laughing. He closes the relating of the incident with, ". . . I praised Jesus aloud that He had saved me from my own stupidity. It was by no means *my* victory, but the sovereign intervention of God. I thought of the words of the Psalmist: 'Truly God is good to Israel, but as for me, my feet were almost gone, my steps had well nigh slipped . . . so foolish was I and ignorant: I was as a beast before thee.' "

Four conditions are mentioned in that short quotation used above from Psalms 72: *temptation, foolishness, ignorance, and the animal instinct.* All come into play in this matter of sex.

Temptation is very real. There is (1) the temptation to pursue wrong avenues for fulfilling one's sexual needs; (2) the temptation to fall into the trap set by another. Some Christian men have to go into homes to perform their jobs—plumbers, television repairmen, and the like. Many say it is frightening the situations they run into. They almost feel they should get another job! The woman in the home gives off the signal—the conditions are so conducive—bang! Sometimes there is a real need in the lives of the women involved. Husbands may be giving too much time to business or be on the road too often. Loneliness results. Satisfactions may be sought by both husband and wife outside their marriage.

Then along comes *foolishness.* Some people are in this type of operation just for the fun of it—it is a game to them.

Ignorance, too, plays its part. Even in the light of our early sex education in the schools and exposure in general, ignorance of the actual dangers involved and the strength of human desires once unleashed, can get one into serious trouble.

The phrase, "I was as a beast before thee," has been enacted before the eyes of God so many times that we wonder at His patience with us. In another phrase, this one from the Book of Romans, the writer paints the most painful picture of sexual deterioration ever drawn: "Wherefore God also gave them up to uncleanness through the lusts of their own hearts . . ." (Romans 1:24). Read chapter one of Romans and see how well acquainted the early continuers were with the sexual degradation of the society of their day.

To return to Jesus' treatment of the problem in Matthew 5, we see He begins His diagnosis of sexual sin on this same level—*lust in the heart.* After quoting the command, "Thou shalt not commit adultery," given "of old time" (longstanding and familiar to all), He continues with God's interpretation and understanding: "I say unto you . . . ."

Here He moves to the source of the trouble, "Whosoever looketh on a woman to lust after her . . ." (v. 28). What does the word, *lust,* involve? It is a very strong word and conveys the meaning of uncontrolled desire. This sounds like the progressiveness of anger, doesn't it? There is a similarity, for when a seed of desire is planted within the heart, there are two possibilities—and *only* two! (1) The seed can be stamped out at once; or (2) it can be fed, watered, and permitted to grow into a full-blown act.

So, we are examining a principle which says, "When a man (or woman) looks with uncontrolled desire upon one of the opposite sex, something needs to be done to bring that desire under control." Before we move into Jesus' suggested measures for dealing with the desire, we need to get a *few facts about lust* out into the open.

Normal desires can be satisfied. Lust cannot. It makes no difference how many men/women a lustful person becomes involved with, there is no lasting satisfaction. There is that increasing desire for more. Ten husbands or ten wives won't put out the fire. It is like drug addiction that moves on out to uncontrolled desire. Promiscuity in any area results in becoming sick and nauseated with the thing one has been lusting after. We all know that an overdose of anything, (including strawberry shortcake), is sickening.

Then there are *several types of persons* whose reactions to any kind of restrictions on sexual behavior need to be analyzed.

One is the person who says, "Well, Jesus says if I look with lust, I have already committed adultery. I might just as well go ahead with the act." It is true that Jesus said the first part of that response, but He certainly did not indicate the latter. He knew if lust were in the heart, lust would drive toward satisfaction of that craving. Jesus wants to get at the root, not to excuse our actions merely because we have strong impulses.

Second, there is the person who takes the pseudo-holy approach and tries to stifle his God-given privileges of being able to enjoy the beauty in one of the opposite sex without lusting. This often results in a life of frustration, becoming irritable and condemnatory. One is apt to lose the normalcy with which sex can be rightly handled.

Here is an instance of right handling. Two men are walking along a public beach—one is in his eighties, saintly but still very much alive to the enjoyments of life. His companion is a considerably younger man. Along come two bikini-clad girls—beautiful exposure! The younger man becomes embarrassed for his generation, wondering how the older man will react. To the former's surprise and delight, the remark, "Didn't God do a beautiful job?" brought the incident to a natural conclusion. This is freedom in the spirit—the looking and not lusting about which Jesus is talking.

A third person comes up with this response to Jesus' differentiation between lusting and looking. "I'm just too weak. God understands. After all, He gave me these urges." Yes, He did and He also gave the way to channel the urges. It is taught in schools, and by many psychiatrists, that sex is only a natural instinct and it was meant to have outlet when aroused. But God did not make men to be left at the mercy of animal instincts, as is propagated by such teachings. God made rules that will keep us safe and set us free. Men aren't meant to operate by *instinct,* but by *command.* They are free moral agents.

There are many and devious ways in which *this third person* operates—that one who attributes his actions to weakness. He may use an engagement ring and after the ring has been accepted, proposition with, "As long as we're engaged—and plan to get married—what's wrong with it?" Sorry to say, it often works.

Proverbs 6:20–26 has some pertinent advice along these lines. The remarks are prefaced with, "My son," giving the impression that the writer may have had some experience with his subject. He begins with, "Keep thy father's commandment . . . for the commandment is a lamp and the law is light; and reproofs of instruction are the way of life: To keep thee from the evil woman, from the flattery of the tongue of a strange woman."

Whether it's the man with the engagement ring (which may have been used on more than one or two occasions), or the one who tries less expensive tactics, flattery is often involved. If you are a lonely widow, he will tell you the things you want to hear. If you are a harried business man, that secretary may try some enticing words about "not being understood and appreciated by your wife." Anyone who wants another for sexual reasons, can weave some mighty honeyed word traps.

In verse 25 of Proverbs 6, we find that word we are working on— *lust*. "Lust not after her beauty in thine heart; neither let her take thee with her eyelids." Looking upon beauty with genuine appreciation and lusting after beauty's possible exploration and exploitation are two entirely different matters. Whether smooth words or long eyelashes, the aim is the same.

Verse 26 puts the aim into a stronger perspective: "For by means of a whorish woman a man is brought to a piece of bread: and the adulteress will hunt for the precious life." This applies to both men and women as being the "whorish" person—that one who purposefully goes about seeking satisfaction for his lustful passions.

Here they are on the hunt—for the "precious" life. Why not be satisfied with seeking out one of their own kind? Two reasons come to mind. One is that a virtuous woman, or a man who is trying to lead a clean life and be faithful to his wife—these persons are a special trophy to the hunter. Second, if you are a person who is trying to live according to Christian principles, Satan takes a special joy in placing temptation before you. If you decide to walk with Jesus in purity, you are going to meet these situations. It is something you will have to face and conquer. Satan would like nothing better than to see you seduced and then laughingly taunt you with, "You don't look much like a citizen of God's Kingdom to me!"

Verses 27 and 29 ask and answer a question that shows this to be exactly what will happen. Question: "Can a man take fire in his bosom and his clothes not be burned?" Answer: "So he that goeth in to his neighbour's wife, whosoever toucheth her shall not be innocent." Satan can use just the smell of smoke or a small spark to start a conflagration.

Eighteen years of observation and counseling along these lines, makes my conclusion coincide with that of the writer of Proverbs. *No one can play with fire and not get burned!* Those who "touch" with lust in their hearts are not innocent—there are guilt feelings that linger long after the pleasure subsides. We are living in a society that is deteriorating to the point where it has become necessary to take myriads of tranquilizers to "forget it all," and the spending of millions of dollars on psychiatrists' visits in the hope of getting some solution to our problems. But unless we can understand release, forgiveness, and healing in God, there can be no lasting solution.

Matthew 5:29, 30 presents the only lasting solution to lust. Divine surgery is necessary and *you* are the only one who can schedule the operation. We cannot do it by ourselves. We have spent quite a bit of time diagnosing the case. But, just as in treating physical ailments, the patient's background and symptoms must be thoroughly investigated and revealed. Then comes the Great Physician's prescription.

Rx: "If thy right eye offend thee, pluck it out and cast it from thee . . . And if thy right hand offend thee, cut it off, and cast it from thee . . . ." Strong measures! Who would want to try getting along with only one eye or only one hand? Yet Jesus continues, ". . . for it is profitable for thee that one of thy members should perish and not thy whole body should be cast into hell."

We know that Jesus' words are not to be taken literally, for that other eye can prove offensive; and the left hand may reach out to "touch" equally as greedily as the right one. Jesus is saying that if there is lust in your heart, you have two problems: the eye and the hand. Both are under control of the heart. If you have the temptation to look with lust, and we hope by now you see that this is not in the sense of, "Isn't she a beautiful woman—or isn't he handsome?" but the roving eye that penetrates beneath the surface—get rid of that eye! If you have the temptation to touch things that don't belong to you—and this includes heavy petting—get rid of that hand! For these temptations will eventually lead to the destruction of the whole body. This may include your business, your marriage (or prospects of marriage), your health, your spiritual progress—total!

The Constitution and Bylaws of the Kingdom of God were instituted to salvage men from total destruction. Jesus went to the cross and sacrificed His life that we might come into the Kingdom and live according to its concepts and precepts. Here is available forgiveness —acceptance—deliverance—healing—hope! "I am come that they might have life, and . . . have it more abundantly." This is Jesus speaking in John 10:10.

Included in that abundant life is freedom from becoming ensnared in another danger to which continuers are particularly susceptible and need to heed warnings. Did you ever hear of "spiritual affinity"? This usually results from mixed-up marriage relationships—a wife whose husband is not saved; a husband whose wife is not interested in prayer meetings, when prayer meetings are first on his list of priorities. Or there is the divorced person—the lonely widower—the young person struggling to stifle normal desires without accepting Jesus' recommendation for proper handling of sexual problems. There may be a real love of the Lord—an anointing—a joining of spirits in praise between two people of opposite sex who strike up an "affinity."

All who have experienced the moving of the Spirit must learn to carefully guard themselves from exposure to situations that could invite or initiate sexual temptations. The reason is that, as the Holy Spirit moves over one's whole being, that one is being quickened and made alive emotionally. The Spirit of the Lord moves over the same nervous system as does the sexual desire. Unless one is firmly established in the rules, this can lead to trouble.

There is even a false doctrine abroad under the guise of the possibility of a spiritual bride—soul mates—or a similar term which describes the affinity one experiences "in the Lord" for one of the opposite sex who is not his legal mate.

The soil for this subtle but effective snare is an obliteration of the distinction of the sexes by a wrong application of Paul's statement:

". . . there is neither male nor female." Thinking ourselves to be *above* sexual temptation and really desirous of the will of God, we assume ourselves safe.

Numerous wrecks and irreparable casualties—some known, but most unknown—testify to the validity of what I say.

Two people pray together (and I would warn against too close a relationship here between either members of the opposite sex, or the same sex), they get a "witness," and developments can be heard in these snatches of conversation: "Oh . . . I think I married the wrong man/woman . . . You and I pray together so perfectly . . . We could be a great witnessing team . . . Why not meet tonight for dinner at 9:30 and we'll go witness on the beach . . . Don't tell your wife, she wouldn't understand . . . We just want to talk about it to the Lord . . . He understands . . . ." The end result? Damage—degradation—default!

These understandings are important if we are going to walk before the Lord in purity. If we purpose in our hearts to follow the commands of Jesus, then even when we are tempted, we will look at the situation from a different point of view. If the law "Thou shalt not commit adultery,"—with all of its implications—is firmly established and accepted as a life-style, we will listen for and respond to the Lord's nudgings with, "Yes, Lord, I see that . . . I understand . . . I will obey."

The Apostle Paul, as well as Peter, stressed this understanding and response. They ran up against these same complications and used the same prescription.

1 Thessalonians 4:2, 3 For ye know what commandments we gave you by the Lord Jesus. For this is the will of God, even your sanctification, that ye should abstain from fornication.

2 Peter 2:1, 2 . . . there shall be false teachers among you, who privily shall bring in damnable heresies . . . . And many shall follow their pernicious ways; by reason of whom the way of truth shall be evil spoken of.

Has the truth ever been evil spoken of because of offenses in this area? We all know of stumbling blocks being placed in the paths of weaker brothers, and even of the trying of stronger faiths.

Yes, the things done in secret have a strange way of being proclaimed from housetops. Disasters have come to my attention that cause me to cry out, "Lord, I hope this doesn't get out!" But Luke 12:2 tells us such news has a way of getting around. "Hey, did you hear . . . ?" Sometimes the hidden secrets must be brought to light before the parties involved are willing to admit their guilt and turn from their sinful ways. The only person who can know the *privacy* of cleansing is the one who will say, "I have sinned—I have betrayed my marriage vows—I have been seduced—Lord—forgive me— cleanse me and heal me." When that is effected, the matter is put beneath the blood and into the sea of God's forgiveness never to be remembered against you. For this we are most grateful. He is a loving and concerned Father. He longs to bring our wills into alignment with His, saving us suffering and shame.

When Jesus spoke of plucking out an eye or cutting off a hand, He was saying, in effect, that there is no action too drastic to avoid the pain and remorse that sexual deviation brings. Is the Bylaw of Purity clearly understood? It is a rule of the Kingdom *for thy good.* If you are lonely—if you have sexual desires that are unmet—or if you are in danger of having lust burst the bonds of control—seek out someone whom you can trust. Confess to them and open yourself up for help and healing. If you are already in a situation that is dangerous, do anything possible to get out of it. Get free. Extract yourself. Nothing is too drastic a measure to insure escaping an adulterous involvement.

Freedom from sexual defilement constitutes a glorious victory. Every person is forced to grapple with this problem. Why not open it up to the Law of Purity and experience the peace and enjoyment God intends and provides?

III THE LAW OF FIDELITY

And he opened his mouth and taught them, saying:

31 It hath been said, Whosoever shall put away his wife, let him give her a writing of divorcement:

32 But I say unto you, That whosoever shall put away his wife, saving for the cause of fornication, causeth her to commit adultery: and whosoever shall marry her that is divorced, committeth adultery.

33 Again, ye have heard that it hath been said by them of old time, Thou shalt not forswear thyself, but shalt perform unto the Lord thine oaths:

34 But I say unto you, Swear not at all; neither by heaven; for it is God's throne:

35 Nor by the earth; for it is his footstool: neither by Jerusalem; for it is the city of the great King.

36 Neither shalt thou swear by thy head, because thou canst not make one hair white or black.

37 But let your communication be, Yea, yea; Nay, nay; for whatsoever is more than these cometh of evil.

Matthew 5

As we move into Bylaw Three, we review some of the principles of Kingdom learning and living. It is necessary from time to time to remind ourselves of the reason why we are so relentlessly pursuing the *intent and implications* of these truths Jesus is teaching. It is a fairly simple matter to surface-read truths and miss much of their value.

The Old Testament laws were engraved on tablets of stone. New Testament laws are to be engraved on the heart. The Old Testament prophets proclaimed that this was the aim of God—to place within the hearts of His people the laws of the Kingdom. Jesus came to make this possible. Belief in and acceptance of His Messiahship brings to man a new heart, which results in a desire to do God's will. The teachings of Jesus show us the way to move from desire to ability to do this will. By applying the rules and running the race according to them, we gradually bring our wills into alignment with God's.

The Constitution and Bylaws of the Kingdom pertain to the activity of God's people. We are to conduct ourselves differently from those outside the Kingdom rule. The new nature we received when we came into the Kingdom develops into new character— which results in Kingdom conduct. This is not an easy transition and must have a strong motive to keep us seeking the interpretation of the Bylaws and putting them into practice in our lives.

That motive was graphically presented by the Teacher in a parable—Matthew 13:45, 46: "Again, the kingdom of heaven is like unto a merchant man, seeking goodly pearls: Who, when he had found one pearl of great price, went out and sold all that he had, and bought it."

Note these key words: *seeking—great price—sold all*. All of them are relevant to our study.

Seeking   Jesus calls by desire. He gives us a choice. This entails knowledge of the price to be paid for involvement, and willingness to pay it. No one can put discipleship standards on another. Each person has to willingly accept them and walk in them.

Great price   Righteousness, peace, and joy—the pearl—is costly. Alignment of the whole man brings the pearl, but we must realistically take a good look at the price tag and decide if we are willing to make the sacrifice necessary to execute the transaction. Embracing the Bylaws is going to cost you—no discount prices or partial payment!

Sold all   This means top priority. All of us have many desires, demands, interests, opportunities—just as the pearl merchant had
many precious gems. But when we see—truly see—what God
has for us as presented in His Word, the possibility of attainment
becomes overwhelming and we gladly sell all and seek, thus obeying Jesus' command, "Seek ye first the kingdom of God . . ."
(Matthew 6:33).

In studying the *Bylaw of Fidelity,* it is not our intention to present a doctrinal thesis on marriage and divorce. We are approaching this high-blood-pressure area from the angle of relationship to
the Laws of the Kingdom of God. The Laws of Anger and Purity
have been investigated and if you have received new light on these,
you are well on the road to discovering the freedoms to be found
through applying the Law of Fidelity. Right in the middle of the
road, though, stand those three familiar roadblocks: Rebellion,
Resentment, and Independence. They are not impassable hurdles
once we are willing to pay the price for getting over them (or under
them—or around them), depending upon the particular needs and
abilities of each of us as individuals.

Jesus approached the teaching on Fidelity from the marriage/
divorce angle. It was a natural transition from the interpretation of
the Seventh Commandment, "Thou shalt not commit adultery."
Fidelity can be defined as faithfulness or trust. If fidelity were the
generally accepted law of the land, we could do away with many laws

which man has had to make to protect himself and his property against the worthlessness of his fellow man's word.

When someone comes to me and says, "I don't understand all this talk about rules. I've always heard about freedom *from* rules —that the truth would make us free from rules," I reply, "You are right: truth will—when applied!" Read again Galatians 5:22, 23 relating to true freedom. When we walk in the Spirit as Paul pictures, we will have no need for rules. But by learning the rules, as presented by Jesus, and applying them—then we free ourselves by aligning our wills with God's. This insures His ultimate aim—and ours—freedom. *This is the pearl of great price secured at great cost.*

One of the costs is coming down from our self-erected tree of protection. Any situation which involves more than one person, demands some common ground from which to move toward settlement. In marital problems, almost invariably the husband is up his tree and the wife is up hers. Neither will consider coming down until the other makes the first move toward giving in or giving up. A buildup or a flare-up can send one or both parties scurrying for a vantage point of self-defense. Resentments, rebellions, and independence can blind eyes, harden hearts, and unfit us—not only for a satisfactory marriage—but for any satisfactory degree of Kingdom living.

Divorce—or the legal dissolution of the marriage contract—is not only more prevalent today than in any other generation of human history, but it is also big business. The next ten years will bring increasing attack on the marriage relationship. Husbands and wives will suffer such a strain on their relationships that only those marriages where fidelity is the foundation stone will have real chance of survival.

As marriages continue to fall before Satan's onslaught, the basic structure of society is being destroyed. The fabric of society is interwoven and held together by the threads of home and family relationships. Many teachers in the social studies are saying that the family is no longer a viable institution. This battering at the ramparts of marriage is damaging enough but now many Christians and non-Christians are promoting the idea of dissolving the family relationship by entering into communes and living together. Problem marriages usually produce problem children. Pooling problems is not the solution, neither will a superficial concept of community act as a panacea. We must get to the source. Faithfulness and trust are necessary to satisfactory solutions.

God intended that marriage be a lasting relationship. When questioned about this later in His ministry, Jesus answered the query of the Pharisees with, ". . . What therefore God hath joined together, let not man put asunder" (Matthew 19:6).

One of the strongest barriers to harmony in our churches is the disharmony in the homes. The body of Christ is made up of cells, similar to the human body. Husband and wife form one cell, with its nucleus and protoplasm. If we have three hundred "cells" in a church and two hundred fifty of them are infected—the body is diseased. We might call this cell inflammation *cellulitis*. Most church groups suffer from spiritual cellulitis!

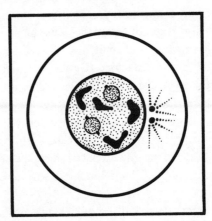

Fidelity is essential to cementing any contract into a working instrument. A lawyer friend once said to me, "Bob, I don't know of any legal contract that a person cannot get out of if he wants to badly enough." This reminds me of a personal experience which has all the overtones of a marriage contract.

As far back as I can remember, I wanted to join the navy. My family background was navy. I kept scrapbooks as a boy and could name many of the ships—knew how much weight and armament they carried—I could hardly wait until I was old enough to join up— and I spent time worrying that they might not take me. But they did!

A fellow I knew signed up at the same time I did. First thing on the agenda was a swearing in. After questioning us to be sure we knew what we were doing, came the Constitution—the flag—the witness. "Do you solemnly swear . . . ?" "Yessir, I do!" And we were in!

Then came boot camp. Most everyone knows what that involves. There were times when we wondered if we would survive. One of us didn't. After eleven months, the other fellow was discharged—undesirable discharge. It was his desire—his attitude—that resulted in the dissolution of the contract made at swearing-in time. He hated the navy—the drill instructors—the food—everything and anything. It was *attitude*. We were both subjected to the same pressures but one was full of resentment, rebellion, and independence. There were times when one or all of these three hindrances faced me. But how we met these reactions made the difference.

One day I said to myself, "Mumford, you are in this thing for four years. You are either going to have to yield to it or let it get the best of you. You are going to have to break, or the navy is going to break you." I made my choice to stay and before long I was "navy" all the way.

Marriage is like a hitch in the navy in many ways. It's a good idea to go into it with your eyes open. We've all been exposed to the institution of marriage and have some idea of the responsibilities and rewards. After the decision is made to sign up, along comes the swearing in. "Do you solemnly promise . . . ?" "Yessir, I do!" Then it's boot camp for both. Here, too, attitudes make the difference.

Attitude regarding the marriage relationship falls into two categories. The first one is the *attitude* with which a couple *enters into the marriage contract*. If the two feel the marriage is the will of God for their lives, then the fact should be accepted that God knows just what kind of life partner you need. If he/she doesn't turn out to be what we *thought* we needed, we ought to give God credit for know-ing what we needed. Husband and wife are meant to complement— or complete—one another. Husband, that wife is tailor-made to bring about the best in you. Wife, believe it or not, that husband will provide all that is lacking in your personality and makeup. (I dealt extensively with this in *Living Happily Ever After*.)

Second, the realization of the oneness depends upon attitude. The way in which you meet the frictions and fractions that you two may face as your lives merge, will form the proving ground for God's perfect will. If you feel the going is too rough, you can do as my navy buddy did—get an undesirable discharge. We might liken di-vorce to military service AWOL—Absent Without Leave. You can bail out. Our civil laws make this a fairly simple matter.

Divorce laws in Israel, A.D. 30, were very permissive. Listen to Deuteronomy 24:1, which was still in effect:

> When a man hath taken a wife, and married her, and it come to pass that she find no favour in his eyes, because he hath found some uncleanness in her, then let him write her a bill of divorce-ment, and give it in her hand, and send her out of his house.

(That term, "uncleanness," covered a lot of territory. She might not have ironed the pillow slips or fixed the pottage like her mother-in-law. Just write it on a paper saying, "You are now divorced," and send her out of the house.) What about remarriage? Deuteronomy 24:2–4 goes on to say:

> And when she is departed out of his house, she may go and be another man's wife. And if the latter husband hate her, and write her a bill of divorcement, and giveth it in her hand, and sendeth her out of his house; or if the latter husband die, which took her to be his wife; Her former husband, which sent her away, may not take her again to be his wife . . . .

Both parties of the divorcement were free to remarry, except to be remarried to each other, after another marriage had been in effect.

The Jews of Jesus' day liked their divorce laws. It was a very convenient arrangement. In Matthew 19:3–8 some of them came to Him asking questions on this matter—hoping His reply would get Him into trouble for trying to make changes in their easy way of nullifying the marriage vow. And that is just what happened.

QUESTION   Is it lawful for a man to put away his wife for every cause?

ANSWER   Have ye not read, that he which made them at the beginning made them male and female, and said, For this cause shall a man leave father and mother, and shall cleave to his wife: and they twain shall be one flesh? What therefore God hath joined together, let not man put asunder.

QUESTION   Why did Moses then command to give a writing of divorcement, and to put her away?

ANSWER   Moses, because of the hardness of your hearts, suffered [or permitted] you to put away your wives: but from the beginning it was not so.

Are you beginning to understand why the scribes and Pharisees were so anxious to do away with the new Teacher and His kind of teaching? Jesus had told them He had come to fulfill the law—give it the true intent of God. God never intended divorce—from the beginning it was not so!

Why then Moses' divorce laws? Jesus made it clear why: *because of the hardness of men's hearts.* Do you see that divorce is not God's intention, but because of man's contentions?

What about today's divorce laws? Still due to man's hardness of heart! This, in turn, causes many bleeding hearts. And when you deal in human problems and emotions, it is too complex to be solved by one answer. Hardness of heart produces complications too deep to be solved with legalistic Band-Aids. Some of the approaches we, as Christians, take to the situations caused by hardness of hearts add to the difficulties rather than aiding those who find themselves "put away for every cause."

Jesus was after a deeper principle in this matter. Let's go after it. Going back to Matthew 5:31, 32, we find Jesus giving only one exception clause for dissolving the marriage contract, ". . . saving for the cause of fornication." Do you remember we said both the words adultery and fornication were used, in their broader sense, to mean all forms of sexual sin? If the marriage partner was unfaithful, that, according to Jesus, permitted divorce.

Jewish wives were very seldom unfaithful to their marriage vows. The penalty for unfaithfulness (adultery) was stoning to death. When divorce was so easy and punishment for adultery so severe, it is understandable why wives, as a rule, were faithful to their husbands.

In the Old Testament a wife could be "put away" for anything— if she just did not any longer find favor in her husband's eyes. Jesus said they were not permitted to do this anymore—not in Kingdom living, at least. He told them God had intended that they go into marriage with their eyes opened to the fact that this was a lifetime commitment.

Also in the Old Testament the penalty for adultery was stoning. Jesus said when a mate is unfaithful, you can "put her away," for if that mate transgresses the marriage vow, that one is just as good as dead. There is to be no stoning right on the spot (taking judgment into man's hands). The right to judge and punish is in God's hands in the new Reign. In fulfilling their laws, He *restricted* the reason for divorce to unfaithfulness, and also *lessened* the penalty— reserving it to Himself. He is going to administer—not man—with his limited understanding and possible hardness of heart.

Paul handled some problems arising from man's hardness of heart in 1 Corinthians 7:12–15 (AMPLIFIED). He is speaking to those "un-equally yoked together"—believer to unbeliever.

To the rest I declare, I, not the Lord [for Jesus did not discuss this], that if any brother has a wife who does not believe [on Christ], and she consents to live with him, he should not leave *or* divorce her. And if any woman has an unbelieving husband,

and he consents to live with her, she should not leave *or* divorce him. For the unbelieving husband is set apart (separated, withdrawn from heathen contamination and affiliated with the Christian people) by union with his consecrated (set-apart) wife; and the unbelieving wife is set apart *and* separated through union with her consecrated husband . . . . But if the unbelieving partner [actually] leaves, let him do so; in such [cases the remaining] brother or sister is not morally bound. But God has called us to peace.

Paul saw what Jesus was driving at in His teaching on the Kingdom. He realized that an unbelieving partner could make life very difficult. But there was always the possibility of helping the unbelieving one come into a new relationship to God through love and understanding. Also, in showing love and understanding, the believer is being changed, too. Paul says, in effect, "Don't bail out. Stay in there as long as you can. You will find that Jesus will do something in your life that will more than compensate for not throwing in the sponge." As the believer trusts God, the unequally yoked marriage can be brought into harmony. Opportunity is being afforded for Him to break all hardness of heart on both sides and transform the marriage.

Only Jesus knows the hearts of men—the hardness—the hurts —the possibilities for change. He knows, too, that attitudes make the difference. Perhaps this paraphrase of His interpretation of marriage will impress us enough to engrave the meaning of it upon our hearts—married and unmarried alike.

God said, I made these two—male and female—so that she would leave her family and he would leave his, and they would come together and forsake all others, that they might become one flesh—no longer two, but one. It was my desire that they should become so completely "one" that no man could separate them. This is what I intended from the beginning, but because

of the hardness of your hearts, you want to do it another way.
Go ahead—if this is what you really want.

Matthew 19:4–8 (paraphrased)

That last sentence is a sad commentary. The one desiring release
from the marriage vow may triumphantly shout, "I'm free at last!"
But really he is not. All he holds in his hand is an undesirable discharge—bailed out without changing—the loser—in the heat of the
battle, a dropout. There are complications and complexities that result. There may be another attempt at marriage. Some have the
third . . . fourth . . . fifth go-round—usually resulting in the
same old story because of the same attitude.

*If you are still in there hanging on, ask the Lord to change your
attitude, if it needs it.* Search out the situation until you get some
solidity under your feet—then stand upon that conviction. *Attitude
gives latitude for God to effect change in both parties.*

Moving from the teachings on fidelity in relation to the marriage
vows, we find Jesus enlarging on the principle to include all other
statements of intent. He began, as usual, with the basis of operation
then in effect. Reread Matthew 5:33–37 of our Law of Fidelity.

Evidently the Jews were undergirding their vows to each other
by calling into witness the holy things of their day: the heaven—
the earth—Jerusalem—their own heads. Today, vows made in public are usually made by placing one's hand upon a Bible; or in common parlance, we hear the phrase, "I swear on a stack of Bibles."
Seems man hasn't changed much, has he?

Jesus again is aiming at attitude. All the swearing by things holy
will never make a man's vow valid. It is the *attitude* with which that
man enters into contract. The Teacher tied it all up with the simple
admonition, "Let your communication be yes or no. Anything more
is unnecessary and is only added to undergird questionable intentions or to impress others with your integrity. It will not change
your character or intent."

We are going to look at advice from three portions of Scripture to see how God pointed out the importance of fidelity in making and keeping oaths.

(1) *Psalms 15* begins with the question, "Who shall abide in thy tabernacle?" In reply, nine qualities of character are listed and the conclusion is: "He that doeth these things shall never be moved." The first three qualities are, "He that walketh uprightly, and worketh righteousness, and speaketh the truth in his heart" (v. 2). This sounds like Old-Testament-Kingdom teaching, doesn't it? David goes on to say, "He that sweareth to his own hurt, and changeth not" (v. 4).

What does this mean to you? To me, it might be illustrated by this incident. One man agrees to pay ten dollars for an item of merchandise. Upon receiving the item, he finds it is only worth about five dollars. But he pays the original agreed-upon price of ten dollars because of his word given at the time of the purchase. However, knowing he is the loser, he most certainly will not enter into agreement with this particular merchant again—unless there is a change in his way of conducting his business.

(2) *Ecclesiastes 5:1–6* has words of wisdom about making vows and the weakness of man to keep them. It begins with a warning, "Be careful when you go before God." (We are paraphrasing and we hope that you will read the words of Solomon the "Preacher," for yourself.) "Don't be rash with your mouth, and don't be hasty to make vows to God. When you do, don't defer paying it, for God has no pleasure in fools. Pay what you vowed. It is better that you should not vow at all than that you should vow and not pay."

Have you ever made a vow to God which you found difficulty in keeping? Beware of a voice that urges you to "make deals" with God. The Enemy is always on the prowl. He would love to have you say, "God, if you do such and such I'll promise to read ten chapters in the Bible every day (or tithe 25 percent of my income) and so forth." Then the Enemy seeks to raise every possible (and seemingly impossible) circumstance to make that vow invalid.

(3) *James 5:12* answers this question. What happens to the one making the vow?

> But above all things, my brethren, swear not, neither by heaven, neither by the earth, neither by any other oath: but let your yea be yea; and your nay, nay; lest ye fall into condemnation.

James's advice came some years later than that of Jesus, but evidently men were still swearing by heaven and earth. James reiterates the advice about letting one's yes be *yes,* and his no be *no.* And he concludes with an explanation on the advice given in Ecclesiastes about it being better not to vow than to vow and not follow through on your agreement. *Condemnation will result.* This can be a set trap. Satan will do everything possible to make it impossible for you to keep your vows.

So, after considering words from David, Solomon, Jesus, and James, we gather it is best to be very careful in making vows. Don't let our mouths get us into trouble; and let us not say we make any vows in error—not realizing all that is involved. Let us live one day at a time, permitting our words to carry weight. Let our words be few, both toward the Lord and toward men, for our whole society hangs on the worth of men's words!

It is well, also, to watch loose words and exaggerations. Why? This releases us from the tyranny of trying to recall what we have said to someone in order to impress or persuade. It leaves us free to be constructive in conversation—not defensive or indecisive. Jesus' truths *will* make us free. In turn, so will our own truths. We will never be tied down with unfulfilled vows and broken oaths if we take the Law of Fidelity seriously. Let our yes be *yes;* and our no be *no.*

◇◇

IV   THE LAW OF FLEXIBILITY

◇◇

And he opened his mouth, and taught them, saying:

38   Ye have heard that it hath been said, An eye for an eye, and a tooth for a tooth:

29   But I say unto you, That ye resist not evil: but whosoever shall smite thee on thy right cheek, turn to him the other also.

40   And if any man will sue thee at the law, and take away thy coat, let him have thy cloke also.

41   And whosoever shall compel thee to go a mile, go with him twain.

42   Give to him that asketh thee, and from him that would borrow of thee turn not thou away.

Matthew 5

Are you beginning to feel the probing is getting deeper and problems growing more demanding? If so, you are 100 percent correct! Jesus is placing before His hearers problems which present the necessity for choices in the everyday exchange of life. Through new insights into ourselves, and through a new dependence upon God, we move toward the freedom of Kingdom living. Remember, it is *you* who needs these laws—not the other fellow!

We begin study of this particular Bylaw with consideration of the words flexible and inflexible—and how they relate to us personally. As we have just stated, it is vital that we apply the teachings to ourselves. For, unless we are ready and willing to do this, the seed is falling by the wayside and the canaries—crows—vultures are reaping the benefit instead of permitting the truths to find lodgment, take root, and bring forth fruit for the Kingdom of God. Look now at these words:

> *Flexible: pliable, supple, elastic, yielding.*
> *Inflexible: brittle, hard, unyielding, rigid.*

From just a cursory glance at these meanings, we may be apt to place ourselves in the flexible category; but as we see what Jesus considers true and desirable flexibility, we may change our minds. It is my hope that we may also change our ways.

A dead branch is inflexible and snaps when you bend it. A fossil is a piece of organic matter that failed to make the change and it has become crystallized and inflexible. A piece of hard clay is unyielding —but with squeezing and the warmth of pressure, it can become soft, pliable, and usable. Romans 9:21 asks the question, "Hath not the potter power over the clay . . . ?" God takes us—hard, stiff, and cold—and begins to work on us. As He does, it is amazing how He will take us from one situation into another that will bring us into His desired state of flexibility.

In Philippians 4:11–13, Paul tells us, ". . . I have learned . . . . I know both how to be abased and how to abound . . . . I can do all things through Christ which strengtheneth me." Paul *learned* by the situations in which he found himself to be flexible, finding he could do all things through his Strengthener—Jesus Christ. So must we.

As usual, we find Jesus saying, "Ye have heard . . . ." This time it was the accepted way of handling personal offenses: ". . . an eye for an eye, and a tooth for a tooth." Retaliation is a *natural* response —usually carried to extremes, exacting double or triple for the injustice. This "eye for an eye" was really a restraint—demanding that man not go as far in retaliating as his human nature might drive him. It was, in fact, protection for the one causing the injury, as well as the restraint needed by the offender not to go too far. As was evident in the Old Testament laws for handling divorce, this, too, was permitted because of the hardness of men's hearts. It was not the Kingdom way in which to handle the matter.

Jesus said, "Resist not evil!" That is a difficult assignment. But it is not in the *natural* man to live and act according to the Laws of the Kingdom. That is why man needed a new birth with its *new nature*. The *new nature* is capable of seeing new light and hearing new truth

—and of changing character and conduct. And God sends situations that will effect the change!

The Teacher follows His command to "resist not evil," with four offenses that would *naturally* result in retaliation; a slap on the face —a law suit—mandatory servitude—favor-seeking. Then He follows with four substitute reactions: Turn the other cheek—Give the one suing you more than he requires—Go the second mile—Don't turn away from those asking favors. In the light of such stringent suggestions, are you about ready to decide you are rather inflexible after all? These responses *are not only unnatural—they are almost unthinkable!* Let's examine them one by one.

FIRST SITUATION   If someone strikes you on the right cheek:
SOLUTION   Turn to him the other also.

This true story from the mission field shows the effect of such unnatural reaction. Two heathen Chinese young men found a New Testament and began reading it on their own. In Matthew they found the above situation and solution. The next time they went to one of the mission home meetings, they went up to the missionary and asked, "Sir, are you a Christian?" Upon being assured that he was, one of the youths slapped him on the right cheek. Then they both stood aside—waiting to see what would happen.

Somehow the Lord gave grace to meet the situation and the missionary calmly turned the other cheek toward the offenders. The two began excitedly talking to each other in Chinese and we can imagine the conversation went something like this, "Say, he must be the real thing!" (Which makes me wonder if it had happened to me if I would have failed the test.)

Now, *why* would the Lord ever let someone strike you on the cheek? The Lord sees resentment, rebellion, independence inside and knows how to get these reactions to manifest themselves. Sometimes we are oblivious to the fact that there are buried areas of this type and we must have proof before we can accept that fact. When they surface, we are afforded opportunity to free ourselves from a spirit

of revenge. Wouldn't it be great to be permanently freed from the seething desire to avenge ourselves—free to accept situations that, under natural circumstances, would spill hate and vengeful desires into the stream of our lives?

God permitted a situation to develop in my life which brought home forcibly my own resentment, resulting in a near outburst—and a needed lessson.

We all meet up with persons who don't like us—in fact with some who thoroughly dislike us! One such was a member of a church where I was pastoring. One day she came to me and let loose her dislike with words that sizzled and burned. For a while I stood and took it quite at ease and in control of the situation. She raved and ranted and I took it with an "I am being persecuted for Jesus' sake" look on my face.

Unable to stand it any longer, the woman right out spit in my face. Something within me shifted into automatic! Just out of the navy, I cocked back and clenched my fist—that old navy haymaker was on the way. When I looked down and saw that fist and felt that tensing of muscles, I was overcome with conviction and guilt. For days I could scarcely believe that reaction had been within me. All my life I had nurtured a protectiveness for woman—with a mother and five sisters at home! Anyone who would ever hit a woman was less than a man in my estimation. And yet I came that close! God wanted to show me what was deep within my spirit. No one could have ever convinced me of its presence—but the situation did. *God sends situations to teach and reveal.*

But do we always learn? Who needs to turn the other cheek? The one who retaliates. Why? There is something within that spirit which needs breaking and correcting. We must keep turning the other cheek *until* we are delivered from that response. God wants to free us from a spirit of revenge, and this Bylaw will insure results. Remember, it is we who need this law.

Two situations from Scripture will help us to see how this law works.

John 18:22, 23   "And when he had thus spoken, one of the officers which stood by struck Jesus with the palm of his hand, saying, Answerest thou the high priest so? [*And Jesus turned the other cheek*.]" (No, that is not what the Scripture tells us. Here is how the story goes): "Jesus answered him, If I have spoken evil, bear witness of the evil [tell me what I have said]; but if [I have spoken] well, why smitest thou me?"

Acts 23:1–5   "And Paul, earnestly beholding the council, said, Men and brethren, I have lived in all good conscience before God until this day. And the high priest Ananias commanded them that stood by him to smite him on the mouth. [*And Paul turned the other cheek*.]" (Again, that is not what we are told. Let us pick up the story in verse 3): "Then said Paul unto him, God shall smite thee, thou whited wall: for sittest thou to judge me after the law, and commandest me to be smitten contrary to the law? And they that stood by said, Revilest thou God's high priest? Then said Paul, I wist not, brethren, that he was the high priest: for it is written, Thou shalt not speak evil of the ruler of thy people."

Here are three men—Jesus, Paul, and Bob Mumford. Why didn't Jesus turn the other cheek? He didn't need to. There was nothing in His spirit that needed changing. There was no resentment, rebellion, or independence in his response. He was free; and without any inward spirit of retaliation, He could call His offenders to task.

What about Paul? In the first instance, his response—though sting-ing—was not uttered in a spirit of resentment, rebellion, or independence. Before God, it was a justifiable reaction in calling to task his offenders. In the second instance, when he was accused of reviling God's high priest, Paul apologized and stood under the law of his people.

Do you see that had I responded with the same words in the same situations there might have been burning resentment at the treatment I was receiving? *Attitudes determine acceptable responses.*

SECOND SITUATION   If someone sues you for your coat:
SOLUTION   Give him your cloke also.

When we are served notice that someone is taking us to court to sue us, what is the natural reaction? Get the best lawyer we can and show them a thing or two! Listen to what Paul has to add on this subject in 1 Corinthians 6:6–9: "But brother goeth to law with brother . . . . Now therefore there is utterly a fault among you, because ye go to law one with another. Why do ye not rather take wrong? why do ye not rather suffer yourselves to be defrauded . . . . Know ye not that the unrighteous shall not inherit the kingdom of God . . . ?"

Well, why not? There is something within us that rises up and says, "Who does he think he is, treating me like this? I'll show him!" Those same old hindrances to Kingdom living—resentment, rebellion, and independence.

Suppose my neighbor thinks my property line is two feet over the line of his property; and he proposes taking me to law about the matter. My first inclination is to prove in court his guilt in the assumption. But the Lord says, "Better get a surveyor and give that neighbor four feet." Why? Better for me—better for my neighbor.

Suppose I sell a friend a used car for two hundred fifty dollars. He thinks I said two hundred dollars and refuses to pay me any more. Shall I take him to small claims court and get my rightful price? or, if my spirit is one of revenge, would it be better to offer him the fifty dollars' difference?

Recently, our younger son was hit with a car. The hospital expenses were all taken care of by the party in the offending car. But then our lawyer who was handling the protective procedures, said, "Well, shall we take him to the cleaners?" I had to beg off of that one, for I knew if such action were instituted, I would be the one who would be taken to the cleaners in the long run. Are you beginning to see how this works? Let's look at our next situation/solution.

THIRD SITUATION   If someone compels you to go a mile:
SOLUTION   Go with him two miles.

This situation actually existed in Jesus' day. His hearers knew very well what He was talking about—and how unlikely such a response would be!

Palestine was under Roman rule and a Roman soldier could rightfully compel a Jew to carry his pack for one mile. The soldiers were self-contained units and the pack carried was heavy. We can well imagine the burning resentment with which a Jew stooped and shouldered that pack. The whole mile was probably spent grumbling and cursing; and when it was completed, the pack would be thrown on the ground with more cursing. This would elicit a laugh from the soldiers, for they delighted in the compulsory servitude.

Can you picture the surprise of one of the Roman soldiers if at the end of one mile the Jew came up with, "Do you mind if I carry this another mile? I haven't obtained the victory over this yet." There probably isn't one person reading this book who hasn't found himself in a situation where a second mile wasn't needed *to be able to accept what seemed to be an injustice.* But Jesus tells us this second mile will result in "righteousness, peace, and joy!"

I found this to be true while helping to dig the foundation for a new church. I was pastor, and about fifteen of us had agreed to work on the foundation. For a while we all pitched in and the pickaxes were swinging. Then one man left . . . then a couple of more . . . until I was the only one still swinging. The axe handle got closer to the ground with every swing (along with my disposition). "Who do they think I am . . . !" About that time the Lord spoke to me and

inquired for whom I was digging. I assured Him that it was for Him
—but I kept on letting anger mount with every swing.

Finally the Lord returned and asked, "Bob, if these men never
came back and helped you, would you dig on?"

Then it dawned on me what He was saying to me; and I replied,
"Lord, I am not a hireling. Nobody can hire me. I'm doing this because You asked me to do it. Thank You for the privilege of digging
for You." Joy welled up within me and even though the fourteen men
returned to pick up the work, it really wouldn't have made any difference if they had or not. Joy had come to my heart!

> FOURTH SITUATION   If someone persists in asking favors
> from you and borrowing from you:
> SOLUTION   Continue to give and lend to him and do not
> turn him away.

All of us have possessions which we particularly cherish and hesitate lending to others. With me, it was my car. And it seemed anyone
and everyone was wanting to borrow my car. It wasn't easy to graciously hand over the keys, but I kept at it until I was free from that
resentment that would rise within me when a request came. But the
law worked. You see, *we* need to keep giving until we are free from
reaction; then we can say *no* with complete freedom—knowing we
are not in bondage to a fear of loaning our car. Now when a request
comes to borrow my car, and I feel the person is not responsible, I
can say so with all genuineness—no resentment. No need to lend if
circumstances dictate to the contrary.

How about a housewifely illustration? A knock comes on the door,
"I'm the lady next door. Can I borrow a cup of sugar?" Of course
the answer is yes. But suppose this same knock and this same request
comes every day or so. Soon the housewife finds herself wondering,
"Don't you ever go to the store?"

Have you caught the intent of this Law of Flexibility? Do you see
that to make the law work, you are required to give cup of sugar after
cup of sugar until *you* get the victory and there is finally no resent-

ment when the familiar knock and request come? About the tenth day and ten cups later, you find yourself saying, "Hi, it's good to see you [and mean it]. I've been a little hostile about all this borrowing, but I want you to know that I really love you and don't have to give you sugar any more. I'm free."

These four situations, with Jesus' solution, form the Law of Flexibility. The Lord keeps working in these areas until He knows we are free—and we know it, too. Jesus and Paul knew there was no resentment, rebellion, or independence in their responses. They were free to respond in love—and yet in the sternness which the situation demanded. The response Jesus had in mind was not a "Well, I am a Christian and I can't talk back" response. We can talk back if our spirit is right and the situation calls for a stand or explanation.

This lesson is learned progressively. Its learning will help you in everyday situations and each time you gain a victory, you find yourself increasingly freed from little irritations and big confrontations as well. Once the pattern is established, responses are natural in the unnatural realm. You will find yourself living in an atmosphere of *"I'd rather take the loss and learn the lesson!"* There will come a time when you will not need to turn the other cheek—give your cloke—go the second mile—or continue to lend. You will be able to meet every situation free of resentment, rebellion, and independence. Then you will be free to decide what solution is in the best interest of the Kingdom when situations arise. If turning the other cheek will help your brother, you will do it—not because there is any need to, but because your spirit directs this is the best plan of action for the situation.

The Law of Flexibility offers wonderful compensations. You will lose all dread of people and problems, for through Jesus' strength you can meet life head-on and experience personal victory. This is worth every slapped cheek, lost cloke, or second mile!

V THE LAW OF IMPARTIALITY

And he opened his mouth, and taught them, saying:

43 . . . Ye have heard that it hath been said, Thou shalt love thy neighbour, and hate thine enemy.

44 But I say unto you, Love your enemies, bless them that curse you, do good to them that hate you, and pray for them that despitefully use you, and persecute you;

45 That ye may be the children of your Father which is in heaven; for he maketh his sun to rise on the evil and on the good, and sendeth rain on the just and on the unjust.

46 For if ye love them which love you, what reward have ye? do not even the publicans the same?

47 And if ye salute your brethren only, what do ye more than others? Do not even the publicans so?

48 Be ye therefore perfect, even as your Father which is in heaven is perfect.

Matthew 5

Probably the first response to a command given to a child is, *"Why, Daddy?"* As adults, this is likewise our instant reaction. When a law is enacted, we want an explanation before we obey. The responses, whether to the child ("Because I said so."), or to the adult ("Because the government deems it necessary."), are seldom enough in themselves to motivate compliance.

Jesus seems to have taken these human reactions into consideration in giving this *Law of Impartiality*. He interjects into this presentation very specific reasons for being impartial.

First of all, the *why* of the Kingdom Bylaws is for one purpose— to reveal ourselves to ourselves. *Why* is this necessary? We are all prone to evaluate our actions and motives according to the human or natural basis. God wants to show us how our motives and actions look to Him—according to the new nature, character, and conduct of Kingdom living. The initial incision, and the picture we get of ourselves under His microscope, can be most painful. But this new view affords the springboard for change.

In the *Law of Impartiality,* we have a barometer which registers the degree of maturity to which we have attained in the Kingdom. It is how we treat our enemies that reveals the changes that have been taking place in our lives—thus indicating the degree of maturity which we have reached. Here is an outline of the method Jesus used in handling this lesson.

(1) Law of Impartiality—vs. 43, 44
(2) Reason for the Law—v. 45a
    [Illustration—v. 45b]
(3) Comparison of Two Levels of Treatment—vs. 46, 47
(4) Concluding Command—v. 48a
(5) Comparison to the Ideal—v. 48b
(6) Summary

(1) *The Law of Impartiality* begins in the now-familiar way: "Ye have heard it hath been said . . . ." At the time of this original law, "Thou shalt love thy neighbor and hate thine enemy," the line of demarcation between neighbor and enemy was dramatically drawn. When the children of Israel moved into the Promised Land they found "enemies" all around as they laid claim to the territory into which God led them. Anyone who interfered with their progress was considered an enemy; those who accepted the newcomers were categorized as neighbors.

Over the years the line of demarcation became erased by the human element. Anyone who displeased or provoked a person could find himself tagged ENEMY. We are always on the alert to protect our personal property and private pleasures. We come to "hate" anyone who interferes with personal progress. Friends and neighbors can quickly become enemies if they offend—do not agree with us—or irritate us.

Notice the progression of the responses Jesus recommends, as well as those of the enemy's actions.

Love—bless—do good—pray for them.
Those who curse you—hate you—despitefully use you—persecute you.

Notice, too, that Jesus starts His list of responses with *love*. We might think this a backward approach—that we would gradually learn to love if we started by praying for our enemies and trying to do good toward them. Not so, says Jesus.

There are four different Greek words used for our one English *love*. Jesus made His choice of the four very plain. For the benefit of comparison, we look at the four.

(*a*) *Eros:* this begins in the emotions (usually associated with the sexual desire) and bends man's will.
(*b*) *Storgos:* family or mother-type of love.
(*c*) *Phileo:* brotherly, friendly love. It is reciprocal in function.
(*d*) *Agape:* God's love! *This begins in the will and bends the emotions*—just the opposite of *Eros*. If we begin with God's love, then by His grace, we will determine to love that person because of a desire to please God. Soon our emotions are changed, and we find we are truly loving that person.

Can you see how utterly impossible the task would be if we started out with any of the other three kinds of love for an enemy? How could we bless that one—pray for him—do good toward him? It would only be surface placation; there would not be true love motivating our actions. But when we have God's love, *agape,* as the beginning—the praying, blessing, and doing good bring about the change, and we find hate is not an element determining reaction or action. It has been erased. Love is a command and God is not telling us to do something we cannot do. Why should He want us to bless someone who is persecuting us? *To free us from hate, which is a debilitating response.*

Loving isn't always easy. In fact, it seldom is. But it has its rewards. During one of my summer vacations from college, I took a job with a surveying crew. I was the new man on the job and they delegated to me all the unpleasant assignments. Somehow I got all the yards where people had dogs—where the poison ivy grew—and other distasteful assignments. Sticky situations? Mumford was it! I even got to the place where I questioned, "God, are You sure You gave me this job?" Cursing, spitefully using, and persecuting were the order of every day.

Before the end of the summer I had come to the place where I could pray for them, asking God to bless them, and looking for opportunities to help them. Coming home one evening several days before I was to return to Bible college, one of the three men in the truck said to me, "Mumford, we've watched you all summer. We want you, that's what He will do." As he walks out the front door, he trips self." It took me three months to earn the right to witness to those men. God's love overcame all barriers and spoke through me.

There is another extremely important side to this Law of Impartiality. *I refer to it as "damage joy."* A reading of Proverbs 24:17 may help bring this into focus: "Rejoice not when thine enemy falleth, and let not thine heart be glad when he stumbleth."

Have you already begun to get the implication of this word of wisdom? Here it is in action. My friend and I are having a heated argument and he leaves in a huff. I say to myself, "The Lord will get you, that's what He will do." As he walks out the front door, he trips over the sill, falling, and breaking a leg. Isn't a natural response to this, "Oh, that's terrible!" (with tongue in cheek, of course!).

That simple little illustration demonstrates a sizable and sneaky reaction. It is very easy to find joy when your "enemy" gets in trouble. But that reaction will get you into trouble with God. He sees that first stirring of, "Well, he finally got what he deserved! He had it coming!" We need to watch this carefully.

If you rejoice when the girl who stole your boyfriend gets worse grades than you do—or when there's a layoff at work and that fellow who has been making life miserable for you gets a little pink slip—be careful! There are future report cards and layoffs.

Another example: The church around the corner burns down. There has been quite a competitive spirit between the two of you. Will your thought be, "Well, all those members won't have any place to go. Now maybe they will come and join us. Isn't that too bad!" or will you suggest that your church take up an offering to help the burned-out membership repair, enabling them to carry on their work?

A situation somewhat similar to the above actually occurred in an Eastern city. Two churches had been having difficulties over the charismatic movement. The anticharismatic church found itself in financial difficulties—facing possible foreclosure. The second church took up an offering and sent over to their "enemies" seven hundred dollars of the needed one thousand dollars to stave off their creditors. This brought to the troubled church a living demonstration of the Law of Impartiality. It also brought a step forward in the maturity of the assisting church. They had just studied the Laws of the Kingdom and thrilled to see them enacted right before their eyes.

Watch your attitudes—be alert for reactions. To be partial means self-will is still in control. The Laws of the Kingdom bring release from the tyranny of self. *Why* is this discipline so necessary? Here is Jesus' reasoning on the subject.

(2) *The Reason for the Law of Impartiality* is that we may become the children of our heavenly Father (*see* v. 45). Phillips and the Revised Standard Version put the reason this way: ". . . so that you may be the sons . . . ." In other words, we are to mature into the same attitude as that of the Father. John 1:12 tells us: "But as many as received him, to them gave he power to become the sons of God, even to them that believe on his name." We might add "and receive His teachings" for that is included and implied in the process of believing.

One mark of maturity is impartiality. Children are inordinately partial. They have their pet friends and tend to operate in small circles, to the exclusion of others—often using ridicule to keep out siders in place. As adults we, too, have our cliques. We limit our activities and favors to family, business acquaintances, and those from whom we may possibly reap personal benefit. Even in our Christian associations, we are apt to limit ourselves—drawing denominational or other man-made lines. This, God does not tolerate. He is aware of its interference with our progress in Kingdom living. It keeps us from "growing up."

(Jesus follows the reason for impartiality with an illustration, showing the Father's way of handling relationships. Verse 45b pictures God showering His blessings: the rain and sunshine so necessary to human existence, on the just and the unjust. This is to be our example.)

Aren't you grateful for this aspect of our God's dealings?

(3) *Comparison of Two Levels of Treatment*   Verses 46 and 47 give us more food for thought. We must ask, *what about me?* Jesus compares the accepted mode of treatment in daily relationships (using the publicans as examples) with God's way.

Publicans were placed on a very low level of society due to their tax-collecting connections with the Roman government. Jesus is asking His hearers what is the difference between the actions of the despicable (in their sight) tax collectors and their own? The publicans loved those who loved them, and saluted those who acknowledged them. Is this the level on which Kingdom citizens should operate? Unthinkable! We are children of the King—and are to be like Him. Then comes the answer to the questions Jesus posed (in the form of a command) plus the motive for carrying out the order.

(4) *Concluding Command*   "Be ye therefore perfect . . . ." What can He possibly mean by perfect? Does that seem to be asking too much? The Greek word, *teleios,* as used here, means to come to full end. We might consider a grain of wheat—the young shoots coming from the seed—the maturing blossoms—the full head—complete! Maturity—that is the Father's aim for each of us. He wants to bring us into our full inheritance in the Kingdom as mature sons.

How we treat our enemies is a mark of either immaturity or maturity. Isn't it the desire of most earthly fathers to see their children come into maturity?

Maturity in its fullest meaning encompasses preparation for being able to accept responsibility, to take a place of usefulness in our world, to know righteousness, peace and joy. Our heavenly Father offers these in their highest and purest forms.

(5) *Comparison to the Ideal*   ". . . even as your Father which is in heaven is perfect." What a standard to hold before us! But He is so much more than an ideal and the standard; He is the Way. In telling us of the Father's desire that we grow up and act like Him, Jesus also tells us the Way—He shows us the Way: Himself.

These teachings are presented to bring us to maturity. God is going to help us grow up. Retarded children in His Kingdom are just as much a heartache to the Father as they are in the earth's social economy.

(6) *Impartiality Summary*   Keep an eye on how you treat others, friend and enemy alike. For if there is any difference in your treatment of them—you are showing partiality—immaturity.

This Law, like the others, brings a challenge to change. "Be ye therefore perfect . . ." is not an imaginary ideal or an illusion. It is a possibility—even a necessity; and it is within the reach of every Kingdom citizen.

VI THE LAW OF PURE MOTIVES

And he opened his mouth, and taught them, saying:

1 Take heed that ye do not your alms before men, to be seen of them: otherwise ye have no reward of your Father which is in heaven.

2 Therefore when thou doest thine alms, do not sound a trumpet before thee, as the hypocrites do in the synagogues and in the streets, that they may have glory of men. Verily I say unto you, They have their reward.

3 But when thou doest alms, let not thy left hand know what thy right hand doeth:

4 That thine alms may be in secret: and thy Father which seeth in secret himself shall reward thee openly.

5 And when thou prayest, thou shalt not be as the hypocrites are: for they love to pray standing in the synagogues and in the corners of the streets, that they may be seen of men. Verily I say unto you, They have their reward.

6 But thou, when thou prayest, enter into thy closet, and when thou hast shut thy door, pray to thy Father which is in secret; and thy Father which seeth in secret shall reward thee openly.

7 But when ye pray, use not vain repetitions, as the heathen do: for they think that they shall be heard for their much speaking.

8 Be not therefore like unto them: for your Father knoweth what things ye have need of, before ye ask him.

9 After this manner therefore pray ye: Our Father which art in heaven, Hallowed be thy name.

10 Thy kingdom come. Thy will be done in earth as it is in heaven.

11 Give us this day our daily bread.

12 And forgive us our debts, as we forgive our debtors.

13 And lead us not into temptation, but deliver us from evil: For

131

thine is the kingdom and the power, and the glory for ever. Amen.

14 For if ye forgive men their trespasses, your heavenly Father will also forgive you:

15 But if ye forgive not men their trespasses, neither will your Father forgive your trespasses.

16 Moreover when ye fast, be not, as the hypocrites, of a sad countenance: for they disfigure their faces that they may appear unto men to fast. Verily I say unto you, That they have their reward.

17 But thou, when thou fastest, anoint thine head, and wash thy face;

18 That thou appear not unto men to fast, but unto thy Father which is in secret: and thy Father which seeth in secret, shall reward thee openly.

Matthew 6

The teaching given on the *Law of Pure Motives* is probably the most detailed and descriptively presented of any of our Fifteen By-laws. Jesus lists what not to do, what to do, gives illustrations from life, lists results of both approaches to the situations he is probing, and, as always, leaves His hearers faced with choices.

For the lesson on Pure Motives, Jesus discusses *three areas* of religious ritual, routine, and practice. To many people *giving, praying,* and *fasting* represent only prescribed disciplines of their church or belief. They are performed perfunctorily, grudgingly, or even resentfully. They may, though, be performed meticulously and graciously—giving an outward appearance of acceptance and satisfaction. But Jesus is talking about what is going on inside a man—not what appears on the surface. *Motive,* or *intent,* determines the ultimate good or evil in every transaction of life.

In civil law, motive is the hinge upon which the verdict hangs. Lawyers strive to substantiate proper or improper motive. Did this man intend to murder his wife when he reached for that gun? Did this company intend to defraud when they laid plans for this investment? What must be proved is intent. When man puts his own interpretation on intent, he can come up with almost any answer. But when God places His client on the stand, divine wisdom lays bare men's intents.

Jesus wants us to put ourselves on the witness stand, look at the facts, and determine our intent in the areas of giving—praying—fasting. These are not meant to be merely "religious" acts. These would have deep spiritual impact upon the growth of every believer. In the most simple terms, what Jesus is teaching here is: *It is not what you do, but why you do it!* Are you ready to examine yourself under the probe of Kingdom perception? Remember, the Judge already knows you better than you know yourself. Be careful of your defense!

First, look with me at a principle which may help us as we weigh our progress in Kingdom living. We have discussed the inner alignment that is needed to come into true freedom. How do we straighten

NATURE
DESIRE
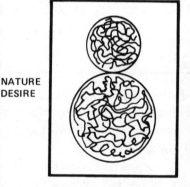 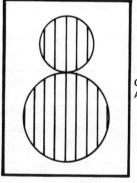
CHARACTER
ABILITY

out the kinks? By adhering to the Bylaws in a given circumstance. And who directs the circumstances? God. He knows that as our wills become aligned with His will, we can know the freedom Jesus taught and lived.

Some people wonder why they don't make greater progress in their Christian walk. The reason could be their motives. For when we make a certain measure of progress, there is always the danger that we may become self-satisfied and feel that we have arrived. We may have arrived at a certain plateau; but God desires that we move on up the mountain. That is why He doesn't permit us to become too satisfied with any one step of progress. There is always that next venture which promises *more!* We have to keep open eyes and hearts to keep up with our Guide.

Many Kingdom travelers crack up on this spiritual journey because they attempt to impress others with their progress and attainments. We overextend ourselves—trying to be something we haven't grown into yet. Adolescents battle this problem constantly—wanting to appear adult—trying to act adult—when their physical and mental growth just does not allow for the realization of their projected images. Here is one of the most subtle traps on our journey. Perhaps we can better catch the implication from this diagram:

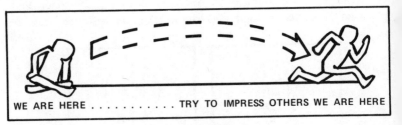

WE ARE HERE . . . . TRY TO IMPRESS OTHERS WE ARE HERE

It is often easier to fool others and ourselves in the spiritual realm than in the physical. We must build carefully and face ourselves honestly. It is fairly simple to create an impression—but it proves a nasty assignment trying to live up to that impression.

The temptation to casually (for few of us would be blatant in advertising our virtues!) drop remarks that would color a listener's thinking, giving the impression, "My, he is a great prayer warrior— the way he gives to God's causes certainly puts me to shame—fasting has accomplished great things through his perseverance!" The one who makes the above deductions from our conversation soon becomes a conveyor of our spirituality; and others embroider on the story. Soon we find ourselves almost believing we *are* something special. This, in turn, may engender a feeling of independence on our part. Who needs God when he is so well thought of? or it may cause resentment when God lowers the boom on our self-styled halo.

Before you get to the place where your whole spiritual life starts to come unglued and you feel it's no use struggling any longer, consider your building procedures:

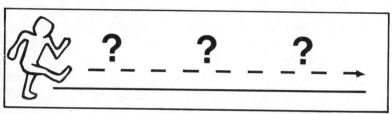

Take inventory. Learn one lesson before tackling the whole course. You can't take a student out of third grade math and give him trigonometry assignments. At least, you can't expect right answers to result from that foundation in the subject. False impressions can build a facade that covers inner bewilderment, confusion, and failure.

Join Jesus as He moves behind men's facades—not to embarrass them, but to show them the truth about themselves, and point the way to enjoyment of God-endowed avenues for self-expression and self-sacrifice. Pure motives determine the results. The opening statement of the lesson is a warning: *Take heed!* Jesus links the three areas in which He issues this warning with the words "and . . . moreover." Motive is the lesson and warning is issued in each area.

GIVING: Reread verses 1 through 4.   Webster defines *alms* as a free gift. Wouldn't you think a free gift would be enough to insure proper credit? No. The giver is more important in God's economy than the gift. There is nothing wrong with the gift—it may be used to alleviate suffering—build a new church—pay the pastor's salary. But that's it! There is no, "Well done, thou good and faithful servant." Not even if you had to forego a new dress or a chocolate malt? Your friends may appreciate your sacrifice, but what about God?

Verse 1 warns not to give to be seen of men. If you do, you have no reward from your heavenly Father.

Verse 2 illustrates the act of giving to be seen of men as a common sight in Palestine. Much fanfare often accompanied Jewish giving. It could happen in the place of worship—making a resounding an-nouncement of one's generosity as the coins dropped into a metal container. Or it could be on the street corner—with weeping of turtle tears and flourish of kindly concern for the poor ragged beggar de-pendent upon his richer brother. The conclusion of that type giving? "They have their reward."

What is their reward? The gasp of the gathered worshipers in the temple at the size and sound of the proffered gift. The smiles of ap-probation of other street passersby. Their commendation is reward. You received your money's worth. Enjoy it!

This reminds me of a friend who loved to get out his wallet as the offering plate made its rounds. With an habitual snap of a crisp one-dollar bill, and a gentle placing of it on the plate, my friend waxed warm and fed by the even more gentle dropping of coins by those whose dollar bills were more hard to come by. My friend had his reward. The glory of men is a strong motive.

Why do we so often have our building fund drives when the con-gregation is gathered together? "Is there anybody here who would like to give one thousand dollars toward the erection of our new edifice?" It's easy to fall into that trap. "I might as well show every-one how much the Lord has been prospering me—let them see how interested I am in bringing about the success of this venture."

To the acclaim of my peers for that thousand dollars, I get the picture that I am not such a bad fellow after all. I have just purchased a thousand dollars worth of reward. God will take my thousand and use it for His glory—but what about me? I have glory, too—the glory of the men before whom I made my gift—to be seen. When the glow of their glory begins to wear thin, where is that spiritual satisfaction I may have been expecting? I may even be sorry for my hastiness in making my pledge—and paying it may turn into drudgery.

Verse 3 tells us how to give—why—and what reward we may con-fidently expect when we follow His recommendation. The admonition not to let our right hand know what our left hand is doing is often grossly misinterpreted. No sleight of hand is going to fool God—or ourselves. This does not mean that we are to avoid Internal Revenue

Service records of our giving. Proper records might be the means of having more to contribute to His cause. Nor does it mean being so secretive about our giving that it poses a problem to us and those with whom we are associated in Kingdom business. We are discussing motives—pure motives—God-directed and inspired motives. The conclusion of the matter? God will openly reward every gift made with the right motive. You will receive evident recompense—and others will be able to benefit, too.

PRAYING: Reread verses 5 through 15. Verses 5 and 6 go through somewhat the same procedure as the "take heed" for giving. Notice the word *hypocrite* used again. A hypocrite is one who is playacting. This is the core of Jesus' teaching. One is playacting that he is giving or praying or fasting out of pure motive—when all the time it is to be seen of men. The performance may be perfect—but curtain time is a disaster!

Again, there was much fanfare in A.D. 30 praying. Onlookers were apt to be impressed by the length and loudness of the prayers made both in synagogue, temple, and on the street corners. What devotion! What depth! What a sham! (would be more like it!). But God will grant the desires of your heart. Isn't He good? You want to impress others with your prayer power? He will grant that desire.

Prayer is to be upward to God—not outward to man. That may be one reason why some prayers never get off the ground. Have you ever had someone go into lengthy prayer, asking God to bless Brother Brown, and then go on to delineate his faults and failings—just to be sure he knows that you know what God needs to do about it? or, "Dear Lord, bring us back to church tonight"; or, "Give us a good meeting next Tuesday"; or, "Place it upon the hearts of our elders to be present at tonight's session." Is this making our requests known to God or making announcements and jogging memories? You may have your reward: good attendance at meetings—*worthy offerings*—and improved behavior from Brother Brown. You may have the commendation of your fellow workers for the comprehensiveness of your prayers—but where is the warmth derived from standing in God's presence—the growth in your own faithfulness and behavior?

Prayer is not flowery dissertations—displays of knowledge of Genesis to Revelation. Nor is it ornament and decoration of *canst—shouldests—wouldst nots*. These may bring some reward from men; but it may also bring a measure of inferiority to other men. What about that fellow who feels tongue-tied when asked to pray? His words may not flow as fluently, nor his English be as King James; or another may feel he is not as spiritually qualified to pray if he cannot come up to the standard set by the more verbose brother. Prayer that goes upward to God lifts others. They respond and forget themselves and their thoughts soar upward, too.

A. W. Tozer, a mighty man of God, was once called upon to offer prayer at the funeral of a fellow minister. Everyone was expecting a eulogy to the deceased. The refreshing prayer, "Oh, Lord God, we thank You that You own both sides of Jordan," was a means of bringing us into God's presence and spanning Jordan with our brother. These few profound words did more than a thousand flowery ones would have done.

In this second area—praying—we have an admonition that is as misinterpreted as the left-hand/right-hand words of warning about giving. The prayer closet can prove a trap. One may think he cannot pray acceptably unless he is in quietness—darkness—away from everyone and everything. *The only door one needs to shut is the door to creating impressions.* A freeway, a Greyhound bus, a political rally —any of these places may be a prayer closet if the world is shut out and prayer is sent upward. The rewards of this type prayer are promised. I like that "reward thee openly." As with giving with the right motive, prayer brings God's approbation in such a way that we will recognize it—and others will be aware of it, too.

Jesus adds some further thoughts on prayer, using the heathen (or unbelievers) as examples. The listeners were acquainted with the practices of those who prayed to heathen Gods. Much ado was made in bowing before their dumb idols. Many words were poured into their deaf ears. Vain repetitions are often offered up to the living God and some of us may even hope to receive answers for our "much speaking."

One such problem was faced and denounced by Paul as he called to task the believers in Corinth. Here was an evident case of trying to impress men with the spirituality one had attained. These new converts had just come out of the heathenism to which Jesus referred. They had been involved in much speaking and vain repetitions. Upon coming to Jesus Christ, and receiving the Baptism in the Holy Spirit and a new prayer language, they retained some of their former ardor and practices. In their adolescence, they wanted to impress others with their maturity in the new way of life.

Paul tells them (1 Corinthians chapter 14), "Yet in the church I had rather speak five words with my understanding, that by my voice I might teach others also, than ten thousand words in an unknown tongue. Brethren be not children in understanding . . ." (vs. 19, 20). Paul knew the value of the secret closet and there spoke his ten thousand words, that before men he might present the claims of Christ. "He that speaketh in an unknown tongue edifieth himself . . . . I thank my God, I speak in tongues more than ye all" (vs. 4, 18).

Verse 8 in Matthew's chapter six may raise some questions in your mind. Why pray if your Father knows what you need before you ask Him? We mentioned independence being one hindrance to entering Kingdom living. Prayer, even though God knows our needs, shows our dependence upon Him as the Giver of every good gift. Also, why does God often wait until the last minute to grant some of our requests? Again, He wants us to realize our dependence. If He answered sooner, we might claim the credit. What is greater even than the answer to one particular prayer? The joy of getting to know God in a more intimate way by acknowledging our dependence. This opens the way for greater fellowship—our reward!

In verses 9–13 Jesus becomes more specific. He tells the disciples how to pray. We often refer to this as the Model Prayer or the Lord's Prayer. Very few portions of Scripture are more familiar to us than these words. Perhaps they are so familiar that we miss some of the implications.

After addressing our Father and acknowledging His holiness, the truth about which we are teaching is expressed: "Thy kingdom come. Thy will be done . . . . " The Kingdom has been established, and His will is being done as we come into alignment with His will.

Then come three petitions which show our need for dependence upon the Father: for our daily bread—for forgiveness—and for protection from the evil one. The prayer closes with again making mention of the Kingdom, along with the power and glory that are the King's prerogatives.

Two verses (*14 and 15*) stress the truth we brought out as we considered anger and its adverse effect. We must forgive those who trespass against us in order to know forgiveness and healing in our own lives.

FASTING: Reread verses 16 through 18. Here Jesus teaches on a practice which was accepted and common in His day. In fact, the Jews had practiced fasting from the days of their formation into a nation. In many sections of the established churches today, fasting is an unknown (and sometimes even questioned) discipline. Again, the motive is of primary concern.

The Pharisees had reminded Jesus on more than one occasion about *their* faithfulness *in* fasting. But evidently they didn't have to remind anyone *when* they were fasting. Their outward appearance announced their compliance with set rules and regulations. Jesus chided them for disfiguring their faces. He told them to wash them instead. Wipe away all outward signs of your inward withdrawal from daily food and drink. God is the One who is interested in your sacrifices. If you fast to gain the attention and commendation of men for your faithfulness—you have your reward.

It is a tremendous temptation to try to impress others with our spirituality. I am on a twenty-seven-day fast. That is three meals a day—total of eighty-one foregone meals. It is easy to put on our martyr complex and start talking. "I had this burden . . . ." Gradu-

ally the twenty-seven-day fast finds its way into the conversation—
and you have your reward! There goes eighty-one meals down the
drain—expensive recompense!

In review, let me ask: Did Jesus show concern with pure motives
while He ministered among men? What about His commendation of
the widow who put her mite into the offering plate? He contrasted
her motive of "giving her all," with the giving of those who gave from
their abundance (Mark 12:42–44). He also contrasted two types of
praying (Luke 18:10–13). The Pharisee prayed with himself, telling
himself about his faithfulness in fasting and giving. The publican
confessed his sins and asked for mercy. The former had his reward
—seen and heard of men. The latter? He "went down to his house
justified." Then there was the occasion of a visit in the house of
Simon of Bethany when a woman poured out upon Him from her
treasure—a very costly ointment. Again note Jesus' discernment
(John 12:3–8) as he rebuked those who questioned such an expensive display of appreciation and commended the woman for her pure
motive.

The words "Thy father which seeth in secret" offer both encouragement and cause for caution. Being aware of the fact that God sees
beneath the surface, makes us increasingly conscious of what is
transpiring inside. God knows our intents and He acts accordingly.
No need for us to tell Him—He will even see changes in our attitudes
before we are conscious of them ourselves.

God sees and rewards: the woman who has seven children and is
almost engulfed with keeping up with their needs—and just throws
her apron over her head and finds herself in her "closet of prayer"
for a few moments.

God sees and rewards: the man who genuinely feels a burden to
such an extent that he gives up eating and drinking for a certain
length of time—but who continues to present to the world a smiling
countenance and quiet assurance.

God sees and rewards: the unassuming contribution made to a

Kingdom cause—given from a heart of compassion. No need for fanfare.

The matter of motive is very delicate. *One condition that must be guarded against is false humility.* You are asked to play the piano. Your response may be "Oh, I'm too humble to get up in front of all those people—I don't want to be seen of men." If you can play the piano—do it! Being seen of men does not rule out the reward of your Father. If anything is done in the right attitude, it *insures* His reward.

Here are two guidelines:

(1) Don't ever cease from doing anything *because* you are seen of men.
(2) Don't ever do anything in *order* to be seen of men.
    Father knows the difference.
    You usually do, too!

One attitude which should be developed is that of gratitude. Giving, praying, and fasting will be a natural outgrowth of this attitude. They will then spring from a pure motive. If you are grateful for a good bed, a car that runs, a nation where freedom is permitted—*praying* will be motivated and you will not care if anyone hears you expressing your thanks to your heavenly Father or not.

With an attitude of gratitude, *giving* is one means of showing thanks for the goodness of God. It will not matter who is watching. But if someone sees your generosity, this will be opportunity for you to attribute your thankful heart to God's goodness.

Fasting, too, will become a joyful experience. No need to put on a long face when you turn down that invitation to a steak dinner. A smiling explanation of your desire to give yourself in a spiritual discipline need not carry with it any superior overtones—not if you are truly trying to please God.

To be seen of men: earthly recognition;
To be heard of men: earthly reward;

To be accepted by God: pure motive and the Father rewards openly!

The temptation to create impressions before others that we are more spiritual than we really are is always with us. Don't pass over this lesson lightly.

Take heed!

Take stock!

Take Jesus' words to heart—and enjoy your reward.

◆◆

VII THE LAW OF LIBERALITY

◆◆

And he opened his mouth, and taught them, saying:

19 Lay not up for yourselves treasures upon earth where moth and rust doth corrupt, and where thieves break through and steal:

20 But lay up for yourselves treasures in heaven, where neither moth nor rust doth corrupt, and where thieves do not break through nor steal:

21 For where your treasure is, there will your heart be also.

22 The light of the body is the eye: if therefore thine eye be single, thy whole body shall be full of light.

23 But if thine eye be evil, thy whole body shall be full of darkness. If therefore the light that is in thee be darkness, how great is that darkness!

Matthew 6

This particular law might be also labeled the *Law of Finances*. Does this mean that Jesus is stepping out of the spiritual realm when He deals with worldly matters? Not at all. Even though our world is money-oriented, this is no indication that money is not a concern in the Kingdom of God. In fact, Jesus taught many lessons on money matters. He was vitally interested in every area of life that was of interest to man. He became a man that He might identify with every temptation, reaction, and transaction that we might ever encounter. That is why He qualifies as the most able of all teachers.

This *Law of Liberality* logically falls into two separate sections. *The first emphasis* is on the futility of storing up treasures upon earth, as over against the value of storing them in heaven. *The second emphasis* deals with cause and effect—money being the context of the teaching.

Verses 19–21 center around the word "treasure." In the first century, gold, silver, precious gems and large land holdings had just as much fascination for men as they do in the twentieth. There may not have been as much monetary exchange then as there is today, but the exchange of time and service for payment has always been the order of the marketplace. That is why we say money is spiritual. It represents time. Time is life. Life is man—and man is God's concern. When a person puts five dollars in the offering plate as it goes by, he may be putting in two hours of his life—if he earns $2.50 per hour.

Reading these verses makes it apparent that first-century men and women also had some of the same problems we battle today—moths, rust, and thievery. Personally, Jesus was not as much interested in the loss to the treasure, as He was in the spiritual loss and damage involved by putting one's emphasis on the material rather than the spiritual values of life. The punch line is, "For where your treasure is, there will your heart be also."

That truism might be reversed: "Where your heart is, there is your treasure." Some people put their money in automobiles, some in travel, others in their homes and furnishings. Art collectors, stamp collectors, big game hunters, surfers—you name it—there is the heart and pocketbook going hand in hand. Why not take a look at your checkbook stubs occasionally and see where your heart is leading you?

The literal translation of "lay up for yourselves" is "lay up in your own interest." Does this bring the laying-up a bit closer home? If our interests center on earthly treasures and activities, our time and money will be spent in following wherever they may lead us. If, on the other hand, we are giving to Kingdom purposes (not to be seen or impress anyone), but with pure motive—we are laying up to our eternal interest. Each of us must ask, *What percent of interest are our investments bearing?* Are we sending our treasure on ahead of us, with the assurance of finding worthwhile dividends? or are our treasures showing signs of corrosion and pilfering?

Right here we might ask: Why does God recommend the tithe—a minimum of one-tenth of our income—to be given to Kingdom causes? We touched on the answer to this question in discussing the

Law of Pure Motives. Of course, Kingdom causes require financing, but more important: *The Lord wants us to be dependent upon Him.* If He asked 5 percent, that might make giving too easy—20 percent may be too steep. Ten percent is just enough to show the Lord that we do depend upon Him for taking care of our needs.

Sometimes when expenses pile up for me, and I squirm a bit at my responsibility in giving, the Lord has a way of reminding me of my obligation to Him. The man who gives to the Lord is saying, "I need You. I depend on You to make my 90 percent I have left cover my needs." And He does. The twenty-year roof lasts thirty years—the car keeps running—and the children's teeth don't have as many cavities at checkup time. The reverse cycle is true, also. That family which neglects the tithe seems to have emergencies all the time. Where your heart is—so goes the money!

What about leaving what is left over in a will? Leftovers for Kingdom causes won't do *you* any good. You have to send it on ahead. Of course, if your motives are pure and you manage to have some funds that didn't quite make it "up there" as soon as you did, that might throw a little different light on the matter. But if you reason, "Lord, I've only got forty thousand dollars to last me—but after I don't have any more use for it, You can have it." He might reply, "I'll take it, thank you. But if you want it to meet you 'over here,' you will have to send it on ahead." Again, *the reason is dependence.* The Lord doesn't take my estate and add it to my account. That way it doesn't cost me anything.

We need to have discernment, as well as dedication, in the handling of our finances. God holds us responsible for how we use, not only His, but our entire substance. We cannot sectionize our hearts; they are either 100 percent His, or we are still in control. It is for the alignment of man that Jesus is teaching—not for treasure.

In 1 Timothy 6:10, Paul reminds us: "For the love of money is the root of all evil: which while some coveted after, they have erred from the faith, and pierced themselves through with many sorrows." *Neither Paul nor Jesus taught that money, or treasure, in itself is evil.* It is man's *response* to abundance—or lack of worldly belongings—

that causes the trouble. This thought brings us to the second phase of the Law of Liberality.

Verses 22 and 23 shift the emphasis in wise use of earthly possessions from the heart to the eye. These two organs, which are of such vital importance to man's daily welfare, are closely tied in the physical as well as in the spiritual. Remember, the context of the teaching on the "single eye" is money.

We return to the Parable of the Sower (Matthew 13) and see how money matters can complicate the progress of Kingdom fruit-bearing. Jesus was speaking to "a great multitude" gathered at the seaside. Later the disciples asked Jesus why He taught in parables when addressing the multitudes. His reply was, "Because it is given unto you [the disciples—continuers] to know the mysteries of the Kingdom, but to them it is not given" (v. 11). Continuers with Jesus are privileged to move into Kingdom truths. Others cannot grasp their meaning.

Jesus had said that some of the seed sown (which represented Kingdom teaching) would fall among thorns; and the thorns would spring up and choke out the good seed. In amplifying the teaching to His smaller group, this thought-provoking warning is issued in Matthew 13:22:

He also that received seed among the thorns is he that heareth the word; and the care of this world, and the deceitfulness of riches, choke the word, and he becometh unfruitful.

Trying to protect one's treasure from moth and rust and thieves could be classified as the "care of this world and deceitfulness of riches" in my thinking. How about yours?

One's eye could scarcely be considered "single" if it were so busy watching out for protection and distribution of one's treasure that his view of God and Kingdom purposes became distorted. The "evil eye" referred to in verse 23 of our Law of Liberality is an eye that is turned away from God to lesser interests. The eye does not need to be looking *for* or *at* evil (sinful) matters. Preoccupation with any-thing less than God causes darkness and confusion in the whole scope of not only giving, but also living. Great is the darkness if the single eye becomes clouded with the deceitfulness of that which God in-tended to be a blessing—riches. Cataracts can develop, and surgery may be required to restore single vision. Remember the recommended surgery of removing an eye or cutting off a hand if the offending member endangers Kingdom growth?

Can confusion arise in the use of money even when the person is desirous of channeling his money into *worthy* causes? Dozens and dozens of causes may be considered worthy—depending upon the vision and perception of the one weighing the situation. This is where keeping one's eyes upon God is important. Sin may not have been involved in the thorns which sprang up and choked out the Kingdom teaching in Jesus' parable. There may just have been the prick and prodding of continual demands and requests for attention in con-nection with one's riches that was deceitful and caused eventual un-fruitfulness. *Kingdom productivity is the fruitfulness which Jesus is weighing.*

God's children are often likened to sheep—and like sheep are often led astray. It is easy for someone to come along with a super-project and with superoratory convince some "sheep" that theirs is the supreme need of the moment. Appeals for contributions to an orphanage may touch the hearts of those with a deep feeling for homeless and handicapped children. Suffering may be alleviated by our support, but is it in the interest of Kingdom fruitfulness? Radio and television may bring many requests for investments in varied ministries. Bible-quoting preaching does not necessarily insure that the interests of God's Kingdom will be met.

Keep your eye single. Ask for divine wisdom in the use of your finances. Pray and seek God, investigating the many calls that come to you. Once you are convinced that God is leading in a certain direction, keep your eye single. Don't close your eyes to enlarging horizons, but don't be diverted into detours or blind alleys. Once you take that route—great is the darkness!

You and I are building for eternity. We need to watch the building materials we choose. Are they hay, stubble, wood, or stone that will build to withstand the onslaughts of Satan? He is interested in bringing this matter of finances into gradual confusion. He will begin in a small way. Watch for the little leaks. Before long, the dike may break and you will find yourself in over your head—with an "evil" eye and a darkened outlook on life.

It does matter how you evaluate possessions, both the keeping and the spending. Let me tell you of the darkness that enveloped a friend of mine. We shall call him Jerry.

Jerry was gloriously saved one night. The Lord brought him joy and release after his repentance and acceptance of Christ as his Saviour. For three weeks Jerry shared with everyone who would listen his new freedom. Then the Lord said to him, "Son, I want you to assess all of your holdings and take 10 percent and give it to your church." This was a request Jerry had not anticipated. How did he react to it? Why did the Lord ask it?

To answer the latter question first, the Lord was putting the *Law of Liberality* into operation. Where Jerry's treasure was—there still was his heart—in spite of the joy from his newly acquired freedom. There was still a clinging to the security of riches. The Lord knew this and wanted to completely free Jerry.

Jerry? He argued—complained—asked everyone for advice. But he took no advice except the advice of his double eye. The dollar sign overshadowed the King's request. Twilight set in and before long, darkness settled. Jerry lost his joy and freedom—still a child of God—but wandering in the blackness brought on by his double vision.

These are sobering teachings. We may love to be considered liberal, and receive great enjoyment from giving to others. But we are not to be giving to feel good; we are investing our money, time, our lives in fruitfulness in Kingdom causes. It is important to God that we grow. The use and misuse of our treasure (be it great or small) contributes to our alignment and growth. Those three hindrances—rebellion, resentment, independence—rear their ugly heads when we start figuring budgets, tithes, requests. For where our treasure is, there are our hearts. If the light in us is darkness, how great is that darkness! And that exclamation point is not the author's but the Scripture's. The Living Bible concludes the teaching on the *Law of Liberality* this way:

If your eye is pure, there will be sunshine in your soul. But if your eye is clouded with evil thoughts and desires, you are in deep spiritual darkness. And oh, how deep that darkness can be!

Matthew 6:22, 23 LB

VIII   THE LAW OF REDUCED INTEREST

And he opened his mouth, and taught them, saying:

24 No man can serve two masters: for either he will hate the one, and love the other; or else he will hold to the one, and despise the other. Ye cannot serve God and mammon.

25 Therefore I say unto you, Take no thought for your life, what ye shall eat, or what ye shall drink; nor yet for your body, what ye shall put on. Is not the life more than meat, and the body than raiment?

26 Behold the fowls of the air: for they sow not, neither do they reap, nor gather into barns; yet your heavenly Father feedeth them. Are ye not much better than they?

27 Which of you by taking thought can add one cubit unto his stature?

28 And why take ye thought for raiment? Consider the lilies of the field, how they grow; they toil not, neither do they spin:

29 And yet I say unto you, That even Solomon is all his glory was not arrayed like one of these.

30 Wherefore, if God so clothe the grass of the field, which to day is, and to morrow is cast into the oven, shall he not much more clothe you, O ye of little faith?

31 Therefore take no thought, saying, What shall we eat? or, What shall we drink? or, Wherewithal shall we be clothed?

32 (For after all these things do the Gentiles seek:) for your heavenly Father knoweth that ye have need of these things.

33 But seek ye first the kingdom of God, and his righteousness; and all these things shall be added unto you.

34 Take therefore no thought for the morrow: for the morrow shall take thought for the things of itself. Sufficient unto the day is the evil thereof.

Matthew 6

As we began our study on the *Law of Liberality,* we asked ourselves if Jesus were stepping out of the spiritual realm when He began His teaching on money matters. We came to the conclusion that He was not, since everything related to man is related to the Kingdom of God. The Kingdom is made up of men—redeemed and remade by the Teacher—our Saviour and Lord.

Jesus now moves from money to discuss some of the items we consider necessary to life—and they *are* in their rightful place and proper perspective: food—drink—clothing. These are all legitimate items but none an end in itself. The "eat, drink, and be merry" philosophy of life majors on physical satisfactions. Jesus wants to re-relate us to these issues of life, acknowledging their importance, yet teaching us dependence upon our heavenly Father in all things.

These matters (meat, drink, clothing) are very earthly—nothing heavenly here. It isn't that these material necessities are immaterial, but that He desires we have an understanding of their place in our lives. This will afford us security and stability. My earlier understanding on these more mundane demands of life was, "Do your best to get to Heaven and God will take care of the rest of your needs." I have come to realize that the Father's objective is not to get us *to*

Heaven—but that His desire is to get Heaven *in* us! The Kingdom of God is here—and now—seeking to be established in all who claim to be members of the family of God.

Let's see what Jesus is after. He talked earlier about the singleness of heart and eye. Pretense is one hazard we need to be particularly careful to screen from our lives. If we try to act spiritual in areas where we have not fully grasped the implications of Jesus' teachings, we open ourselves to darkness; we fool ourselves, and perhaps some others, but never God. We must not *pretend* to trust God in material matters unless we truly do. A proper understanding of the philosophy Jesus presents will bring security and release from the tyranny of "things."

There are some conditions involved in establishing this security. *Verse 24* lays down a principle that allows for no exceptions: *No man . . .* and *. . . Ye cannot.*

Verses 25 through 32 lay out the problem in beautiful detail. The references and language form one of the most quoted sections of Scripture we have.

Verses 33 and 34 bring the lesson to a logical conclusion with definite instruction on how to solve the problem. Jesus never left His hearers hanging or in doubt. His explicitness is exceeded only by His perception into the tendencies of man.

Here is the ultimatum: "No man can serve two masters: for either he will hate the one, and love the other; or else he will hold to the one and despise the other. Ye cannot serve God and mammon."

The word *cannot* has two meanings: prohibited and unable. The latter is the one used here. One is *unable* to serve two masters. This would be quite evident in a master/slave situation, which was common in A.D. 30. You can only take orders from one master. So it is in the internal realm. A man decides his goal in life is to become a millionaire by the age thirty-five. From whom does he take his orders? To what center does he relate every happening and person that comes across his path?

Notice, also, that Jesus said we could not serve God *and* mammon.

154 THE KING AND YOUTHE KING AND YOU

Mammon could be defined as earthly interests: money, meat, drink, clothing. If we establish an inner god, we are bound to serve that god—first priority—loyalty—love. *Cannot* has to do with ability—not desire. *Once our desire is fixed, our ability is limited.*

To help us see the finality of that word *cannot,* note that it is the same word that is used in John 3:5 where Jesus told Nicodemus, "Except a man be born again, he cannot enter the kingdom of God." We often glibly quote that verse, not realizing that Jesus placed the same distinction upon *advancement* in the Kingdom as He did upon *entrance* into the Kingdom. "Ye cannot serve two masters." So we must choose one.

Jesus asks eight questions in the next few verses (25–31) and all of them have to do with the futility of undue concern over material supply and the evidence God has provided, showing His desire to care for His creation—among which man is the most valuable.

The admonition "take no thought" is repeated with the presentation of each comparison of the Father's care for those objects of His care—the fowls of the air and the lilies of the field. Dozens of books are on the market dealing with the subject Jesus is stressing—*worry!* He might be saying, "Do not give way to anxiety. Your heavenly Father knows you have needs in these material realms." And your heavenly Father wants you to realize your *dependence* upon Him for supplying the needs. When you seek God's will and His care, He takes over the responsibility.

Overconcern in the material realm reflects a lack of faith in God as Provider. If He has given you life, can He not take care of the lesser needs? As always, attitude comes first. When we are rightly related to our heavenly Father, we experience *contentment.* Dependence on God does not result in a careless approach to the needs of the physical. In fact, the appreciation of the proper satisfactions of the physical takes on new meaning. We are masters of them instead of their being our masters.

In developing a personal philosophy of the physicals, there are some complexities that beset us. We shall discuss three of these.

(1) The Poverty Complex
(2) The Success Ethics Complex
(3) The Wilderness Complex

These all present hindrances to God's desire for us as His children.

(1) *Poverty Complex*   This is the attitude that says: *If I am poor then I must be spiritual.* Or conversely: *My neighbor cannot be spiritual because he drives a new Continental.* It says: *Jesus was poor. He rode a borrowed donkey and had nowhere to lay His head.* These people forget Jesus had a Father who owned the cattle upon a thousand hills and that He had power to turn stones into bread. Jesus was poor that we might be rich, and He died that we might have life and have it more abundantly.

(2) *Success Ethics Complex*   Here the attitude is that if one is rich, he is so because God has blessed him for being spiritual. Success, by the world's standards, is no sign of spiritual blessing or special favor of God. It can be—but it isn't necessarily so.

Neither of the two above approaches to evaluating is valid. Neither affluence, nor lack of it, is an indication of one's spirituality. Nor does it form a standard by which to judge others. Please ask God to set you free from either of these two complexes if they have a grip on you. There are times in our lives when God can and does bless materially; there are other times when God deals along opposite lines. *It is always God's desire to bless as we are able to receive.*

(3) *The Wilderness Complex*   This reasoning runs something like this: As long as I stay out here in the wilderness and am being dealt with by God, it is safe—because if I come into the land of plenty, and God begins to bless me, I am apt to backslide. It asks the question: Who could ever be spiritual with a new car, a swimming pool, and an American Express card? Who would need God?

Do you remember Paul's saying, "I know both how to be abased, and . . . to abound" (Philippians 4:12)? He had become rightly related to "things," and having them, or not having them, did not affect in any way his relationship to his heavenly Father. This is what

Jesus is driving at. He wants to establish in us an *attitude of dependence* that can accept the material blessings without becoming independent and developing the "Who needs God?" approach. Equally anxious is He for us to come to the place where we do not always need to be in a financial crisis to have a feeling of dependency.

It is not God's intention to leave us out in the wilderness. He wants to bring us into the Promised Land. Hear Him as He tells of this same desire to the Israelites. (By the way, it took them forty years to learn lessons that would permit them to make the move into God's desire for them as given in Deuteronomy 6:10, 11!)

> And it shall be, when the Lord thy God shall have brought thee into the land which he sware unto thy fathers, to Abraham, to Isaac, and to Jacob, to give thee great and goodly cities, which thou buildest not, And houses full of all good things, which thou filledst not, and wells which thou diggedst not, vineyards and olive trees, which thou plantedst not . . . .

If God wants to bless so richly, why doesn't He? He knows what would happen if He did! Should He bless you as He wanted to, it would destroy you. Prosperity to some people would be a curse. John D. Rockefeller once said, "Seldom have I found a man to whom I could give without hurting him." God probably feels this way about most of His children most of the time.

Not too long ago we had a $2500 printing bill—which represents a sizeable sum! Those of us in the office would gather around the desk and pray for the funds. Three days later I received this letter.

> Dear Bob: I was praying today and the Lord told me to put the tithe money from an inheritance I recently received in the mail to you.

And the letter was dated the day of our most fervent prayers. Enclosed was a check for $2618! We all nearly came unglued. What a thrill to see such a concrete answer to our prayers. And who wouldn't like to make a method out of an answering service like that? But it doesn't always work that way, does it?

God knows how to create dependence, as well as knowing how to bring us to a security that is deep and lasting through accepting the teachings of the *Law of Reduced Interest.* He is working for eternal results rather than the temporal. Paul, in 1 Timothy 6:8, says this: "And having food and raiment let us be therewith content." If you can learn the lesson of *contentment,* along with *dependence* upon Him as Provider, He will bless you as you are able to stand it.

It is interesting to note that two people can make the same salary and one of them will be able to have a nice home, car, and never seem to have financial troubles; the other (on the same salary) will always be in hot water. He may be late in paying the rent, car payments, even to the point of borrowing to make ends meet. What makes the difference? The philosophy of money. Some invest wisely and spend when and where needed. Others waste theirs and have little idea of the true value of money.

How many of you know that human sympathy can get you in trouble? Not only you—but the one to whom that sympathy might be misdirected. Is it possible to give to the man who is a waster and only be contributing to his profligacy? We can be teaching him to be a parasite. Some try this route under the *disguise of faith.* This is not God's evaluation or philosophy. Wisdom is needed in handling *all* of His gifts. They are to be invested—not wasted! We are not to "think money" for the sake of money, or what it will gain for us personally—but we *do* have a responsibility. We are to relate our thoughts to how money can serve Kingdom purposes.

This brings us to *verses 33 and 34.* After making it very explicit what we are *not* to have uppermost in our thinking, Jesus gives the positive command, "Seek ye first the kingdom of God and his righteousness . . . ." He, also, gives the result of such thinking, ". . . and all these things shall be added unto you."

The food, the drink, and the clothing are guaranteed to those who first seek the Kingdom. This is our aim in these Bylaws: seeking to learn how to live and act and think as Kingdom citizens. When we learn these lessons, here is our assured reward: The Father will be looking out for our every interest—wanting—waiting to supply our every need.

Jesus is saying, "I want you to seek My Kingdom." And this does not mean going to heaven. It means, "I want you to seek for Me to rule over your life. Sign up!" The minute that we do, we become of special value to Him. He can and will supply according to our willingness to permit Him to have rule over our lives.

This reminds me of what happened to me when I joined the U.S. Navy. Once I signed up and was sworn in, I was their property—for four years! They welcomed me with open arms and open hands. First, they put me in line, took my suitcase with all my shaving articles and clothing. There I was standing—stripped of everything I called my own. Next they even took my hair. I mean, I was *their* property!

Then I was told to join another lineup. Here I received underwear, shoes, clothes, seabag, blankets. They said, "You don't have to worry about anything anymore. If you have to travel, we'll take care of you. If you become ill, that is our responsibility." From then on out, my ID card was my supply line.

Why this stripping procedure—then the supply? There was a psychological need for a definitive situation whereby I understood that I was no longer my own. I belonged to the navy. Does that have a familiar ring? "What? know ye not that . . . ye are not your own? For ye are bought with a price . . ." (1 Corinthians 6:19, 20).

Some people panic when they are going through a stripping process. They think it is the Lord's desire to make them poor. It isn't. The object is to strip away the old loyalties and then give you new ones related to your newly acquired understanding or dependence upon your new Ruler. *God is required to re-relate us to everyone and everything.* Then things and people take their rightful place in the sphere of Kingdom living. One is not trapped by money or friends. Some people, because of possessions, live imprisoned lives.

The story is told of a man who had a beautiful art collection worth several million dollars. While he was in Europe the building where it was kept burned to the ground—nothing was salvaged. It was expected the owner would lose his mind when he learned of his loss. Instead, as he looked over the charred remains, his reaction was, "Ah, free at last!" Only he knew what a slave he had become to his collection.

It seems a human tendency that when we have a little of something, we are driven to desire more, and become obsessed with protecting each gain. We may never collect art objects, but meat, drink, clothing, cars, boats—these can become masters instead of assuming their rightful place—serving us, as *their* masters. Once a car may have owned you. Now you can own the car.

"Seek ye first . . . ." Let me give you my translation of this verse: "Reduce all your interests to this—seek first the Kingdom of God and all these things will be added to you." Notice "thing-*s*"—plural! Materialism has a mighty strong pull. Jesus' words of warning at the opening of the lesson were, "No man . . . Ye cannot!" (*See* v. 24.)

Seek first the Kingdom; let everything be related to that one objective. Whether it is house, land, cars, people, trips, family, ask: "Lord, how does this affect my relationship to You and the Kingdom?" Thereby hangs the decision.

Let me relate some instances from my own experience that will help you, I hope, to see that this principle is workable. It does not work in the same ways for everyone, but the principle stands unchangeable—for it is from the Word of God. I have been walking in this way for nearly fifteen years and recommend it to you.

About middle way in this new walk, God used me in an unusual way to help a man who had quite a bit of money. One night about ten o'clock he phoned me at the Bible college where I was a professor, earning about one hundred dollars a month plus meals. He told me he felt the Lord had led him to call and ask me what I needed—*anything!* I felt like Cinderella!

I put my hand over the receiver and asked, "Lord, God, what do I need?"

He replied, "Nothing." I couldn't believe my ears and tried rebuking the answer, and even asked the question again. The answer came back the same.

"But, Lord . . . ahh . . . ." I thought, what do I need? The rent was paid, we had groceries on the shelf, the bills were taken care of, my car ran and I didn't need tires. So I had to say, "Sir, I really do appreciate your call, but I actually don't need anything."

My benefactor assured me that I need not be bashful, but my decision had been made. It got mighty quiet on the other end of the phone because here was a man with money, who finally met somebody who didn't need anything. We both learned some lessons. About ten months later, God used this man in a very remarkable way in our lives.

Another time, I was driving down the road (I remember the car, a 1962 Falcon station wagon, black and red). God had been meeting every need in our lives and I was rejoicing—when suddenly the presence of the Lord came into that car. He said to me, "You can expect an increase in your provision." Now I don't know how many people ever got a pay raise from the Lord, but I did! Our provision took a little leap from that day, and we have never lacked since. Do you see that God has an investment in you and He wants to increase the dividends as He knows you are able to wisely handle them? He knows just when and how to deal with us—how to keep us humble—how to bring situations into our lives that will test our dependence.

One such occasion came when I was asked to go on a teaching mission to Japan. The invitation came by phone; and, again, I turned to the Lord. "Do You want me to go, Lord?" An affirmative reply came, and I told the inquiring friend that I would accept the invitation.

Then the friend said, "Bob, I forgot to tell you, you'll have to pay your own way." (The plane ticket alone was eighteen hundred dollars!)

But I assured him, "I'll be there . . . ." That assurance was worked out by the One who had told me He wanted me to go. From one source came five hundred dollars for the trip—three hundred dollars from another—total twenty-one hundred dollars! So I left on a Pan American overseas flight—ticket paid in full and three hundred dollars in my pocket. On that plane were executives of U.S. Steel, General Motors, and at least one citizen of the Kingdom of God. When I was asked what work I was in, I could reply, "Well, I am an ambassador and I've got my papers in here." My attache case contained His Word and the promises of Kingdom provision.

Remember the stripping process of the navy? The Kingdom has the same procedure. We must be brought to the place where we recognize our dependence and accept it joyfully. The object is that you are stripped of the old and receive the new. And along with the change comes the re-relationship to all that one possesses.

If clothes are Number 1 on your priority list and God says, "Can I have those clothes?" Your response may be, "Anything but that, Lord." He knows just where to put His finger. It may be giving up an unnatural attachment for your children. We often need re-relating in that area. It is sometimes difficult to trust God for our children's welfare. We feel we can do a much better job—being right here on the premises where the needs are!

We have referred to the words of the parable about the seed falling among the thorns (Matthew 13:22) and the end result fits right here, too. "The ground covered with thistles represents a man who hears the message, but the cares of this life and his longing for money choke out God's Word, and he does less and less for God" (LB). Such a man didn't lose his salvation. He didn't go to hell. He was just left with his Mercedes-Benz, and the Lord put them both on the shelf. Unfruitful for Kingdom use. Enjoyable? Yes. But useful? No.

The Law of Reduced Interest can be boiled down to this: We eliminate everything in our lives that doesn't add up to, or relate to, the Kingdom of God. We don't have a lot of things to worry about that we worried about before. We only seek His Kingdom and then God begins to provide as He sees fit.

The closing verse (34) can be paraphrased: "Don't borrow to-morrow's trouble . . . the interest rate is too high."

Have you come to see three emphases in this Law?

(1) Singleness of purpose
(2) Simplicity of trust
(3) Sincerity of intent

If you have, you are one more step closer to the freedom Jesus has for each of us.

You shall know the truth and the truth shall set you free.

◆◆◆

IX   THE LAW OF TOLERANCE

◆◆◆

And he opened his mouth, and taught them, saying:

1   Judge not, that ye be not judged.
2   For with what judgment ye judge, ye shall be judged: and with
what measure ye mete, it shall be measured to you again.
3   And why beholdest thou the mote that is in thy brother's eye,
but considerest not the beam that is in thine own eye?
4   Or how wilt thou say to thy brother, Let me pull out the mote
out of thine eye; and, behold, a beam is in thine own eye?
5   Thou hypocrite, first cast out the beam out of thine own eye;
and then shalt thou see clearly to cast out the mote out of thy
brother's eye.

Matthew 7

In moving from the realm of the tangibles of The Law of Liberality
and The Law of Reduced Interest (money, clothing, food, and drink)
into what might be termed the intangibles discussed here, Jesus shows
us again the comprehensiveness of His teachings.

Whether talking about the need to carefully weigh our responses
to outside stimuli that could cause anger, sexual irregularities, the
breaking of one's word, or the hardening of one's heart—or talking
about evaluating the treasures of this world, Jesus always revealed
His knowledge of the natural tendencies of man. This perception
brought Him into the very heart of every matter He introduced.
How could He so completely relate to men of every background,
age, and temperament? Could this statement be the key?

For in that he himself hath suffered being tempted, he is able to
succour them that are tempted.

Hebrews 2:18

Every single one of the Bylaws centers around temptations and responses that are common to man. This is one of the reasons why multitudes thronged to hear Him. At one such session, the multitudes lingered so long that before they realized it "the day was far spent." In fact, it was so far spent that the disciples came to Jesus requesting that He send them away to get something to eat. Read about this incident in Mark 6:34–36. There were five thousand men present— plus women and children.

The listeners at the teaching session we have been sitting in on were by now well aware of the manner in which the Teacher identified with their needs. Are you?

The attitude which elicited the *Law of Tolerance* was one to which they were constantly subjected—callous judgments. They were also guilty of indulging in the same type activity—at the expense of their fellow men. Jesus Himself was victim of the venom of this practice as the religious leaders of the day sat in judgment on both His teachings and His acts of mercy.

What framework does Jesus erect this time in placing before them the problem and its solution?

Verse 1   Here is stated a bald command, "Judge not," which is followed by a resulting consequence for its disregard.
Verse 2   Next is laid out the principle controlling the consequence of disregarding the command.
Verses 3 and 4   Two questions are offered for consideration. Both are couched in graphic but easily understood language.
Verse 5   The lesson closes with a recommendation for the solution of the problem.

Right here lies one of the secrets as to the lasting quality of Jesus' teachings. The answer is plainly spelled out and spoken so that we may grasp the possibility of making it our very own. Yet, upon more than one occasion, Jesus added the awesome words, "He that hath ears to hear, let him hear." This implies another possibility: *that of being "in class" and going out unchanged.*

If you can grasp the intent of this particular Bylaw, you will save yourself much pain, as well as lessening the chance of inflicting pain upon others. Involved in these few brief verses is a principle that will make you yearn to move out into the freedom it offers—*if you really see it!* Keep your eyes and ears opened.

Have you ever wished there were some built-in warning system or alert that would bring caution to you as you go into action with your tongue and lash out, or let loose, with words you would give almost anything to recall? If so, here is help for you.

Being critical of others, judging them, speaking derogatorily of them is a curse. It might be called a disease that grows as it feeds on itself. Somehow, the thing sticks to us like flypaper! We want to see why this is so tenacious a habit—how it functions—and how we can get free from it.

The Kingdom of God is made up of people. And most of them are imperfects. In fact, in our private estimation, some of them may be rejects! But, once the *Law of Tolerance* is put into operation in our lives, there will be less hasty judgment—putting on others our convictions—speaking our minds as to their ways of doing and not doing things. Again, we have before us a "learned" procedure.

I almost called this Bylaw the *Law of Breathing Room.* Can you see why? We need to give our brothers and sisters some space for differings. Why do we always want to set ourselves up as the self-appointed sheriff of the Kingdom of God? It is a strange way in which most of us operate. Once we come into a new spiritual truth, or get one of our own kinks aligned, we jump on our horse and ride roughshod, trying to straighten out everyone else on the range. "You shouldn't do this . . . What's the matter with you . . . Can't you see the results?"

Much of our difficulties today are caused by those who are sporting railroad ties sticking out of their eyes going around looking for specks of dust in their brothers' eyes. This is the actual meaning of the words which Jesus employed to get across his point of reference: Read verses 3 and 4.

Why do we so quickly forget the months, or perhaps years, of struggle we had while seeking to come into new light? The minute we learn to "do it right," we feel duty bound to press upon all who will listen (and many who won't listen come in for even *worse* criticism) our own criteria. Somehow, highlighting the faults of others makes us feel even more spiritual! Please let me remind you once again that spiritual alignment is God's prerogative. He knows the *when* and *where* and *how*. That is why He gave us this law.

The Old Testament writers referred to this tendency in people as "pointing the finger." Hear how Isaiah states the evaluation of God on the so-called religious people of that day:

> Which say, Stand by thyself, come not near me; for I am holier than thou. These are a smoke in my nose, a fire that burneth all the day.
>
> Isaiah 65:5

Those people who were saying, "Stand by thyself . . ." were polarizing themselves from others whom they judged to be inferior in religious matters. They were the hypocrites of their day. God said He considered this attitude as smoke in His nose—irritating. Upon another occasion, He spoke of their offerings as being "a stench in his nostrils." Jesus had equally vehement words for the hypocrites of

His day. Would it be well for us to check and see if we fall into this category in our day?

Before we go any further in this matter of "Judge not . . ." we must face the fact that there is a time for rightful judging. We shall call this *value judgment*. We need to establish some understanding as to that which *does not constitute judging as Jesus was decrying here*.

Value judging does not mean we are to be opinionless in matters. We maintain our own ideas and will in *matters where God has dealt with us*. It does not mean being overly indulgent of others, either. We are not to be tolerant of sinful situations. Do you see this calls for divine discernment?

When, then, are some times that we may be called upon to make value judgments?

We are warned that we must be alert to the possibility of false teachers and prophets. How else would we know if a man or woman is a false teacher or prophet than to hear what he says, look at his life, find out how he measures up according to the Scriptures? Always there are "ravening wolves" roaming among the sheep. Also in matters such as the choice of a marriage or business partner, in forming close friendships, matters of educational and recreational participation, right judgment is important. In fact, having a rightly aligned basis for making *value judgments* makes one's life more rightly aligned to God's will in every sphere in which we move.

What are some standards for making valid value judgments? Remember the "law of measurement" is put into motion when you make value judgments for "with what measure ye mete, it shall be measured to you again." Be sure you are willing to be measured by the same standards you apply to those whom you question. How about looking at some standards from God's Word? They are the only certain basis for operation.

John 7:24 "Judge not according to the appearance, but judge righteous judgment." These are Jesus' words given to some Jews who questioned His doctrine of teaching. What may "appear" right or wrong to us must be taken before God for help in reaching a conclusion. Don't depend upon self—take it to the Judge.

1 Corinthians 2:15 "A man who is spiritual learns to judge, to discern, to evaluate things as they are" (paraphrased). No superficial judgment here. Remember, "All that glitters is not gold." Learn the art of divine penetration. The Kingdom Bylaws will aid in this art. Judging properly is vital.

1 Timothy 5:24, 25 "Some men's sins are open beforehand, going before to judgment; and some men they follow after. Likewise also the good works of some are manifest beforehand; and they that are otherwise cannot be hid." Here we are told that some men's sins are out in the open; other men's sins are of a "hidden" nature —they are more sneaky! We are warned to discern the true situation. We often joke about "a gift of suspicion"—but, joke or no— it is wise to evaluate carefully.

Take your suspicions to God. He will reveal what a man is really like. How many of you know the devil is forced to play his hand? Just stick around. He always overplays it! Right at the beginning of Creation and the entrance of sin into that perfect Creation, we find these words: "I will put enmity between . . . thy seed and her seed . . ." (Genesis 3:15).

Value judgments are necessary. Never let someone say to you, "You can't judge me." Your reply can be, "My brother, I am required to make a value judgment on how you line up to the Word of God. I seek to judge with righteous judgment. I believe God will expose anything needful. Truth will prevail."

I have literally prayed this way: "Lord, there seems to be something wrong here. I am asking you to expose what is really in there." Have patience. If you have any doubts, take them to the Lord. This type of judgment is sorely needed. Too much goes on under the guise of "situation ethics and brotherly love." But just as we need *more* righteous judgment, so do we need *less* of the self-appointed Kingdom sheriff-type judgment.

Sometimes using the first two words of our Bylaw of Tolerance,

"Judge not . . ." is only used as a smoke screen for sinful actions. This can be true in our own reactions at times, as well as being found in those whom we would question. When one's response to questioning is, "Remember, you are not to judge . . . Matthew 7:1 . . ."—this may be interpreting the admonition not to judge much as a person would take a Fifth Amendment appeal. ("I won't answer your questions for it might incriminate me.") If one has nothing to hide, no defense is needed. True, there may be extenuating circumstances and the welfare of others involved. Here, again, divine wisdom is needed.

Let me give you three pitfalls to be aware of in making your value judgments. Care is needed; so is love. It is not easy to do and there are times when we make mistakes. God will guide and direct *if our motives are right*.

(1) *Our knowledge is incomplete.* In other words, when we judge we do not have all the facts. Acknowledge that only God knows all. Only He knows the condition of a man's heart and his progress in Kingdom living. We may see a person who seems so right in every way. Another person seems to continually make mistakes, causing difficulties for himself and others. Yet the former seems "cut off"— as far as spiritual advance goes, and the latter muddles along. We tend to say, "God, why do you deal this way with the one and in such a different way with the second?" God may reply, "I know all the facts. Don't touch that person. I know his heart. I deal differently with you."

CAUTION: Seek to obtain as many *facts* as possible if you are required to make a value judgment.

(2) *Remember you judge others from your own heart.* This is a most serious consideration. It needs to be accepted as a fact before we can move further into this matter of judging—both as to value judgments and as Jesus was condemning (critically). Most of the time, we judge people *by the way we would act if we were in that particular situation*. Here are some brief illustrations.

"I saw those two alone out in a car and I know what they did because I know what I would have done if I had been there."

Another may say, "Red dresses are sinful." (Why would a man say that? Red dresses "turned him on.")

Still another may always be accusing others of dishonesty and maneuvering for money. "This fellow is out for all he can get . . . Watch out for that group, their motives are questionable . . . ." From personal experience, I found out why these money-oriented remarks found their way into that man's conversation so often!

Strange, but often the people we have the most trouble with are those who are the most like us. It may be difficult to accept our temperament—*in others!* Psychology refers to this as *projection*.

(3) *You may be going behind the blood of the atonement.* God has made provision for taking care of the mistakes of His children. If He had not, what chance would any of us have?

There is the initial repentance of sin and acceptance of Jesus as Saviour—the new birth—which makes one a member of His family. At this time, past sins are placed behind the blood line drawn by the death of Jesus upon the cross. Then follows water baptism, at which time there is a burial between the old life and the new life. There is also the provision for forgiveness of sins and cleansing for the believer. Thank God for 1 John 1:9: "If we confess our sins, he is faithful and just to forgive us our sins, and to cleanse us from all unrighteousness." This transaction is part of the alignment we have been talking about. Showing us our sins—forgiving us when we put them away—and cleansing us from guilt, as well as showing us the way He wants us to live, and giving us the strength to overcome sins in the future—these are all part of Kingdom alignment.

The actions we are judging, or questioning, in another may have been confessed, forgiven, and are now in the process of realignment. Let's give our brothers and sisters breathing room. Remember, even Satan is not permitted to go behind the blood line.

Now we'll go back to Jesus' words in Matthew 7:3, 4 and try to establish what constitutes judging our brother's speck of dust in the eye—from a vision distorted by a railroad tie in our own eye. Remember the drawing showing the comparison? What is this judging of another which carries such certain recompense: ". . . with what measure ye mete, it shall be measured to you again." Before we list our *Guidelines for Measurement* for judging, here are two possibilities which need to be taken into account.

(1) There is judgment which is influenced by our personal feelings —our love for the one needing judgment. Too much goes on in the name of "love" which, of a truth, is only indulgence. Is it possible for parents to neglect proper discipline out of an inordinate family pride or fear of alienating the child? Yes, there is a *kind* of love that believes the object of his love can do no wrong.

(2) There is also the kind of judgment which stems from an attitude that blinds us to the possibility of anyone doing anything right— even those whom we love. If you are harboring the feeling that nobody can do anything right except yourself—watch out! Why is it that some people feel they are not getting a square deal in life—that nobody understands them—that they are not really appreciated? Could these responses be linked to their judgmental attitudes toward others? Jesus says you are setting the standards by which others will judge you.

Example: A very dear friend of mine is continually afraid to stand up in public and give a personal testimony. Do you know why? Whenever she hears another person testify, she immediately goes into gear and raises criticisms, questions, and doubts about what was said. She is, by virtue of this response, actually expecting that should she testify, others would react the same way. Do you see how she is limiting herself—tormenting herself? She cannot give out or receive.

All right, here are *Five Guidelines* for investigating the possibility of a critical, censorious attitude in our judging of others. Be careful— *you* are looking at *you!*

(1) *The tendency to jump to conclusions* Do you have a tendency to interpret all matters and persons with a questioning, critical censorious attitude? "Why I always did think there was something fishy there . . . I never really did trust that person . . . Who does he think he is?" Wait a minute . . . if you have this tendency, recognize it right now and ask God to help you get rid of it. There is nothing ahead for you but more trouble.

Let me relate an incident in which I was involved. I had been to the dentist for surgery, taken gas for anesthetic, had two teeth extracted. Coming out of the office, I was still groggy and decided I needed a cup of coffee. Even getting across the street to the drugstore posed a problem.

I staggered over to the glass entrance door and didn't see either the door or the glass handle. Result? I walked right into it. Further result? My nose started to bleed and my head began swelling up.

Suppose one of those judge-nots—one of those toward whom Jesus was aiming this command—had seen me. I can hear the words now: "I saw it myself . . . he was drunk . . . spaced out. I saw him stagger . . . ran right through a glass door . . . bottle in his pocket . . . blonde on his arm." And all I was trying to do was get a cup of coffee!

The matter of *value judgment* could be involved here, too—had the circumstances really been as pictured by our "sheriff." If I really had been drinking, it would have been wrong to cover me in the act. I would need to be judged and disciplined. I would be saved further transgression had I been exposed, judged according to my actions, and disciplined. If my brothers don't love me enough to discipline me, who does? By the same token, making a superficial judgment and elaborating on it, can bring reproach to an innocent party and hinder progress of the Kingdom.

We must have all possible facts. Go to the person involved, if necessary. But, please, heed these words of Proverbs 18:13: ". . . he that answereth a matter before he heareth it, it is folly and shame unto him."

(2) *Possession of a generally critical attitude* Think carefully before you rate yourself on this one. If your conversations are splattered with: "The government is no good . . . the church is going to the dogs . . . my neighbors are unfriendly . . . the quality of workmanship today just isn't what it used to be . . . children are getting worse every day . . . the coffee isn't any good this morning . . . what is the world coming to?" Do you see general attitude here? Let me point out some steps downward into this abyss of continual criticism.

First, it begins in self-righteousness. It stems out of a self-righteous attitude—which says, *Others are wrong and I am right.* If you are like that, I pray you will have the courage to say, "God, smash that!" I admit it isn't easy to do, but if you acknowledge it and ask God for help, He will respond. He will send His Ways and Means Committee your way.

Next, a self-righteous attitude makes you despise others. In other words, a despising tendency develops. You plant the seed, water it, and you are bound to grow a crop of what you plant.

Then, the attitude will evidence itself in your speech. All expressions will take on a derogatory film. "Out of the heart, the mouth speaketh" is not idle philosophy but fact. The words come out and you cannot stop them; that is, until you recognize the source and go to God for cleansing.

A still further development is the one we quoted from Isaiah 65:5: "Stand by thyself, come not near me; for I am holier than thou . . . ." This attitude of contempt brings for you some of the most severe dealings of God that can fall the lot of any man.

Take my advice: Start with the *first* signal of trouble—if at all possible—and spare yourself the mounting steps downward. Does this sound like double-talk (mounting—downward)? It isn't. We can build to our downfall just as surely as we build for advance.

(3) *Refusing room to breathe* You can tell if you need to go to God for help on this one. If you find it next to impossible to give other people room in which to differ from you—you need help! Look at this from Romans:

As for the man who is a weak believer, welcome him [into your fellowship], but not to criticize his opinions *or* pass judgment on his scruples *or* perplex him with discussions.

14:1 AMPLIFIED

I would like to word that last phrase, ". . . but not to straighten him out." Grant that weaker brother growing room before you lower the boom! In verses 2–6 of Romans 14, Paul lists some of the points of difference, as well as the futility of trying to make others conform to our understandings. Matters of proper eating habits and certain days on which to worship are mentioned. There are so many others —the Rapture—Millennium—Lord's Supper. Paul later adds, "For meat destroy not the work of God. All things indeed are pure . . . whatsoever is not of faith is sin" (vs. 20, 23).

You see your neighbor's wash on the line as you start out to church Sunday morning. Right away, "Couldn't she find another day to do her laundry?" There may be sick children—and only a limited supply of sheets.

Don't put on your sheriff's badge before you give a little margin. Bells—smells—liturgy—tambourines. Do you see that all these things can be considered marginal and in the realm of the "minors"? Again some words from Paul come to mind: "Now we see through a glass, darkly . . ." (1 Corinthians 13:12). Nobody knows it all; nor does any one group have it all. The essentials of our belief— the deity of Christ—His Atonement—the Resurrection—major on these and allow for differences in the minors. Permit God to do His own work in the lives of others.

(4) *Most judgment comes from the area of my strength* Analyze this in your judgment of others. Do you use the areas of strength in your life (your strong points) to compare the weaknesses of others in this area? Did you ever stop to think you may have some points of weakness, and others may be strong in those same areas? In our walk with God, each of us develops certain strengths. These are permitted us so that we can help those who need help in that realm

—not so we can, from our vantage point, disparage others who have not realized the same strength.

The person who has faith for healing has a tendency to judge others who are sick. One who has faith in the field of finances may be particularly judgmental of others who flounder here. The object of the body of Christ is to bring our strengths into our fellowships to advantage—to help that weaker brother. Help must come out of a heart of concern—not from a feeling of superiority for our own attainments. The weaker brother senses the difference. He is probably well aware of his weakness—and, perhaps, even of our strength.

(5) *Expressing ourselves in areas that are none of our business*
You can pretty well tell whether or not you are critical or not by the fact that you have an opinion about everything.

"They should never have put a red carpet in the church. Green would have looked much better . . . I don't think our pastor should ever have bought that new car . . . I know you don't like to hear this, but I'm going to tell you anyway. It's really for your own good. You wear your dresses too short . . . too much lipstick . . . your hair is too long . . . on and on . . . ."

If you swing at every ball that comes your way, you'll soon strike out and find yourself benched as far as usefulness in the progress of the Kingdom goes.

These ABCs are rather sobering to say the least! That is what we call the boomerang principle of *Matthew 7:2:* "With what judgment ye judge, ye shall be judged: and with what measure ye mete, it shall be measured to you again." It is constant in operation and plays no favorites. Anyone who is acquainted with the way a boomerang works, knows it never comes back to us in the front. It always returns and hits us in the back of the head—*Zap!* Once we realize that we set the standards by which other people treat us and evaluate *our* actions, it isn't hard to see why some people are always in trouble.

How many of you have ever been to a ball game and a particular player comes up to the plate as if he were the immortal "Casey at the Bat." He brushes the dirt . . . goes through all kinds of contortions . . . and readies himself to swing. There is a strange reaction in us that makes us long to see that man strike out. I used to think there was something wrong with me when I had that reaction. Then I learned the truth of "The Lord humbles the proud and gives grace to the humble." Even in small matters, we need to let Him be the Judge and dispenser of judgment.

Now when I realized that I was going to set the standard by which I was going to be judged, I made the standard very low. I have stumbled and fallen and have needed grace—both from God and my brothers. Once we understand this principle, the temptation to be critical, judgmental, censorious takes on a new dimension.

Can you see how this frees us? When I teach I can have great freedom—because I don't judge you. That is why I can expect mercy and acceptance. There was a time when, because of a timid nature, I would get nervous in front of crowds and expend useless energy on concern as to how I would be received. Now I do not need to worry. I can be myself and teach the way I want to teach—and I don't expect you to judge me. That freedom only comes to a person who is willing to give the same freedom to others. I seek not to be judgmental, consequently there is less criticism and judgment coming upon me.

Moving on into the eye surgery described in *verses 3 and 4,* we find some warnings for both those who desire to perform the surgery and those upon whom it is to be performed.

In the physical, eye surgery is a very delicate operation. It is, likewise, in the spiritual realm. Be careful in your choice of a surgeon, should you need one. Place yourself in the care of a qualified party. If someone comes to you and offers to operate on you, ask: "How is your vision? Any beams to interfere?" *Here is a need for value judgment.* Check him out with Scripture; and take a look at how the lessons and counsel he seeks to give is applied in his own daily living.

Then, if we want to operate on others, here there is need for caution, too. We can be desirous to help, and yet be so clumsy that we stumble into situations beyond our abilities. Just as the physical eye quickly closes at the wrong approach, so does the spiritual eye. It might take weeks . . . months . . . even years before that person who was approached with blunted instruments or unskilled hands will submit himself for surgery again.

While in medical training for missionary service, my wife and I scrubbed for an eye surgeon. We learned about the intricacies of removal of the eyeball, transplant of corneas, eyes burned with acid, putting a new lining in the eyelid—as well as the care needed to remove a foreign object from the eye. Jesus drew upon a live issue at this point, "Let me pull out the mote [speck] out of thine eye . . . ." The desert winds carried dust and sand into many eyes. Helping a fellow traveler remove a speck of sand could result in permanent damage if attempted by a person who was careless or had diseased hands. Applying this to the spiritual—be sure to scrub up and move in with skill if and when you offer aid. Don't be too quick to come to the rescue. On the other hand, don't let fear or accusation deprive you of opportunities to serve others.

Verse 5 ". . . first cast out the beam out of thine own eye; and then shalt thou see clearly to cast out the mote out of thy brother's eye." This offers the recommendation that will free us to make *proper value judgments—and* qualify us to remove foreign objects from the eyes of others.

First we must take into consideration the words with which Jesus prefaced His recommendation: "Thou hypocrite . . ." and admit there may be something interfering with the 20/20 vision we need. Be willing to place yourself for an eye examination under the all-seeing examination of the Great Physician. If He shows you a railroad tie, or even some smaller obstacle in your eye, ask Him to remove it. Then you will be free to see others as He sees them. You can offer assistance in His Name and move with confidence, under His leadership, to perform surgery in this very delicate area.

Another caution to heed is that cleansing of the eyes must be a daily procedure. Every day brings its own film formed by the pollution of the environment in which we live. Specks of dust are swirling around us all the time. Provision has been made to protect physical eyes. The eyelid is intricately designed for that purpose. But if we were to keep the eyelid closed all the time, we would shut out our view and limit our abilities. Strive for balance. Operate in the realm where God has placed you. Don't try to overextend yourself.

Do you feel free-*er* already? Just reading these words of Jesus should have that effect. I can assure you that when you begin to put the teaching into actual practice, you will find yourself facing each day and opportunity with the exhilaration of a mountain climber who has reached one more plateau in his effort to touch the pinnacle and catch a view of his expanded universe.

Jesus knew that once a man breathes the invigorating air He offers, and sees the vistas ahead, nothing can hinder him from attempting to move on up the mountain. The further climb to see and embrace Kingdom principles will claim priority in his life.

X THE LAW OF SPIRITUAL TRUTH

And he opened his mouth and taught them, saying:

6 Give not that which is holy unto the dogs, neither cast ye your pearls before swine, lest they trample them under their feet, and turn again and rend you.

Matthew 7

Wrapped up in this one short verse is a lesson that will prove invaluable to everyone who is interested in the Kingdom of God. Yet, it is often overlooked, either because dogs and swine and pearls seem less related to Kingdom living—or because the previous lesson on judging and the one following it (which is on asking and receiving) seem so much more practical.

However, here in verse 6 is a key to one of the reasons why more progress is not made in the "practicals" (we are apt to categorize teachings). Jesus did not place His lessons in categories. He moved slowly but surely toward building understanding of the freedom possible in Kingdom living. Are you holding before you His words, ". . . If ye continue in my word, then are ye my disciples indeed; And ye shall know the truth, and the truth shall make you free" (John 8:31, 32). This is His aim!

In our study on the Law of Tolerance, we mentioned the wide scope of Jesus' teachings and the universality of their implications. But whether He is producing a manifesto on morals, or merely interjecting a word of wisdom (as He does in verse 6), His intent is always to put before us truths necessary for our progress into freedom. *Did you know that we must all learn certain disciplines before we can venture very far into the realm of the spirit without danger of causing damage to ourselves and others?*

The Law of Spiritual Truth, which we now investigate, discloses the answer to questions you may be raising in regard to the above statement. But we *can* limit our own progress, as well as limiting the progress of others. This Law helps us learn how to handle the spiritual truths God reveals to us. We shall see how intimately and personally God works with each individual. It should also encourage us to approach new truth with a heightened appreciation for the privileges and responsibilities involved. *Newly discovered treasures bring with them problems, as well as pleasures.*

Jesus linked "that which is holy" with one of the most precious jewels of His day—pearls. We referred earlier to a parable He used in illustrating a truth on values (Matthew 13:45, 46) in which He speaks of a "pearl of great price" and selling everything in order to possess that treasure. His audience was familiar with the price of pearls, their merchandising, and the manner in which a pearl is formed.

The waters in and adjacent to Palestine cast up oysters in which the precious pearl had been formed—at cost to the oyster! They knew the process of formation from the grain of sand working its way into the oyster and setting up irritation—the oyster starting to cover the grain of sand with one layer of mucous after another in order to alleviate the irritation. Finally, the pearl is formed—by tribulation! Tribulation is not pleasant to the oyster; neither is it to the thinking of the Christian. But it is necessary in both cases. Paul and Barnabas linked tribulation and the Kingdom of God in their words to believers in Lystra, Iconium, and Antioch.

> Confirming the souls of the disciples, and exhorting them to continue in the faith, and that we must through much tribulation enter into the kingdom of God.
>
> Acts 14:22

Have you ever experienced tribulations in hearing and accepting new truths? Usually when God places before us some truth we have not seen before—at first it sets up all kinds of irritations. *How many of you realize that truth is negative when it first comes to you?* It is apt to upset past understandings. It is apt to upset present life-styles.

It may affect your future plans. You may even find yourself desiring to reject it. But the seed of that truth gets down inside you, much as seed does in the soil. It is watered, fertilized, warmed by God's sunlight—and before long it germinates and begins pushing other things aside in order to come into being. The uprooting and struggles prove to be tribulations.

Finally the truth is *formed* in us—just as the pearl was formed in the oyster. We say, "Glory to God! I never saw that before!" And what is our first inclination? To run and tell everybody—or anybody who will listen—about our discovery. This is where the *Law of Spiritual Truth* goes into operation. *You must learn how, what, when, and with whom to share your "treasures."*

Yes, new truth will make you increasingly free; but it does not carry with it the freedom to fling "holy things" to dogs and hogs—as Jesus so picturesquely portrays our natural tendencies. Part of the confusion across the whole body of Christ today is caused by people who come into new truths and then share them out of time—out of school—and in the wrong way.

Just as there is a penalty for breaking laws in the secular realm, so there is in the spiritual realm. Laws are made and enforced for the protection of individuals and principles in both realms. If we knowingly, or unknowingly, break this *Law of Spiritual Truth,* there is a price to pay.

First, the Lord, the One who reveals truth to us, has a way of withdrawing Himself from those who treat lightly or carelessly His treasures.

Suppose He comes to you with some personal, intimate revelation —and after a period of time, during which He builds up your trust in Him and your love for Him, you are able to make it your very own. Do you become so excited that, in your undisciplined condition, you spill it all over? I am not talking about private revelations or new doctrines, but the illumination of eternal truths inherent in the Scripture.

At times Jesus referred to the relationship established between

Himself and His followers as a "bridegroom/bride" relationship.
This is the most intimate of all life's relationships and was easily
understood by all who heard Jesus' teachings. No bride shares all of
her joys and experiences with others. Can you see how, in this comparison, the Lord might withdraw, saying, "There were some things
I wanted to share with you, but now I see I cannot."

This brings to my mind the first time the truth of 1 Corinthians
10:13 became real to me. I had read it before, but now it was mine!

> There hath no temptation taken you but such as is common to
> man: but God is faithful, who will not suffer you to be tempted
> above that ye are able; but will with the temptation also make a
> way to escape, that ye may be able to bear it.

Lights began flashing—bells began ringing. I rushed to my pastor
and expected the same reaction from him. Instead of, "Oh, Bob,
that's wonderful!"—all I got was a consenting grunt. Why wasn't he
as excited as I? At that particular time, that particular illumination
was for me personally. It was a love note from the Bridegroom. After
I simmered down, the Lord said to me, "Be quiet. That's between
you and Me. I want to minister to you personally. I want to share
some things and every time I do, you have to run to someone and
spout off." Has anyone ever been guilty of that—except me?

What is one of the reasons why we want to broadcast our newly
acquired treasures? Could it be that we are trying to impress others
with our spirituality? Is not this in itself a sign of immaturity? *When
the Lord shares anything with you, keep it to yourself; let it work
in your life and people will see the fruits.*

How do we curb our desires to share, running the risk of having
our treasures ignored or tossed aside and trampled underfoot? How
do we learn the discipline necessary—and the wisdom of when, how,
and with whom we are to share them? As always, we ask Him—only
to find He has spelled out the answer in His Word. Look with me at
Isaiah 50:4 for some specifics.

The Lord God hath given me the tongue of the learned, that I should know how to speak a word [what to speak] in season [when to speak] to him that is weary [to whom to speak]: he wakeneth morning by morning, he wakeneth mine ear to hear as the learned.

Do you see the One who teaches us—the how, what, and when? The right thing—to the right person—at the right time—and in the right way. This is so important! And what is the way we learn these lessons? Morning by morning. Not all in one sitting. *We need to say, "Lord Jesus, show me today!"*

A popular song goes, "Tell me tender . . . ." To some people, we will need to use that type approach. To another, at a certain time in his life, we may need to speak bluntly. To a third person, a story with a moral may serve his purpose. The "right season" is also an important factor. God has to create the need; then He will send someone to fill that need. You may be the one—if you are listening that morning and have your tongue consigned to speaking His words. *He never wastes words. He waits until you are listening!*

This lesson has been made flesh and blood to me many times. Once when I had boarded a plane following a speaking engagement, I was "peopled out." I didn't want to see anybody or talk to anyone. The plane was almost empty. It was a night flight and I found myself two vacant seats, put my briefcase on one and told the Lord, "Thanks. And I just don't want to talk to anybody or have anybody talk to me."

About that time a girl about twenty-two years of age came down the aisle, stopped next to me, and asked, "Is that seat taken?" I could hardly believe it! In reply to my reluctant *no* and removal of the briefcase, she settled in. I was sitting there grumbling to myself and protesting to the Lord. Shortly she turned to me and the conversation went something like this:

"Say, can I buy you a drink?"

"No, I don't feel like a drink."

"Well, do you mind if I have one?"

"No, be my guest."

Silence for awhile . . . then:

"Do you drink?"

"Why do you ask?"

"I thought maybe you were one of those religious fanatics."

God had set the stage. Now it was my turn to take over. For three hours I ministered His Word to her. I learned she had opened her heart to the Lord as a young girl in a little country church. The years had brought many changes. She cried and I cried. I tried to bring her to a commitment to Christ but she resisted. But God was after her—she was weary—and He spoke to her through me.

Being sensitive to God's directions also includes knowing when to answer questions. Just because someone comes to you with a question—this doesn't necessarily mean He wants you to get out your jewel box and begin scattering pearls. Suppose a person comes to you merely wanting to start an argument. You aren't duty bound to do battle with him. I have learned that all the proof texts in the world aren't going to convince someone who is looking for an opportunity to flaunt *his* treasures and question yours! If a person is "anti" anything, God has to open the heart. The Bible alone will not *prove* anything. When Nicodemus came to Jesus (John 3:1–21), he came with a question. Jesus carefully explained spiritual blindness to him in these words, ". . . Except a man be born again, he cannot see the kingdom of God" (v. 3).

Jesus explained this principle of operation to His disciples later.

In that hour Jesus rejoiced in spirit, and said, I thank thee, O Father, Lord of heaven and earth, that thou hast hid these things from the wise and prudent, and hast revealed them unto babes; even so, Father, for so it seemed good in thy sight . . . And he turned him unto his disciples, and said privately, Blessed are the eyes which see the things that ye see.

Luke 10:21, 23

The *wise and prudent* to whom He referred were those who were *wise in their own conceits* and so careful to protect their own beliefs that they could be considered *prudent in their efforts.* The *babes* were those, who in their *trust and simplicity,* were able to accept the Master's teachings as truth. God knows from whom to hide holy things, as well as those who can be trusted to receive them.

There are times when we cannot see—times when you cannot convince others—times when the situation is in reverse. Think back on your own experiences. When you were prepared to receive truth, God sent somebody. That somebody may only have been part of the journey into new truth. Then along came somebody else. The light finally breaks through.

There are possibilities of meeting with hostility. Remember we said truth may come first in a negative form? What you offer another person, under God's leadership, may be only a springboard for another approach from an entirely different avenue and person.

So, we have seen *first, that the Lord hides His treasures.* He reveals them as one is able and prepared to receive. Let me give you a twentieth-century classroom example.

While in Bible college, one of my professors often would ask the class: "Class, are there any questions? If you don't know enough to ask questions, I will not volunteer the answers." Talking about a frustrating quandry! At last a student asked, "Sir, why did the angel visit Mary?" This elicited the reply, "I'm so glad you asked that." Then followed twenty minutes of enrichment for all of us. How much I missed by not even being able to ask questions.

A second hindrance to receiving truth is found in John 16:12. Jesus was talking to the smaller group of disciples. It was the night of His betrayal and He was desirous to share with them all that He could before He would be leaving them for awhile. This is His last Word to them: "I have yet many things to say unto you, but ye cannot bear them now."

This, too, is a frustrating situation. But it is one of God's principles of operation. There are some truths that we are not able to bear *yet.* However, we may be assured that as we grow and mature, He will

open these truths to us. Why give them to us when we cannot receive
—masticate—digest—and make them operative in our lives? He
knows our capacities and will enlarge them as we ask Him to do so.
Please don't be intellectually curious about the Word of God. Don't
try to force the Scriptures to yield something to you! Love His Word.
Bow before it. Honor and respect it. As you do this, He will honor
and respect your desires and give as you are able to receive.

Just as God reveals His truths to us as we are able to receive, we
must seek to become sensitive to the abilities of others to receive.
Little by little we learn how to handle God's truth in relation to
others: when to keep quiet—when to speak—and how much to
share—and what!

A third hurdle is presented in 1 Corinthians 3:1. Paul is telling the
believers to whom he had preached God's Word the reason why they
were not able to receive and make use of the goodly pearls God
wanted them to have:

And I, brethren, could not speak unto you as unto spiritual, but
as unto carnal, even as unto babes in Christ.

Here we find that the believers were not walking in the truth they
had been given. They had permitted themselves to be blinded by the
"carnals" of life. Paul delineated these to them and begged them to
see that those who persisted in this type of living could not make
progress in the Kingdom of God. They had no love for the truth they
already had, and consequently Paul was unable to communicate further spiritual truths. Do you see what the Corinthians had done with
present truth—and what they would have done with additional pearls?
They would have trampled them underfoot. Paul was taking seriously
the words of Matthew 7:6. We need to do likewise.

Value judgment is needed before we "throw holy things" to others.
Not only are God's truths desecrated, but we are maligned. We ren-
der ourselves vulnerable to hurt when we don't learn how to handle
the precious truths entrusted to our care.

Let's share some illustrations of how the Law of Spiritual Truth works.

We know there is a right time to share every spiritual truth. That is what they are given for—to benefit God's children. If you have caught the deep implication of this Law, you will pray: "Lord Jesus, show me the right time to talk with my husband—my employer —my neighbor—my child. I am asking You to give me the right occasion to tell others what has happened to me." When I pray this way, before long it "happens" that a friend will come to me and say, "Bob, could you spare me a few minutes? I want to talk with you . . . ." *Then I have confidence that this is it!*

In the discussion of the Law of Impartiality, I told of an incident which happened during one of my summer vacations when I was attending Bible college. May I repeat it again here to demonstrate how God directs.

For three months I had been subjected to many unpleasantries as "new man on the job." The three men with whom I worked on a surveying crew were Christ-rejecting, cursing and callous. My prayer was, "Lord, will You give me an occasion to share with these guys?" As we set out on our last ride home from the location where we had been working, the driver of the truck said to me, "Bob, we have watched you for three months. We've decided we want you to tell us about yourself." That was my cue. An hour and a half later those men got out of that truck as if they were leaving a cathedral!

Now, which proved better? Leaving a tract under their lunch buckets every day or waiting on God's timing? There is a place for tracts and tract ministries—street work—mass evangelism. But as you go on in God, you must seek Him for timing and means for sharing what He has given you.

Along with being sensitive to the *when* of sharing, we also need to cultivate an awareness of *how much* to share.

Example: Here I am—saved, baptized in water, baptized with the Holy Spirit—and recently received healing of a gall bladder condition. My employer becomes curious and starts asking me questions. Where do I start and how much do I share? Too much of the wrong beginning might turn him away completely. He may just blow a fuse and I'll blow my opportunity. The *Law of Spiritual Truth* tells me I must be sensitive to his needs. I pray, "God, help me to know if I should talk to him about being born again—or start at the other end and tell him of my healing." Do you see that I could bungle—offend him—and he would reject the entire package?

We can have our testimonies so pre-pared that it is almost like pulling a string and out of a puppet comes a set of words that have little relation to either the person or the time. This is not walking in maturity. It is not the way to handle spiritual truth. Sometimes the Lord permits others to "rend your pearls under foot" in order to open your eyes to the way He is trying to bring you into the workings of this Bylaw.

We have learned that if we speak out of turn, the Lord will close up on us. It may be some time before He can trust us with further illuminations from His Word. Why not ask Him for permission to share when you are in doubt. "Lord, this is really rich. It has blessed me. Please give me opportunity to share this blessing with others." You can be sure the writing of this book is a result of such a prayer!

We have learned, too, that along with seeking His guidance in sharing, we must be alerted to timing—how to present His truths—and what to expect if we fail in some instances. These are truths one does not learn in just a single lesson. They are skills often made real to us through trial and error. That is why Jesus warned His disciples to be expecting possible rejection of their witness.

In closing, we shall take a look at the *Law of Spiritual Truth* in actual operation in the life of the One who was teaching the lesson. The Teacher was preparing His disciples for the time when they would be presenting "holy things" to others.

Here are some verses from Luke, chapter 8, which set the scene and bring out the truth we have been sharing.

And it came to pass that he went . . . preaching and shewing the glad tidings of the kingdom of God: and the twelve were with him . . . .

V. 1

And when much people were gathered together . . . he spake by a parable.

V. 4

And his disciples asked him, saying, What might this parable be?

V. 9

And he said, Unto you it is given to know the mysteries of the kingdom of God: but to others in parables; that seeing they might not see, and hearing they might not understand.

V. 10

Take heed therefore how ye hear: for whosoever hath, to him shall be given; and whosoever hath not, from him shall be taken even that which he seemeth to have.

V. 18

Jesus is conducting serious business with the disciples. He wanted them to know why some people would turn from their witness and trample underfoot truths that had become the light of their lives.

Jesus wants us to take just as seriously these truths that are presently ours because of the faithfulness of the disciples of that first teaching session.

The King and you! You have a responsibility as you read these words. Take heed how you read.

XI THE LAW OF THE FATHER'S WISDOM

And he opened his mouth and taught them, saying:

7 Ask, and it shall be given you; seek and ye shall find; knock, and it shall be opened unto you:

8 For every one that asketh receiveth; and he that seeketh findeth; and to him that knocketh it shall be opened.

9 Or what man is there of you, whom if his son ask bread, will he give him a stone?

10 Or if he ask a fish, will he give him a serpent?

11 If ye then, being evil, know how to give good gifts unto your children, how much more shall your Father which is in heaven give good things to them that ask him?

12 Therefore all things whatsoever ye would that men should do to you, do ye even so to them: for this is the law and the prophets.

Matthew 7

We move from the serious business of how, when, how much, and with whom we should share Spiritual Truth (Bylaw Number 10— The Law of Spiritual Truth, which presented our relations to others) to the even more serious business of *how* the Father relates to us in this matter of sharing.

Again, we would emphasize the fact that Jesus is building carefully and cautiously. All teachers realize that they can only bring their hearers into the presence of truth. The element of *acceptance* or *rejection* has to be taken into consideration. That is the chance a teacher takes. Jesus met with both of these responses.

No one ever taught with more candor or confidence than Jesus. He laid it on the line and left it there. *Are you beginning to sense that freedom is not free?* We speak of the free will of man, and rightly so. Man is free to make choices. But once the choice is made, the

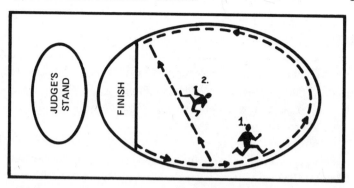

responsibilities begin. How about going back over our diagram of
the race track, the two runners, and the Judge? Do you see that both
runners are free to decide whether to abide by the rules and run the
course from start to finish as directed? Or there is the possibility of
cutting across the grass and reducing the running time. But both
must face the Judge as they come to that finish line. The one who
shortcuts is disqualified. In the end, he will have to pay the penalty.
The Judge decides the penalties, as well as making the rules. Here
are some principles we learned He has made operational in the realm
of Spiritual Truth.

(1) *God tends to withdraw Himself from those who handle carelessly or lightly His revealed truths.* Notice the word is *with-
draws*—not *forsakes.* The Spirit of the Lord becomes grieved
and, in tenderness, He just moves away, leaving us sitting alone
in our coldness and blindness.

(2) *No man can see spiritual truth until he meets the stipulations
set by God.* Recall, if you will: "Except a man be born again,
he cannot see the kingdom of God." This is Jesus speaking in
John 3:3. That word, *cannot,* does not mean that man is prohibited from seeing, but that he is *unable to see.* In other words,
we establish our own inabilities.

Had I been setting up the Kingdom of God, I would have put it
on an island—put a big fence around it—supplied it with big search-

lights and police dog guards. I would have a sign: NO TRESPASSING UNLESS YOU ARE BORN AGAIN. But God? He puts the Kingdom right in the middle of society—and unless our spiritual eyes are opened, we simply cannot see it. Someone gets up and talks about Kingdom living; and the response is, "What Kingdom?"—or "I don't see any Kingdom." You can walk all around it and hear all about it and never step into the freedom it affords.

The law of responsibility says: It is how you handle the truth He gives you which qualifies you for His giving you further truth. *This amazing mechanism we shall call the Law of the Father's Wisdom.*

The first two verses of our lesson text for this Bylaw form a definitive trilogy. You will note, also, that they form an acrostic.

A - ASK
S - SEEK
K - KNOCK

Each one of these three represents prayer. Each one expresses an attitude in prayer. Each one insures its own particular type answer. Each one, as it is explored and embraced, affords the avenue to proceeding to a new height of attainment and usefulness in Kingdom living. Let's investigate.

We begin by presenting another principle of operation. *God always places His treasures just out of reach.* Why does He do this? To understand why, we will need to understand the growth factor.

First, "Ask and it shall be given you." This is the gift realm. What is the first thing you think of when we speak of gifts? Yes, Christmas. Here is a Christmas tree laden with beautiful gifts—yours for the asking: salvation, healing, wisdom, daily bread, finances, forgiveness, Baptism in the Holy Spirit, many others.

There are one or two hazards in this receiving business. Many of us have watched our children come down on Christmas morning. They see the tree—the gifts. Some children will immediately become so wrapped up in the gifts that they forget the giver. Others drop the gift and run to father or mother. They may spot the new bicycle and say, "Oh, what a beauty!" Then without even touching it, hurry to express their thanks with a hug and kiss. What joy this brings! Two different attitudes are evident here. Has giving joy to the Giver of every good and perfect gift entered your thinking?

Some people live their entire Christian lives in the gift realm— asking and receiving. Their needs are provided. They feel no further needs. *But God desires to create needs so that He may reveal to us spiritual advances.* There is more for us than the knowledge that He loves us and supplies our needs as we ask Him. We may never grow out of the asking realm, *but there is more!* Yet some not only fail to realize the *more;* they are still learning lessons in the ask/receive realm.

Two reasons why a believer is not enjoying the abundant life and the blessings made available to him are discussed in James, chapter 4: He begins by saying

". . . yet ye have not, because ye ask not" (v. 2).

and

"Ye ask, and receive not, because ye ask amiss . . ." (v. 3).

James continues to talk about our asking "that ye may consume it upon your lusts." Strong words—but reducible to individual motivation. Let us paraphrase what He was saying, "You ask and do not receive because you ask to satisfy your own lusts." He also talks about humbling oneself before God—about God resisting the proud—submitting ourselves to Him—resisting the devil—and purifying our hearts. *This will help us to see how we can ask amiss, with the result —no answer!*

May I suggest some reasons why we may fail to ask? Usually it is due to being too formal or too fearful. Sometimes our children ask for things they feel almost certain we will not give them. Yet, because of the love relationship which has been established, they are willing to take a chance. And, sometimes, we parents surprise them and grant the request. This is the way it is with God. Then, the too-formal approach: "Dear Lord: wouldest . . . couldest . . . shouldest Thou . . . ." Just ask. It is a whole new world for many believers. "Lord, You know I really would like for You to do that for me . . . ."

I had a very exciting experience not too long ago. Before me was a situation that appeared absolutely insolvable. One day after wrestling with the problem, I walked to the window and said, "God, You have been so good to me that I can hardly get the courage to ask You about this. But You know all about it, and about my inability to do anything constructive. I really would like for You to take care of that for me." There followed a satisfaction in my spirit—and three days later the whole thing fell into place. God moved. I asked and received.

A young woman related to me this gratifying answer to prayer. She was single—met a certain Christian young man, also single. He was working in the city with a construction crew. This type of work took them from one location to another, not leaving much opportunity to form lasting relationships in one community. But the young

THE LAW OF THE FATHER'S WISDOM

woman went boldly before the Lord and said, "Lord, I'd like to have a chance with that young man." Events "conspired" and the entire construction crew moved back to the scene of action and allowed time for their friendship to blossom into marriage.

Are we apt, in our praying, to communicate to God our doubts rather than our desires? He knows our hearts but He wants us to strengthen our faith and enjoy the results.

Returning to our Christmas tree, if I wanted to give my wife a thousand-dollar diamond ring, do you think I would just hang it any old place? No, of course not. God, also, has some special treasures that He handles on an entirely different plane than the ask/receive plateau. He wants to reveal Himself to us—not to be just the Supplier of our needs. When you come to God's hidden treasures, this demands a different attitude of prayer.

The second attitude of our trilogy is: "Seek and ye shall find."

Webster uses these strong verbs to define seeking: go in search or . . . look for . . . pursue . . . aim at . . . entreat. Quite different from merely asking, isn't it? There is a time to ask—and a time to seek. Some things we ask for—others we must seek for. Listen to some commands where we are specifically told to seek:

Matthew 6:33 Seek ye first the kingdom of God . . . .
Psalm 27:8 When thou saidest, Seek ye my face; my heart said unto thee, Thy face, Lord, will I seek.

How many of you see that you don't *ask* for the Kingdom, or for His face. You exert more than a request. There are other treasures that are set before us for the seeking, too:

Colossians 2:3 In whom [Christ] are hid all the treasures of wisdom and knowledge . . . .

You won't find these hanging on a Christmas tree! Why didn't the Lord hang all the treasures of wisdom and knowledge where you could just run up and grab them? Why does He require us to seek for them?

Seeking is an *attitude*—a strong desire. In the seeking we stretch ourselves—become spiritually mature. Thus, we come into a place whereby God can give us treasures from His Word that do not injure us. We must all learn certain disciplines before we can venture very far into the realm of the spirit without danger of causing damage to ourselves and others. God is protecting His children, as well as His treasures. The Law of Spiritual Truth brought us to these conclusions, as well as giving us these words from two teachers.

JESUS   I have yet many things to say unto you, but ye cannot bear them now (John 16:12).

PAUL   And I, brethren, could not speak to you as unto spiritual, but as unto carnal, even as babes in Christ (1 Corinthians 3:1).

The Lord may say to me, "Bob, separate yourself for awhile and *seek* my face. There are some things I want to share with you." And I get away. It may be possible that I can actually "get away" and have time alone in prayer and study. Fasting, too, may be possible. Again, family schedules and demands may require other arrangements. The "getting away," however, involves removing ourselves from other interests and desires. This presupposes obedience, dependence, spiritual hunger and *sufficient spiritual maturity to establish priorities*. All of these have been touched upon in our Bylaws. Are you beginning to see the absolute necessity for building along with Jesus?

Jesus told the disciples not to cast their pearls before swine; and we shared the meaning of that simple statement. God also exercises caution with His pearls. He knows just what to share—with whom—the right time and the right way. The manner in which He shares with you may be entirely different from the one in which He shares the same truth with another.

So we sit down with our Bible—God's truth. We open it with a seeking attitude and He responds. This involves much more than being a "finger-pointer." Some have based their "missionary call" on a finger pointing at "The isles wait for thee." Off they go to Tasmania. We will be investigating this approach when we move into the third command of the Law of the Father's Wisdom, which is *to knock.*

"Keep on asking . . . keep on seeking . . . keep on knocking." That is what Jesus is teaching us. You may feel this is frustration or spiritual intensity. No, it is neither of these. It is a principle that is operative in every sphere of our lives. Someone has said, "You can have whatever you want if you want it badly enough." Be it education —development of skills or the arts—money—or the spirituals. There must be desire, goals, expending of energy, and discipline. God knows we need stretching out and enlargements inside. We need certain maturity lest the very thing that God speaks to us becomes our undoing. It is better not to know the truth, than to know it and turn from it.

There are some things that the Lord spoke to me recently that I had been seeking for ten years. I said, "Lord, why didn't you tell me that way back when . . . ?" To which He replied, "You wouldn't have known how to handle it then." How right He was!

The seeking attitude reveals to you and to God your hunger and seriousness to do business. Our society has engendered a "right-now" attitude that doesn't get results in Kingdom living. We put in a quarter and punch a button to get what we want. God doesn't deal in quarters or button-pushing. God is building toward freedom; and we agreed freedom isn't "for free."

Our third attitude of prayer is, "Knock and it shall be opened to you."

Knocking has to do with the right use of truth we have been given. It doesn't seem to occur to many people that we are required to confer with the Lord on what to do with what He has given us. But this is Jesus' recommendation for progression to the next plateau.

What is it we usually connect with knocking? A door. We go to God and say, "God, won't you give me the opportunity to share what

You have done for me—revealed to me—taught me?" or are you the type who says in response to this suggestion, "Well, if the Lord wants to open a door for me, He knows my name and address. He knows where I am." Could that be why many are still waiting, clutching their treasures to themselves—while the treasures and desires gradually diminish?

Then there is the Mumford way. You tear the door off the hinges or pick the lock to get in! I have been in rooms that didn't belong to me and I got there by tearing the door off the hinges. I failed to take His advice and knock. I didn't understand—I suffered—and I said, "Lord, when I get back I will tell others to knock."

"*Knock . . . Knock*—Lord, give me people to witness to today . . . Bring across my path someone who needs to hear what I have to say . . . Lord, open a door." When you knock, and the Lord opens the door (from the inside)—then you can step into that entryway in confidence.

God never opens the door to situations you are too immature to handle. You never get in over your head. The Lord will give you people to listen to your witness—to sing to—minister to with power and authority—*if you knock*. There are opportunities waiting for each of us. But don't knock too soon. You must be sure you have something to offer first. That is one hazard. Two others are: that of not knocking at all (then you become stale); and if you tear the door off the hinges, you get into a realm that doesn't belong to you.

Ask/Receive. Seek/Find. Knock/Opened. This is the Law of the Father's Wisdom. When one does not heed the first command, he robs himself of many riches and blessings. Failure to obey the second command, results in lack of progress into the treasures provided for us in Christ Jesus. The third? If you do not understand and apply this portion of the threesome, all Christian service will be done with a human/soulish approach. We are not built to stand that long pull. Many Christian workers start out with only a soulish desire and zeal. Remember our "finger-pointers"? Hundreds of casualties line the battlefield because of failure to knock.

How many of you know God doesn't always answer the door right away? Jesus knew it and proceeds to explain further about the Father's wisdom in handling our asking, seeking, and knocking.

In the group Jesus was addressing at this teaching session there must have been hundreds of fathers. So Jesus flings out this question, "What man is there of you, whom if his son ask bread, will he give him a stone? Or if he ask a fish, will he give him a serpent?" (verses 9 and 10). Surely the agreement must have been unanimous—not one in the crowd.

So the Teacher draws the conclusion: "If ye then, being evil, know how to give good gifts unto your children, how much more shall your Father which is in heaven give good things to them that ask him?"

This conclusion has two important aspects; both of which we need to consider. First, if the son asks for bread or fish, items necessary for life—the father won't give him a stone or serpent. That would be cruel and inconceivable. Second, what if the son asks for something the father knows is harmful or inadequate—a serpent or a stone? No answer—no serpent and no stone.

Do you recall our words from the Book of James about "asking amiss"? He was taking into consideration the possibility of asking for "serpents and stones." There have been multitudes who have prayed seriously and fervently for something and didn't get it. Later they were glad they didn't. As we move into Christian maturity, there are times—looking back—when we are exceedingly grateful for unanswered prayer.

Why did Jesus feel it necessary to undergird His teaching on asking, seeking, and knocking with verses 9 through 11 about serpents and stones—bringing it home so forcibly by appealing to their fatherly responses to requests from their children? It is because, when you *ask, seek,* and *knock,* God's responses may *seem* more like a serpent or stone than the bread and fish you were requesting.

It was brought out in the Law of Spiritual Truth that when truth first comes, it comes in *negative* form—at least in its appearance. It disturbs you—threatens you—and seldom is God's answer what you thought it was going to be.

Consider initial truth about the necessity for repentance and forgiveness of sin. "What? Me a sinner? Going to hell? That couldn't be God!" or consider the Baptism in the Holy Spirit—speaking in tongues—tithing—sanctification. Seeking the Lord for truth and coming up with a slimy serpent. "No," He says, "It's bread." That takes faith—to believe the wriggling answer in your hand is what you asked for. But the Father says, "Even though that looks like a serpent, it isn't one."

One day I said, "God, if You are doing anything in the earth, please let me know about it." Within six months I had lost my church, my ordination, my fellowship—and almost my family. "It's a serpent! God, You betrayed me."

The answer came back, "No, it's bread."

"It is?"

"Yes, that's bread. Just watch."

And slowly and surely that "thing" stopped wriggling and I watched as my Father turned a seemingly evil situation into bread!

Didn't He say, in effect, "I don't know *how* to give a serpent or a stone. If you, being evil, wouldn't do such a thing—would I?"

Aren't you grateful that Jesus stressed this teaching? Now, when you take your requests to Him and the answer comes in a questionable form, you can state with assurance, "That's really bread—that's fish—that's God!"

The final truth in discussing the Father's wisdom is one of the most quoted Scriptures in the entire Bible:

Therefore, all things whatsoever ye would that men should do to you, do ye even so to them: for this is the law and the prophets.

Matthew 7:12

We all have bandied this truism around so much that it has become almost trite—without the teeth that Jesus meant for the admonition to have. He didn't waste words or state pious platitudes. He was presenting a principle so potent that—if adhered to—it could transform society. If men were honest with themselves (and before God) this Golden Rule would eliminate lying, cheating, hasty judgment, and most of the other ills that beset mankind. That is why Jesus prefaced it with, "Therefore"—and added, "For this is the law and the prophets."

This principle works for our good and protection—just as do the others we have studied. God is putting into operation the sowing/reaping assurance. He is doing something in our behalf.

First we are going to paraphrase the statement and then we will picture it. It is fairly easy to come up with words, but putting the words into action takes more understanding. Once we get the idea behind the words, then our words can carry some weight. How about: "Put yourself in the other fellow's place. Deal with him just as you would have him deal with you, should you be in his place."

BEFORE YOU ARE CRITICAL, OR STRIKE UP A DEAL . . .

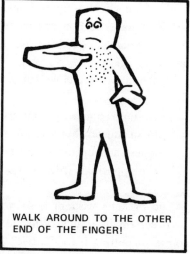

WALK AROUND TO THE OTHER END OF THE FINGER!

Once I was trying to come to an agreement with a man about cutting the lawn and trimming shrubbery. He agreed to do it for twenty dollars. I looked at the task and at the hot, burning sun, and thought, *Boy, I wouldn't tackle that for twenty dollars!* So I said, "How about twenty-five dollars?" And he nearly fell over, as you can well imagine. Now, I am not promoting a giveaway program—just a be-honest program. If you are going to hire a person, hire him for what his work is worth to you. Don't try to beat him down and extract every dollar possible.

Another time, I got into a traffic snarl caused by a teen-age girl in a car with a flooded motor. Horns were blowing—people cursing —and there she sat with tears running down her face. Off I went to the rescue—not because I am so spiritual, but because if it were my daughter in that predicament, I'd appreciate someone helping her.

Let's raise some hypothetical cases that present themselves in one guise or another to all of us. You decide to sell your termite-ridden home, concealing the condition or not correcting it—don't do it! You'll lose any profit you might gain in the long run; or say you sell a fellow a car with a faulty transmission. Then you buy what is supposed to have been a one-owner car—never been in an accident. What happens? You drive around the block and the transmission falls out.

Somehow our principle works two ways.

(1) Do unto others as you would have done unto you—and it doesn't mean that you are naïve or a sucker, but that you are honest and open with all men.

(2) The opposite is true. Do to others and you will get "done" to.

The Father's wisdom is so practical—so universal in application —so certain in results. Why do we have so much trouble when it comes to putting it to the test?

In review, let us remind ourselves that *we can:*

(1) *Ask*—knowing He hears and delights to supply our needs.

(2) *Seek*—knowing He is waiting to reveal Himself to us.

(3) *Knock*—knowing He will open the door, saving us from the

stagnation which would result if apathy should set in, as well as from the fiasco that could result from our stubborn aggression.

Ask . . . Seek . . . Knock—with complete trust in the Father—who says He *cannot* give His children a stone or a serpent.

(4) *Do for others what you would have them do for and to you.*

May God help us to grasp what Jesus is offering us in this lesson of the Father's wisdom—and may we make it our very own.

XII THE LAW OF RE-RELATING

And he opened his mouth and taught them, saying:

13   Enter ye in at the strait [narrow] gate: for wide is the gate, and broad is the way, that leadeth to destruction, and many there be which go in thereat:

14   Because strait is the gate, and narrow is the way, which leadeth unto life, and few there be that find it.

Matthew 7

As we open up the *Law of Re-Relating,* we take one more step toward spiritual maturity. The climb seems more arduous, demanding more skill and surefootedness as we follow on this Kingdom journey. If we have learned the basics in our Kingdom teachings and become increasingly confident in the ability of our Guide, we will welcome each new dimension of understanding. Even when the Teacher takes us by a seemingly devious route, or one with question marks along the way, we will follow on in trust. Yes, there will be some trepidation, for we have never gone this particular way before. Other lessons, if we have learned them, will help us, but each step upward brings its own challenge.

Here we find ourselves faced with a strait (or *straight*) gate and a narrow way that is not particularly appealing. We may be inclined to shrink and turn back. As always, personal choice is the determining factor.

If we caught the import of Bylaw Number 8—The Law of Reduced Interest—we have a foundation upon which to build the "re-relating" Jesus is now throwing out to the disciples gathered to listen to His teachings. Bylaw Number 8 was designed to teach us dependence upon the Father for provision in all things. If we gained from, ". . . seek ye first . . ." the necessity for having a *new center* around

which all things should revolve, we will be experiencing gradual release from the tyranny of "things."

We found out that God is interested in all things that interest man
—for things can form a barrier to the entrance into Kingdom living.
In His economy, He stated without reservation, "Ye cannot serve
God and mammon [things]." Unable! Where is your loyalty? To the
King or mammon? This includes material—intellectual—physical
—*anything you serve.*

If your interests have been reduced, you won't have as much
trouble getting in through the narrow gate. You may be raising your
eyebrows over that statement. We said the desire and purpose of
God in our lives was not so much in getting us to heaven as getting
heaven into us. The spiritual Kingdom is here on earth for us—
right now. True, we are moving toward life with Him in the hereafter, but He doesn't want to wait that long to be with us. His desire is to dwell with men of each generation. And the way He does
it, is by bringing us into Kingdom living, under the rulership of King
Jesus. That is eternal life—a quality of life He taught about, died to
make possible, and lives to actuate.

First, of course, we must come to the decision to accept His offer
of death and life. We refer to this acceptance as being born again,
or conversion. To convert is to turn around and go in an opposite
direction from the one previously traveled. The Lord apprehends us,
presents His claims—and if we accept them, He turns us around.
Now we are going upstream—the rest of humanity is traveling along
with the current downstream. As we move upstream, we come to
another choice. Many experience conversion, change their direction,
but settle only for fire insurance. They don't go on to take out *life*
insurance. That's where the narrow gate comes in.

Here is another misconception we need to clear up. Many have
the idea that the strait gate and the narrow way works like this: They
feel you become converted and enter into a strait and narrow way
that restricts and limits you all the rest of your life—until you finally

reach heaven. Some pray for the day when they may be released from the confines of the narrow way. That is not what God intended.

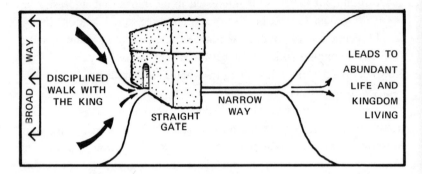

Instead, here is a better picture of the "strait (or straight) and nar-row gate." A *gate* is an entrance into something. A *way* may have two very differing meanings: one, a road or street; the other, a con-dition or requirement. I believe Jesus taught that there is a narrow and "straightening" way into the freedom He was teaching about—the truth shall make you free—bring you into freedom.

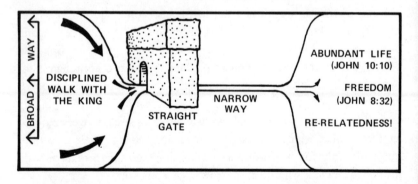

What is this narrow way that Jesus said few find? The Greek language conveys the meaning that the *way is made narrow by pres-sure*. If you are interested and pray, "Lord, I know there is some-thing more to the Christian life than trying to keep on the strait and narrow. I want to find out what You really have in mind for me,"

—then be prepared for the pressure. For the narrow gate is only wide enough for two—you and Jesus. It comes right down to that common denominator. No wonder Jesus said so few find it. It takes focus to see that pinpoint in our confusing and cluttered field of vision. There is a stripping process necessary; both in *seeing* what He wants us to become and *how* He wants to get us through the gate.

Gates played a very important role in the lives of those listening. The cities were walled and heavily guarded against enemy attack, as well as wild animals. As darkness fell, the entire countryside was plunged into blackout. No neon light flashing signals to give away

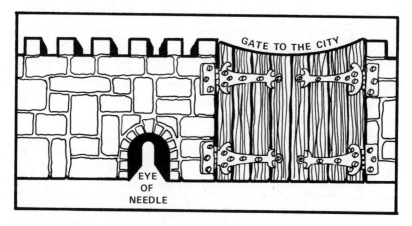

GATE TO THE CITY

EYE
OF
NEEDLE

locations. Was any provision made for the ones who might have been delayed or waylaid and arrived at the city after the large entrance gates had swung closed and been bolted for protection? Yes, there was. Here is shown the narrow gate they provided for such emergencies. If the late-comer arrived by camel, you can see what would have to take place before he could enter the city. All of the baggage or merchandise would have to be removed from the back of the camel. The animal would have to stoop and crawl through on his knees. Then the baggage would be pushed through, and, finally, the traveler would "enter" by the narrow gate.

This entryway, because of its small dimensions, was often referred to as "the eye of the needle." Does this immediately bring to your mind an incident when Jesus made use of this descriptive term? He always used live issues and scenes of the day to bring home a point.

Matthew 19:16–25 records this story. Out of the crowd that was following Jesus, there came a young man of great wealth. He came with a question, "Master, what good thing shall I do, that I may have eternal life?" (v. 16). Jesus laid down the requirement—for him! Remember we said that Jesus personally chooses the requirements for each questioner—in order to face the individual with a choice. The young man was told to "go and sell that thou hast and give it to the poor . . . and come and follow me" (v. 21).

The *follow me* is always the basis for decision, that is a conversion —the turning about. But we gather from the command to "go and sell and give" that riches *had* this young man, rather than his having riches. Why do we say this? Because of the ending of the interview. ". . . he went away sorrowful: for he had great possessions" (v. 22). He would never have made it through the narrow entrance with his great possessions.

Jesus uses the incident to bring home a point. He commented that it was a difficult decision the man had faced and that it was hard for a rich man to enter the Kingdom. The disciples were amazed—for were not the rich of their day the privileged? They asked for an explanation, to which Jesus replied, "It is easier for a camel to go through the eye of a needle, than for a rich man to enter into [through the same eye] the kingdom of God" (v. 24). But note that He added, ". . . with God all things are possible" (v. 26).

The narrow gate necessitates the stripping of everything: baggage —riches—sometimes even dignity (for getting on one's knees and crawling in behind one's camel isn't the world's conception of a dignified entrance), but it is the only way!

God, in His wisdom, knows what *has* you. We spoke of the Father's wisdom in our previous study (Bylaw Number 11). Remember the bread that took on the appearance of a stone when it was first received? And the fish that slithered around like a serpent when we first tried to handle it? Here again the Father's wisdom asserts itself and He puts His finger on the very things that hinder us from experiencing *life* as He designed it.

Referring again to our study on the Law of Reduced Interests, do you recall the stripping that went along with my induction into the navy? Everything connected with the former way of life had to go —even down to my hair. Then came a re-relating: travel—room— clothing—food—all were now supplied by Uncle Sam. I was his responsibility for the duration of my term of service. Some people feel that God's stripping is for the purpose of depriving them, when it is not that at all. *It is to establish a right relationship to the things that were keeping us from true freedom.*

We also mentioned the wealthy man whose priceless art collection was destroyed by fire. Everyone expected him to be destroyed, too. Instead, his reaction was, "Free, at last!" He came to realize what a prisoner he had become to his belongings. Our valuables can eat us —our time—energy—money—desires.

When a person is going through the stripping process, there is every possibility he doesn't understand the purpose and he may put up a struggle. If we could see the end from the beginning and go through the narrow way head first (understanding), that might not prove so difficult. But the Lord usually has to drag us through feet first—then comes the understanding—and rejoicing.

Do you see that the issues under consideration here are not heaven or hell—but life and death? The life is the abundant life Jesus said He came to afford (John 10:10). The death is the sterility and apathy that can creep over the believer who has not been willing to go on to become a follower and come under the discipline of the King.

It was He who said, "Few there be that understand this." Have you understood? Do you have life working in you; or is death evident? When you touch somebody, is the touch of divine life flowing through you? It is soon evident to the one you touch; and to you, if you will be honest with yourself.

As you look at certain things that seem so important to you, you may ask, "Lord, can't I be a Christian and still have these ideas—

habits—friends? That is not the issue. If you want to understand what life is all about and realize the true value of your possessions, tell Him of your desire and then prepare for the stripping process. Once you are through the gate and on the way into the freedom of the city, *He will restore everything that is to your advantage.* And these will take on new meaning. You will then possess them; they will not possess you.

When I returned to my ship after meeting the King in such a glorious way during one of my shore leaves, I found two of my closest buddies had been transferred. We had had many rootin'-tootin' times together and I had looked forward to telling them of my newfound life. So I questioned, "Lord, why didn't You leave them here? I would have brought them around." Me! A new convert—taking on the world! The Father in His wisdom knew best. By stripping me of these two friends, He re-related me to my new Christian life almost immediately. Friends—public opinion—set ideas—all may have to go.

I had a friend whose absorbing hobby was tropical fish. He had every conceivable contraption that went along with the pastime. He spent hours in front of his big aquarium. One day while giving himself completely to the enjoyment of his investment, the Lord said, "Get rid of those fish." Just like that! For three weeks the same message kept coming through. At last my friend acquiesced, and got rid of them. When he put the tank on the closet shelf, the question came, "What are you doing that for?" "UMMM . . . ." So the tank went the way of the fish. Obedience is the *issue*—not fish or tanks or golf clubs or art collections.

Can orders from Headquarters come into the realm of the "good" in order to provide a "better"? Yes, indeed. You may be caught up in helping the handicapped. Nothing wrong there. But continuing and enjoying this "ministry" to the exclusion of listening for further word from the Lord, may necessitate a stripping even of that activity. Counseling—ministry—music—when the satisfactions overrule the flow of life from God through that channel, stripping may become the order of the day.

One night I was praying with a Princeton University student and as we were kneeling together, I heard him say, "I won't . . . I won't!"

Sensing his struggle, I asked, "You won't what?"

I won't give it up! I've studied—worked . . . ."

"Son, what has a hold on you?"

"I won't give up being an astronaut." And he meant it. His desires—ambitions—dreams—these had made him a prisoner. He was in bondage. Everything that came into his life contributed to one goal. But he had to free himself from that all-consuming effort. Otherwise, he and his ambitions would remain outside the narrow gate. He might have gone to the moon—he would have gone to heaven—but he never would have known the joy of Kingdom living. Some of our astronauts reached the moon, taking the Word of God with them—conquerors for the King! Once inside the city gate, there were their goals. They found themselves re-related. But the King came first—the moon second.

Too many people feel God wants them to live "stripped" of ambitions, goals, possessions, and pleasures. He just wants to be sure that we do not become in bondage to the securing of these satisfactions and sit down and revel in them to the exclusion of fellowship and followship with Him. Realizing the joys *available* on the other side of the eye of the needle is as important as realizing we must go through it. When we can say, "I'm free—free from opinions of others—politics—lust—greed—I'm free!"—then all of life takes on a new perspective. Money, sports, holidays, family—all take on new meaning.

God dealt with my wife and me regarding our family. We went through the eye. You know He can deal with any area where His wisdom tells Him stripping is needed—anytime, anyplace, anyway. The gate is obedience—the question is, will we obey?

We were planning on going to South America as missionaries. For about three months before our departure, a voice came to me, "Your two little girls are going to die of blackwater fever in Peru." Judy and I prayed, pleaded, rebuked the devil—but to no avail—

until we were able to say and mean it, "Lord, if we go to Peru and our little girls die with blackwater fever, we will still praise You." We were through the eye of the needle into freedom and have been re-related to our children in a way that has brought us through many emergencies.

There is such a thing as having a *wrong* relationship to our children. Fear, unsubmittedness or unyieldedness can have debilitating effect on parents and children, as well. Recently our young son was hit by an auto and taken to the hospital emergency room. Standing by the side of our seriously injured son, Judy and I were able to lift our hands and voices in praise to God. We knew He was in control. We were free to love our children in a different way.

The Apostle Paul left us some profound thoughts on freedom through re-relatedness. Here are two of them.

1 Corinthians 9:19   For though I be free from all men, yet have I made myself servant unto all, that I might gain the more.

Paul had been through the narrow gate. God had to strip him of many hindrances. When he could say, "I'm free from all men," then he could become the servant of men—not in any *slavish* manner, however much he desired to win all men to Christ.

Can you see that the apostle was not free to be a servant unto all while he remained a "servant" to *himself* (Romans 6:6), to his *religion* (Philippians 3:4–6), to the *opinions* of others (Galatians 2:4–6), or even to some *financial gain* (Acts 20:33–35)? Until the Lord Jesus Christ re-related him to all of these things, he was *not* free to be a servant to others.

It should not be too difficult to understand that a person can look out through the bars of his own personal bondage and, at the same time, experience a great desire to help others—while in prison himself!

Romans 6:16–18   Don't you realize that you can choose your own master? You can choose sin (with death) or else obedience (with acquittal). The one to whom you offer yourself—he will take you and be your master and you will be his slave. Thank God that though you once chose to be slaves of sin, now you have obeyed with all your heart the teaching to which God has committed you. And now you are free from your old master, sin; and you have become slaves to your new master, righteousness (LB).

These words take us back to our discussion on "Freedom or Bondage" in Chapter 4, and the unconscious bondage that we may experience. We concluded that it is the Lord's obligation to show us when and where we are in bondage—for we cannot be free if we are captives to the capriciousness of our "self" life. The strait and narrow gate is the entrance into freedom. Obedience to the Word of God and the Holy Spirit's promptings will precipitate the occasions for us to become re-related to everything and everybody.

Entering in at the strait and narrow gate is not a once-for-all experience. There remains the distinct possibility of coming into wrong relationships to many things in this life. The one seeking Kingdom living, however, must understand that God reserves the right to examine our entire life-style in order to reveal trouble spots. Methodically and rather determinedly, He forces us through the narrow gate —in order to enjoy a freedom we have never known. We could not know this freedom in any other way.

Jesus knew this when He made the simple and straightforward statement: "Enter ye in at the strait gate." He also knew that not many would respond to His invitation to meet Him on the other side of the gate. There must have been an element of sorrow as He concluded with the words: ". . . few there be that find it."

Are you convinced sufficiently to stoop to enter by the way that leads to a re-relatedness? It is a way which will bring recompense and a greater freedom in your walk with the King!

XIII   THE LAW OF ROOTS AND FRUITS

And he opened his mouth and taught them, saying:

15   Beware of false prophets, which come to you in sheep's clothing, but inwardly they are ravening wolves.

16   Ye shall know them by their fruits. Do men gather grapes of
thorns, or figs of thistles?

17   Even so every good tree bringeth forth good fruit; but a corrupt
tree bringeth forth evil fruit.

18   A good tree cannot bring forth evil fruit; neither can a corrupt
tree bring forth good fruit.

19   Every tree that bringeth not forth good fruit is hewn down, and
cast into the fire.

20   Wherefore by their fruits ye shall know them.

Matthew 7

Examples of the teachings of Jesus are part of the curriculum of almost all educational courses in speech and writing. Men recognize the simplicity and clarity of His presentations. These qualities are always a hallmark of effective communication. Here we have a classic selection. We shall look at its structure and then go back and fill in the applications.

One of the beauties of Jesus' teachings is that the applications are always relevant to every age, culture, and personality. Eternal truth has a way of standing the test of the centuries.

Verse 15   The very first word, *Beware,* introduces the intent of the teaching. We are alerted. Of what? Immediately there comes the cause for concern—*false prophets.*

Verse 16   How shall we recognize this danger and be prepared to meet it? "Ye shall know . . . ." Isn't that comforting? If we have time to get our guards up, any danger loses some of its potential. We are told to examine not only outward appearance, but take a look under the sheepskin. No need to have the wool pulled over our eyes if we heed what follows: ". . . by their fruits." The verse closes with a question. Often by raising the ridiculous, we are made to see the valid. Grapes from thorns or figs from thistles? Who would be taken in by such impossibilities?

Verse 17 Here is presented the conclusion in the positive. It is an agriculturally accepted fact. The root determines the fruit.

Verse 18 Now the conclusion comes in the negative aspect. Again Jesus uses the word *cannot* meaning *impossible!*

Verse 19 How to solve the problem? The answer is that of the action of every farmer or vinedresser in the audience, "Away with the unproductive!" All cultivatable soil was guarded with care. There must have been much head-nodding assent to that edict.

Verse 20 Repetition of the major premise closes the lesson. No *ifs, and,* or *buts—by their fruits!*

Anyone who throws out this type challenge must have something to back up his words. On that platform, there could be no question when the Teacher's premise was analyzed in the light of the teachings of the Jewish law and prophets. True, some did raise questions. But fear of change—fear of the new—fear of loss of personal prestige—these were among the attitudes that dared raise suspicion to the lessons being taught from the shores of Lake Galilee to the Jericho Road.

The Law of Roots and Fruits is designed to protect your most valuable possession—that pearl of great price—your spiritual life. Once you have "sold all and purchased the pearl," from then on it is your responsibility to "beware"—there are wolves on the prowl.

Many of the Old Testament writers warned about false prophets. They pleaded with their people to beware. And some of those prophets had to stand by and watch their fellow men be taken captive—slaves because they would not heed the words of the true prophet.

Jesus had many scathing reprimands for those of His day who

were taking captive the lives of men in the name of religion and tradition. There were probably more spiritual eyes blinded to Jesus' teachings because of false religious leaders than there were physical eyes blinded by the ravages of disease. Leaders in the early church continued to sound the warning against false prophets.

100% TRUE PROPHET?

100% FALSE PROPHET?

What about today? How shall we recognize the false prophet? Just because someone turns up in a long, flowing robe, sandaled, and carrying a staff, crying, "Thus saith the Lord," doesn't prove he is or isn't a false prophet. Neither does wearing striped trousers, a plaid sports jacket, and a white tie, identify the wearer as either one or the other. We must say the same for the dark clerical garb with turned-around collar. Jesus' criterion still stands: *By their fruits . . . ye shall know!*

We probably should say a good prophet with a false message is what we need to be alerted to. He may have started out on target but, somehow, became sidetracked by Satan—in other words, a good prophet gone bad.

Should a man come into your meeting and say, "I am a prophet of the devil—hear ye!"—he wouldn't stand a chance to be heard. But when that same devil can get a good man to present untruths, half-truths, or any teaching tinged with self-imposed principles, he may secure quite an audience. By the expression "good man" we mean one who is held in esteem—whose sheepskin appears to be the real thing.

Does every prophet face the possibility of "going bad"? Yes. All of us who teach, preach, and minister in the Name of the Lord Jesus must be on guard against deception. And it is a responsibility of those who are on the receiving end to be "fruit inspectors" and search out the product being presented and thus keep us in line.

Today, as never before, spiritual fruit inspectors are necessary. For many years the church veered away from the supernatural. In our day, however, the Holy Spirit is bringing those who are tuned to His movings into a new realization of God's desire to pour out His signs and wonders. Healings—deliverances—miracles—prophecy—these are part of His workings. Satan, at the same time, is loosing his powers in an attempt to nullify or weaken the effectiveness of God's power at work in the human situation. The occult—false doctrine—drug abuse—distorted teachings on community living—all these are rampant in our society. How am I ever going to find my way safely through the confusion? *First, recognize the need to beware; then, learn to become a fruit inspector.*

One of the first lessons one must learn is that because a man or woman has the spiritual gifts in operation in his life, this doesn't necessarily mean he is holy.

Someone says, "There is a woman here who has a tumor on her left lung. The Lord is healing her now." Is this a valid gift? Certainly. There may be someone present in that condition and she may receive healing. Immediately we jump to a hasty conclusion, "He must be a holy man." We stand in awe and hang on every word. What did Jesus say? By their what? *Fruit!*

Gifts in the Bible are not a sign of spirituality or holiness. Gifts are given to accomplish God's desires. They are given to imperfect people to assist in bringing them to perfection. May I repeat—*gifts are given; fruit is grown*. Let's delineate the difference. Gifts of the Spirit are like tools. Here we see a rack in my garage lined with saw, shovel, rake, and pruning shears. Suppose I bring you into my garage and begin telling you, "See that shovel. I paid twenty dollars for it. That hoe? It was my father's. He was a successful farmer and he gave it to me. Those clippers—been mighty effective in the past."

GIFTS = TOOLS

About that time, my wife joins us and says, "Don't put any stock in all that talk. He hasn't grown anything for years. He just keeps the tools shined up so folks will think he is spiritual." I weakly try to defend myself by bringing up some crops of former years. But all three of us realize tools are to be used to work in the garden and produce some fruits, vegetables, or flowers. *Results are what count!* Gifts are given—fruit is grown. "By *this* shall all men know that you have been using the tools."

How about looking at some fruit that should be in evidence? The gifts (tools) are given by the Holy Spirit. In Galatians 5:22, 23, we find listed some of the fruit expected: "But the fruit of the Spirit is love, joy, peace, longsuffering, gentleness, goodness, faith, meekness, temperance . . . ." You may want a more practical list of items to look for.

All right, how about these for criteria? Remember, they are all the outworkings of the Holy Spirit engendered fruit of love, goodness, temperance, and so forth.

Examine the so-called prophet's home and meet his wife. Spend some time with his children. Find out if his bills are paid. Where does he spend his free time? What about his friends? Does he come recommended from a church fellowship? And does anyone have authority over him in the Lord? We are not violating any constitutional rights in doing this—and we are referring to the Constitution of the Kingdom.

This is the essence of what is referred to as the Love Chapter, First Corinthians 13. Paul says, in effect, "If I have . . . no fruit in my garden . . . ." If there is no fruit, the tools will pass away. Fruit remains through eternity—faith, hope, and love. These three are fruit—not gifts. They are grown. "By this shall all men know that you have been under my cultivation." And the Lord has a way of using the hoe and rake and clippers to advantage.

Besides the responsibility for *fruit-inspecting,* there is the responsibility of *fruit-bearing.* This applies in measure to each of us. We shall take several portions of Scripture which show the Chief Inspector looking for fruit—and the consequences of failure to come up to production standards.

In Isaiah 5:1–7, God is speaking to Israel, His "wellbeloved," and likening her to a vineyard from which He expected choice fruits. He tells of the precautions He had taken, and the wild grapes that came up instead of the expected crop. Verse 4 pictures the heartache of the Vinedresser as He says, "What could have been done more to my vineyard, that I have not done in it?" God's exasperation! Then comes this verdict in verses 5, 6:

And now go to; I will tell you what I will do to my vineyard: I will take away the hedge thereof, and it shall be . . . trodden down: And I will lay it waste: and it shall not be pruned, nor digged; but there shall come up briers and thorns: I will also command the clouds that they rain no rain upon it.

In other words, "Just go wild if you want to. I can do no more." There comes a point of cessation of the digging, pruning, and rains.

Jesus brought this out in the parable recorded in *Luke 13:6–9.* Here we note a *time factor* in the dealings of the Vinedresser.

He spake also this parable; A certain man had a fig tree planted in his vineyard; and he came and sought fruit thereon [*his rightful expectation as a land owner*], and found none. Then said he unto the dresser of his vineyard, Behold, these three years I come seeking fruit on this fig tree, and find none [*Did you realize God was taking account of your productivity?*]: cut it down; why cumbereth it the ground? And he [*this may be you taking the responsibility for cultivation of others placed in your care; or another speaking in your behalf*] answering said unto him, Lord, let it alone this year also, till I shall dig about it, and dung it: and if it bear fruit, well: and if not, then after that thou shalt cut it down.

Do you see that *the Owner hands down the verdict?* Can you see the *time factor* taken into consideration? This should be a comfort, and yet a caution to all of us. For, ". . . if it bears fruit, well: and if not, then after that thou shalt cut it down."

What does God want from you and me? Spiritual fruit! That means that He will love us, deal with us, fertilize, fence us around, rain on us, teaching us to worship, pray, and produce. What is He looking for? *Fruit.* After a certain time and expenditure of divine patience, He may say, "Ah, they are just playing games. Holy Spirit, come on; We'll have to go somewhere else—find someone whose desire it is to bring forth the expected crop."

In the Book of Jude (only twenty-four verses in all), the writer gets right down to where we live. He talks about trees without fruit and clouds without rain. Jeremiah, writing in the Old Testament, used the picture of wells without water. Let's get practical with ourselves.

Here comes Mumford. He *looks* like a big fruit tree—beautiful green leaves—promising fruit. People come running, "Fruit, and are we ever hungry!" You feel through the leaves—*no fruit!*

"Hey, did you hear? There's a well flowing at the church around the corner. Bring your buckets and get filled and refreshed." *No water!*

"Did you hear about the evangelist who is coming to town? He looks like a storm cloud and we need rain." It gets all dark and cloudy; there's lightning and thunder; soon the storm passes away— *no rain on the parched ground.* The object is rain—remember?

Warning: Don't give false impressions. Do not promise others that which you cannot produce. Who is the fruit and water for? The weary and needy. When that needy one comes to you for love, assistance, or advice, don't just give him a New Testament and say, "The Lord bless you." He comes expecting from you something he doesn't have! He may be seeing a need for discipline in his life and come to you because he feels there is something different in yours. Will he find it? If the tools have been used to produce fruit and not just for display, chances are the answer is *yes.*

When engaged in *fruit inspection* of others, or for yourself, always take into consideration the *time factor.* Listen to the writer of Hebrews describe what we are talking about: "You have been Christians a long time now, and you ought to be teaching others, but instead you have dropped back to the place where you need someone to teach you all over again the very first principles in God's Word . . ." (Hebrews 5:12 LB).

Criticism and fruit inspection are two very different matters. One danger involved is impatience with ourselves, and with others. Should we not recognize that a small, green, and sour apple in June is "perfect" for the *time* that it had to develop. Problems present themselves when that same apple is still small, green, and sour in September when it has had sun, rain, and *time* to mature into a beautiful red delicious about six inches across and weighing nearly one pound.

In your fruit-inspecting, remember as well, the Property Owner is the final Judge. All you are to be concerned about is the prevention of your own deception by someone who appears to be what he is not.

Have you ever had a friend who had great potential for spiritual development and yet continued to produce dried up, shriveled, worthless fruit? Have you ever prayed, "Lord, I know he loves You, but

I also know he is only playing religious games. Give me another year to pray for him—dig around and cultivate. Maybe he will come forth with something You can put Your approval on." The end of the year rolls around and the Chief Inspector asks, "How's your friend doing?" I may be forced to reply in sorrow, "Not so good, Lord."

When someone comes to me and says, "Brother Mumford, I think I am going to leave the ministry," I may have to advise—in the light of no fruit, no desire, much pruning, and little results—"You may be right. This may be best for the Kingdom." If you are going to minister, you have to produce.

If you walk into the office where you work like the answer to all the ills and ailments of the entire staff—you had *better* have some fruit! If you let it be known that you have "something," you had better have at least a few pieces of fruit hanging in there among those leaves. Listen to another parable given by Jesus that shows His response to this matter.

> Now in the morning as he returned into the city, he hungered. And when he saw a fig tree in the way, he came to it, and found nothing thereon, but leaves only, and said unto it, Let no fruit grow on thee henceforward for ever. And presently the fig tree withered away.
>
> Matthew 21:18, 19

I don't know about you, but these words of Jesus bring me to my knees. While there I acknowledge that the gifts are given, that fruit is grown. I take a look at the tools in my garage and see if they have the marks of use and effectiveness. I pray that those to whom I minister may heed the words, "By their fruits shall ye know them," and ask that I may be known as a producer of top-quality goods. This all makes me realize anew how important it is to check on the *roots* in my life.

Verses 17 and 18 of our Bylaw of Roots and Fruits stated some facts that we must seriously consider: A good tree cannot bring forth evil fruit; and, conversely, an evil tree cannot bring forth good fruit. What is it that determines whether or not a tree is good or evil? Its roots.

When dealing with roots and fruits, Jesus says, "Beware!" He clearly is suggesting the possibility and danger of deception. This comes in two basic forms: (1) self-deception; (2) being deceived by another. Both are equally dangerous and one cannot escape the responsibility placed upon him in this matter. Understanding and obeying *this* teaching will prevent us from that which is false—in ourselves and others.

There is a certain mystery in the Christian faith which is necessary. As P. T. Forsythe said, "Faith is a religious experience, but religious experience is *not* faith." It is to this distinction that Jesus speaks when He says, "A good tree brings forth good fruit and a good tree cannot [unable] bring forth evil fruit."

Let's clarify the term *religious experience* as we are using it here —that which may result in the deception against which Jesus was warning. Here are some possibilities: human impulse, religious obsession, hypocrisy, illusion, demonic revelation, and impersonation, as well as hallucination.

Since the motives, inner workings, and nature of a person are inaccessible to us (as mere humans), the evaluation of a ministry, person, or experience must be traced back to the source of origin— hence the term, *roots*. We must guard against some immature appeal on our part of "being sincere," or that "Jesus wouldn't let me be deceived." Why do you think He was so vehement in His warnings?

Examination of all religious experiences, both of your own and that of others, must be on the basis of what it *produces*. Keep in mind the fruit of the Spirit as given in Galatians 5:22, 23, and the promised result of Kingdom living—righteousness, peace, and joy. Jesus is teaching that *fruit alone* determines whether or not the experience of a person is born of His Holy Spirit—or out from some other source, human or demonic.

The First Epistle of John deals with this spiritual problem. We are taking several portions to compare *roots* and *fruits*. What the apostle is trying to communicate is that talk or experience that did not *produce* fruit in the life of the believer was of doubtful origin.

It might be well for us to remind ourselves that John was in the teaching session which we have been using for our study. Also, remember that Christ did not come to *teach* us truth, but to *make* us true. Notice the key words John uses in the below: "*if* . . ." and "*he that saith* . . . ." These statements need careful analyzing—not just casual reading. Three are from a positive approach to good roots producing good fruit; the fourth is from the negative.

1 John 2:29 If ye know that he [the King, *see* v. 28] is righteous [roots], ye know that every one that doeth righteousness [fruits] is born of him.

1 John 3:14 We know that we have passed from death unto life [roots], because we love the brethren [fruits].

1 John 5:4 For whatsoever is born of God [roots] overcometh the world [fruits] . . . .

1 John 4:20 If a man say, I love God [roots], and hateth his brother [fruits], he is a liar . . . .

Jesus and John both taught that the object of the genuine Christian experience is *fruit*—fruit of the Spirit, as evidenced by a changed character and a conforming to His image—fruit in the sense of winning others to Christ and affecting them positively for the Kingdom.

When the Apostle John recorded the events of the earthly life of his Master, he penned these words:

> You have not chosen Me, but I have chosen you—I have appointed you, I have planted you—that you might go and bear fruit *and* keep on bearing; that your fruit may be lasting (that it may remain, abide) . . . .
>
> John 15:16 AMPLIFIED

These words were given by Jesus during the last time He met with His disciples prior to His arrest and Crucifixion. Evidently John was one disciple who took seriously the words of the Kingdom Concepts and Laws of the Kingdom which he heard under the tutelage of Jesus.

What about you? Jesus was teaching for eternity and He is still interested in roots and fruits. Bringing forth good fruit requires pruning and cultivation, even when the roots are "good." Cutting back on some of our present so-called religious activities, programs, and plans may be necessary—for the object of this walk is *not* vines—but *grapes!*

XIV THE LAW OF OBEDIENCE

And he opened his mouth, and taught them, saying:

21 Not every one that saith unto me, Lord, Lord, shall enter into the kingdom of heaven; but he that doeth the will of my Father which is in heaven.

22 Many will say to me in that day, Lord, Lord, have we not prophesied in thy name? and in thy name have cast out devils? and in thy name done many wonderful works?

23 And then will I profess unto them, I never knew you: depart from me, ye that work iniquity.

Matthew 7

One of the time-proven principles of good teaching is the necessity for warning pupils of possible pitfalls in applying the lesson. Misunderstanding or misuse of the information must be taken into consideration. Jesus emphasized and *re*-emphasized the importance of *"doing the Father's will."* In this Bylaw, He zeroes in on obedience in no uncertain terms.

As we begin our study on Obedience, in relation to the Father's will, we review the fact that our one English word *will* has two separate Greek words to convey its meaning.

(a) *Boulema* Here it is primarily designated as the eternal counsels of God. These are unfolding through the ages and do not depend upon man's cooperation or obedience.
Example: James 1:18 "Of his own will [*boulema*/purpose] begat he us with the word of truth, that we should be a kind of firstfruits of his creatures."

(b) *Thelema* This indicates God's wish or desire. It depends upon the response of each individual for fulfillment.

Example: Acts 13:22 ". . . I have found David . . . a man after mine own heart, which shall fulfil all my will" [*thelema/* wish, desire].

When Jesus prayed, ". . . Thy will be done in earth as it is in heaven," and when He said, "For whosoever shall do the will of God, the same is my brother, and my sister, and mother" (Mark 3:35), He was speaking of the *wish or desire of the Father.* This is the way in which Jesus is using the word *will* in our *Law of Obedience.*

We also want to review the diagram we used in an earlier study on Kingdom Concepts. It is vital that we see God's desire for us to bring our wills into conformity to His will—and the possibility of this taking place.

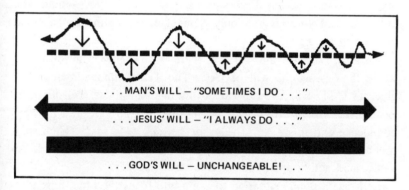

. . . MAN'S WILL – "SOMETIMES I DO . . ."

. . . JESUS' WILL – "I ALWAYS DO . . ."

. . . GOD'S WILL – UNCHANGEABLE! . . .

Do you see God's will? It is the steel bar which never changes for anything, anyone, or at any time. ". . . the Father of lights, with whom there is no variableness or shadow of turning" (James 1:17).

Just above it is Jesus' will—perfectly aligned with the Father's will. In all matters, the Son could say, "Lo, I come . . . to do thy will, O God" (Hebrews 10:7).

Then comes—let's call it Mumford's will. It fluctuates. Sometimes I do His will—other times I prefer to do my own will. When His will *crosses* mine, that is the opportunity for one or more of those three hindrances to please my Father to arise. The three? *Rebellion —Resentment—Independence.*

Jesus came to this earth as a man to do the Father's will (wish/ desire). We are prone to say He came to die to save us from our sins. That is correct insofar as it goes; but it goes further. He came *primarily* to do the Father's will. Becoming the Lamb that takes away sin, the journey through Gethsemane, and the agony and shame of the Crucifixion were all involved in the perfect *will* of God for Jesus!

Our Lord Jesus says to us, in effect, "If you will permit Me, I will work in your life so that your *will* can be lined up with My will— and you will find yourself desiring to do the Father's will, even as I did." This is the essence of the Gospel of the Kingdom. However, the Bylaws are designed to squeeze you—adjust you—mold you until you find yourself, not only doing the will of the Father—but *desiring to do that will.*

We must establish the fact that there is no higher criterion in the world than doing the will of God. The Ten Commandments were given as God's will in the matter of morals and ethics. Tell me, why is adultery wrong? Because it breaks the marriage tie and destroys confidence and trust? No, it is wrong because *God said,* "Thou shalt not commit adultery." Adultery is wrong *because* God's will is revealed and action other than that is disobedience.

Let's use a family situation to bring into focus the often-misunderstood principle which Jesus is presenting in Matthew 7:21-24.

Suppose your ten-year-old son decided to try to be helpful while you were at work. Seeing the family car covered with ice, he decides to help. Braving the cold and taking a screwdriver, he methodically digs all of the ice free from the automobile—feeling quite proud of himself for "helping." On your return, you spot the scratches and digs in the paint. You say, "You didn't . . . !" to which he replies, "Yes, I did . . . !"

Now this wasn't sin—it was primarily due to ignorance. The child, in trying to help, nearly ruined the car. The body of Christ is beset with spiritual children trying to be "Father's little helpers," instead of ascertaining the revealed will of their Father. If we could only understand that He requires only this of us—*seeking, understanding, and doing His will.*

Should we press our illustration further, we would discern that the child scraped the snow with the screwdriver trying to help, while neglecting his *assigned* household chores. In this *Law of Obedience,* we are dealing with disobedient and obedient children of the Father —believers who are faced with choices. Some make the wrong decisions. So, the lesson begins: "Not everyone who says to me, Lord, Lord . . . ."

1 Corinthians 12:3 tells us ". . . no man can say that Jesus is the Lord, but by the Holy Ghost." So, we are not dealing with nonbelievers, but those who do not understand the implications of calling Jesus their *Lord*. We talked about clouds without rain, wells without water, and trees without fruit in discussing the Law of Roots and Fruits. Pretending to have something to offer when you do not—and to be something that you are not—carries serious implications for the pretender. So does calling Jesus, *Lord,* and not meaning it! You had better be able to stand back of your claims.

Some believers, it seems, never progress much beyond the border of the Land of Salvation. For illustration's sake, let's use a geographical setting. Outside of this Land of Salvation is the Land of Outer

Darkness (the land of the unsaved—those who reject our Lord Jesus
Christ). Take this differentiation from Ephesians.

> Once you were under God's curse, doomed forever for your sins.
> You went along with the crowd and were just like all the others,
> full of sin, obeying Satan, the mighty prince of the power of the
> air, who is at work right now in the hearts of those who are
> against the Lord.
>
> 2:1, 2 LB

Military strategists know that most military conflicts begin at the
border—where there are those enemies desirous of taking (by force
if necessary) that which belongs to you.

In the light of this, it always puzzles me *why* those who come to
know the Lord do not seek to penetrate deep into the love, protection, and provision of the Lord. Mysteriously, however, many stay
"just over the line." Saved? Yes. But not really enjoying that which
their salvation provides due to a continual conflict with the world
(outer darkness). Living so close to the world, there is a constant
struggle and internal conflict. Double mindedness, with its consequent
spiritual instability, is very damaging to the progress of spiritual life.

People who "just get inside," who are concerned only with "getting
to heaven," are in constant temptation to go back across the border.
(*See* Hebrews 11:15.) I have come to describe this as "borderline
anemia,"—being the *irreducible minimum*. We might say that if they
had any less of God's provision in Jesus Christ, they would have
nothing!

Then there are those for whom this book is written—the searchers,
hungry to *know* and *do* the whole will of God. This seeker, once he
enters the Land of Salvation, keeps looking, growing, and enjoying
all that Christ has provided for him. He seeks for a *full, New Testament experience*. He knows, instinctively, there is more to this walk
with the Lord than the irreducible minimum. Paul described this desire when he said, ". . . I keep working toward that day when I
will finally be all that Christ saved me for and wants me to be"

(Philippians 3:12 LB). This may be described as the *New Testament Maximum*—the freedom toward which Jesus is teaching.

Are you aware, also, that as long as you limit your commitment to *Jesus as Saviour,* not as much is demanded of you as it is if you say, *"Jesus is my Lord"?* When we are in that first category, we are limited in our presentation of Him to others. We can tell them He is our Saviour and ask them to consider His claims to forgive and cleanse. But we have nothing to offer in the realm of knowing Him as Lord of their lives and entering into that freedom for which He died.

When Jesus is only your Saviour, you disobey and say, "Jesus, forgive me," and He does. You repeat the procedure again and again, pleading the blood and receiving forgiveness. But no change! Is it clear to you the difference between repeated forgiveness and the change of character? I have stressed the difference between this transaction of forgiven sin and that of a changed will. You can *continue* being forgiven and *continue* going your own way. But this is not the Father's desire for any of His children. *His desire is Kingdom living for you and me.*

Once I get tired of repeated failings and forgivenesses, and turn to Him and ask Him if there isn't something He can do about it, then I approach Him as Lord. Once that acknowledgment of Jesus as my Lord passes my lips, everything changes. Acts 2:36 tells us, "God hath made [him] . . . both Lord and Christ." When the Holy Spirit brings us to the place where we come to Jesus as Lord, we come under His *authority.* We must come seeking. He knows when we are ready to come under His rule.

When I confess Jesus Christ as my Lord, I no longer choose where I live—I may not choose my occupation—I am unable to choose in many areas of my life that had not previously come under His control. Now I seek His will—and obey!

Police dogs are given obedience training for one purpose—to make them effective servants of the law. One day while watching them being put through their paces, the Lord impressed upon me a lesson which I have never been able to forget.

The trainer took a purse, gave the dog the scent of it, and then threw the purse into the open field, with the word, "Fetch." The dog took off in a cloud of dust and proudly trotted back with the purse. After several repeat performances, the police officer once again threw the purse, but this time, the command was, "Heel!" I thought the poor dog would blow a gasket as he saw the purse go and he knew he was to stay. For the goal was obedience, not returning the purse. How my heart was convicted as I saw myself racing off after the purse, ignoring the Master's, "Heel."

There is such a condition which we could label "religionholicism." Do you know what I mean? We get so caught up in meetings and programs and the thrill of being used, that we just keep on our merry way, regardless of restraint. We don't develop any concept of "the will of God." All we know is that it is Thursday night at 7:30 and a certain activity always takes place then—and we are urged to be present. You must see that this has nothing to do with sin or back-sliding, although it may result in these; *but it has to do with priorities*.

Recall with me the story of that couple in the early church, Ananias and Sapphira, as given in Acts 5:1–11. They had some property and decided to sell it and give the money received to the Lord. The trouble was some of the money stuck to their fingers and they only brought a certain portion to the apostles, stating this was the entire sum. But Peter, knowing by the Holy Spirit the true facts, confronted Ananias with, "Why hast thou conceived this thing in thine heart and lied to the Holy Ghost?" (*See* verses 3, 4.) His wife was also questioned as to her part in the transaction; her reply was the same— and they both dropped dead.

In this situation, the Lord was not after their money, He was after their obedience. They had called Him their Lord and then acted on their own initiative. The lesson caused fear to come upon other members of the church. I can see why, can't you? If one says, "Lord," there is a way of life that must be embraced—or the alternative of chastisement must be faced.

You realize, don't you, that *merely calling* Jesus, "Lord," does not insure entrance into His Lordship? It does place upon one the added responsibility of obedience—but actual down-to-earth compliance with His commands is necessary for stepping into the freedom inherent in obedience.

Accepting the Lordship of Jesus brings me into a new relationship to the Son of God. Now I recognize Him as King and admit His right to issue commands, which I am expected to obey.

When Judy and I were facing the decision of whether or not to leave California and come to Florida, we went through this crossing of wills. After our visit in Florida, we returned with confidence, "No, sir, we're not leaving California—we love it here!" But one night while preparing for sleep, the Lord quietly said to me, "You know what I told you?" I turned to my wife and barely breathed, "Judy . . . ."

"Yes, Bob . . . ."

"You know what the Lord said, don't you?"

"Yes . . . ." She knew and I knew—and we both knew the other knew!

Now let me ask you, could we have stayed in California in disobedience and have continued an effective ministry? I believe so. Take a look at Matthew 7:22 and let it answer the question for you. Yes, I could have stayed and preached, prayed, prophesied, cast out demons, and done many wonderful works—but one Person saw me disobey. By my disobedience, I would have placed myself in the position of discipline and chastisement in order to teach me God's highest priority is not ministry but obedience.

This obedience is not something one *has* to do. It is not forced upon us. It is something that must be *desired*. Once a person "enters His Lordship," then God begins to establish His Kingdom in that life —at your own request, mind you. Now He can say, "Don't go on vacation this year . . . Better not buy that car . . . Leave those friends alone." Yes, He starts "meddling" in your life!

Another experience my wife and I had came when we were requested to visit a certain home. As we drove toward the address, I could literally feel the restraining hand of God. Finally, I blurted out,

"Honey, I feel like we are driving right out of the will of God." Come to find out, she felt the same way. So we stopped the car and prayed, "Lord, if we are going somewhere that you don't want us to go, we will gladly take the misunderstanding of those who requested us to go. Just let us know Your will." The presence of the Lord filled that car—and we had no further doubts. Turning the car around, we returned. When asked if we had completed our visit, we had to say no, and explain about His priorities in our lives.

Jesus has the right to demand priorities because He always did the will of His Father. He is qualified to judge the actions and decisions of those who come to Him as Lord. He knows the questions—tribulations—sacrifices we may face. He faced them, too.

He knew the agony of decision in Gethsemane. He knew the doubts of those closest to Him in ministry. He learned how to say, ". . . I have meat to eat that you do not know of . . . . My meat is to do the will of [the Father]" (John 4:32, 34). The goal of His life was not ministry but relationship and obedience to the Father.

Therefore, Jesus could say, "Those who merely call Me Lord and do not do My Father's will shall not be able to enter into My Lordship." (*See* Matthew 7:21.) He could also warn them, "Some of you will be surprised to learn that you cannot enter into My Lordship just because you performed signs, wonders, and many wonderful works in My Name. Yes, you had to use My Name for these things could not be accomplished without My power." (*See* verse 22; cf. Mark 9:38–40.)

Then comes the shock! "And then will I profess unto them, I never knew you: depart from me, ye that work iniquity" (Matthew 7:23). These last few phrases of finality are given as worded in the King James Version. Here are some other translations that more nearly bring out the meaning of Jesus' thrust.

He was addressing Himself to those who substituted their own wills for the will of the Father. "I never *knew* you," or, "acknowledged you—approved you—recognized you as being what you claimed to be." *Work iniquity* might better be translated as "those that worked disobedience—lawlessness—without law—or were bent on doing their own thing."

If you can grasp what Jesus is driving at here, you can save yourself many heartaches and disappointments. All three verses could be capsuled, *"If you want to go your own way, don't call Me Lord!"*

Can you equate in some measure this desire of Jesus with the desire of a parent who is trying to bring a child into recognition of obedience as acceptable behavior? Can you see that Jesus is not so much interested in your doing His work as He is in directing His work?

The theme of Christianity for many years has been, "You are saved to serve." Even though we realize that we are not saved by good works, we seem to feel that all God wants from us *is* service. We may not be qualified for certain "works," but because there are needs, along with the encouragement from those who feel new believers will best develop by keeping busy in the Lord's business, we launch out into avenues of our own choosing. Some fall into the trap of serving God in those areas best suited to our natural talents or inclinations. We do not wait before the Lord to see what He has in mind for us—and away we go!

Many are the wrecks that have been picked up on the mission field. Some established missionaries have a special fund set aside to aid these self-appointed "Lord's helpers," who come to foreign countries as "faith" missionaries.

There is, as well, a particular danger in the area Jesus mentioned— prophecy, exorcism, and miracles. These power gifts can prove potential dynamite—not only for those who get caught up in the spectacular, but for those who may be led astray by the willful disobedience of those who feel they are "saved to serve" in this way. Some of this error comes from wrong teaching—some from wrong emphasis— and some from the desire to lay hold on power. *Power without authority and obedience is always dangerous.*

The question each must face is, "Is this the will (desire/wish) of God for me?" It is possible to be engaged in a miracle ministry when it is not the will of God. It is comparatively easy to deceive people through miracle ministries. There are many valid ministries—they are done in His Name, under authority, and in obedience to His command. There are others, performed by good men who have missed the road of obedience and who do not understand the nature of spiritual authority. *It boils down to the Law of Obedience.*

Remember Jesus is the Judge. The will of God is the standard. I trust you will see the necessity for doing His will if you call Him your Lord—and the implications of His words, "Depart from me . . . ."

Ezekiel 44:4–16 tells of God's degree of judgment upon those priests who were serving in His temple. He divided them into two plainly delineated groups: (1) those who were rebellious in the performance of their duties and (2) those who were obedient. The first group were permitted to continue their ministry to the people in the temple; but they were not to "come near" to God. The second group, because of their obedience, were allowed to "come near" and minister to the Lord.

Follow as we pick up threads from the conversation of the Lord to the prophet Ezekiel: "And thou shalt say to the rebellious . . ." (v. 6). "And the Levites that are gone away far from me when Israel went astray . . . they shall even bear their iniquity" (v. 10). "Yet they shall be ministers in my sanctuary . . . they shall stand before [the people] . . ." (v. 11). "And they shall not come near unto me . . . nor come near to any of the holy things . . ." (v. 13). "But the priests . . . that kept the charge of my sanctuary when the children of Israel went astray from me, they shall come near to me to minister unto me, and they shall stand before me . . ." (v. 15).

God is still wanting His servants to "come near" to Him. Those who are walking according to His will—conducting their homes and businesses and their entire life-style in conformity to the Kingdom Rules—these are invited into His presence to worship and fellowship. This is Kingdom relationship.

We are offered the opportunity to come near to Him—to become a part of His Kingdom. Yet, there are times when we get so caught up in the spectaculars and in the doing of our own ministries that we pass by the highest privilege attainable to man—that of coming near to our God and experiencing the joy of walking and working together.

Suppose I come home one evening from a hard day at the office. I am looking for time to be near my wife—be in her presence—enjoy her. And I find her wrapped up in baking cookies for the Ladies' Aid Society and making phone calls for the missionary meeting and getting her bookkeeping in order for the Quarterly Visitation Report. She's too busy to do more than acknowledge my homecoming.

Finally I say, "Stop all that. I don't want to hear about all those activities. I want some attention from you." Her priority is giving her attention to me, as her husband. It isn't that there is anything wrong with all the other claims upon her time, but the issue is that it is taking her away from her duties as my wife. When she is overly occupied with outside activities, something comes between the two of us. This has to be remedied or the breach widens and relationship is affected.

So it is with the King and you. He isn't as interested in what you do as He is in what you are—one of His children. He wants you to come near to Him and spend time with Him. He desires that you find out what it is that *He* wants you to do—and then go out and do it. So often we go off and do things, and then come running to Him for His approval; or perhaps, we find ourselves in the snarl of our own making and come to Him for help in straightening it out.

If we see what is involved in this Law of Obedience, we can then ask, how can I avoid being one of those who call Him *Lord* but do not do the Father's will? I should like to use some of the concluding statements from my book *The Problem of Doing Your Own Thing*.

• Recognize that obedience, like submission, is a discipline. It is something we learn. It does not come naturally. (Hebrews 5:8)

• Take it one day at a time. Never come to the place where you feel you can say, "Glory to God. Look at this obedient servant!" That is asking for trouble! (Luke 9:23)

• Listen carefully to all instructions. Check them out with your three guides: The Word of God, the Spirit, and the authority over you. Ask for a "repeat" if you feel it is necessary. God will always honor that request. (Isaiah 50:4)

• Once you have received your instructions, obey them to the best of your ability. Remember, failure is part of the lesson. (Acts 26:19)

• If you sense even the slightest inward resistance, take careful pains to make certain that you deal with it and that it breaks. (Romans 6:17)

• Be careful of hasty, urgent, demanding voices. Anything that is of this nature, is suspect. I have found that God always begins soon enough to get me to the right place at the right time. Every time I have been on a crash program for Jesus, it crashed! (Colossians 3:15)

• Remember that it is not past experience that counts—it is present attitude. [God desires to reveal pockets of rebellion, resentment or independence that may develop *before they cause alienation.*] (Romans 7:4)

• Examine your own life pattern to find out whether your progress is registered as a series of continual "breakings" [forgivenesses]; or whether you have been broken by God and are walking in humility and obedience—developing a hearing ear and responsive spirit. (Psalms 40:6)

Being continually sensitive to the will of God for your life and having a desire to do that will, is one of the joys of the life of freedom inherent in Kingdom living. The questions, the doubts, the hassles are set aside, permitting righteousness, peace, and joy to replace them.

Jesus stressed these three replacements throughout His ministry: righteousness—peace—joy!

Matthew 6:33   But seek ye first the kingdom of God, and his righteousness; and all these things shall be added unto you.

THE LAW OF OBEDIENCE

John 14:27   Peace I leave with you, my peace I give unto you . . . .
John 15:11   These things have I spoken unto you, that my joy might
  remain in you, and that your joy might be full.

Jesus moved with assurance and purpose throughout each day
because He was walking within the will of the Father. You can, too,
once you become subject to the Law of Obedience.

XV THE LAW OF THE BUILDING CODE

And he opened his mouth, and taught them, saying:

24 Therefore whosoever heareth these sayings of mine, and doeth them, I will liken him unto a wise man, which built his house upon a rock:

25 And the rain descended, and the floods came, and the winds blew, and beat upon that house; and it fell not: for it was founded upon a rock.

26 And every one that heareth these sayings of mine, and doeth them not, shall be likened unto a foolish man, which built his house upon the sand:

27 And the rain descended, and the floods came, and the winds blew, and beat upon that house; and it fell: and great was the fall of it.

Matthew 7

Building Codes are always well defined. Jesus made His specifications for presenting this final Bylaw crystal clear. The basis for judging the compliance with the Code was, "whosoever heareth these sayings of mine and doeth them."

How many hours Jesus sat on the Galilean hillside teaching the truths we have been sharing, no one knows. But we do know He was scattering seeds of truth, which He hoped would take root and bear fruit in the lives of those listening.

It is said over and over again in the Scripture that "He came teaching and preaching the Kingdom of God." He was proclaiming that God searches for a people who want and seek His rulership in their lives. We have seen repeatedly in considering our Bylaws that it is *possible* to reject God's rule over our lives. But when we do, it affects our relationship to Him. It renders us useless in the Kingdom. If we disobey His commands, we lose our righteousness, peace, and joy, which are the basics of the Kingdom of God—those rights guaranteed us in the Constitution of the Kingdom. True, He forgives us, but by now we understand what our disobedience will cost us in Kingdom relationship. This is what the King is seeking to establish —His will in our lives.

We pause here to review one of our principles of operation in bringing the believer to become a *continuer*—thus preparing him to

NATURE
DESIRE

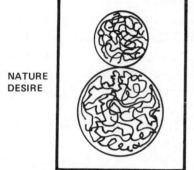

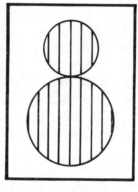

CHARACTER
ABILITY

recognize and receive the truth that Jesus is teaching. Read once again John 8:32. We talked about the *alignment* needed to straighten out the kinks in our wills and the workings necessary to bring them to the place where they are lined up with the wills of the Father and Son. How was that alignment accomplished? By adhering to the Bylaws in a given situation or circumstance of life. After our detailed study of fourteen Bylaws, we ought to be experiencing some change from *nature to character,* and from *desire to ability.* Are you prepared to stand up and take the examination being presented in the *Law of the Building Code?* How have you been building? You are about to find out.

The examination, or test, is pictorially presented. *Verses 25 and 27* describe the testing: The rain descends—the floods come—the winds blow—the house takes a beating. In other words, *demands* are being made upon the house which has been erected. And they are going to be made upon us as sojourners on the earth. These perplexities come to everyone. *It is not what happens to us in life, it is how we react.* As Kingdom citizens, how are we expected to react? Differently from those who make no claim to citizenship in His Kingdom? Yes.

Will your house stand or fall? What determines this? In one word —it is *foundation.* Can you envision in our diagram on alignment the differences in foundation? The life with all the kinks and instabilities of self-will and immaturity doesn't offer much in the way of ground-work upon which to depend. But the ramrod, straightened lines of the life brought into Kingdom relationship does.

Some people feel that because they are Christians they are immune from the catastrophes and calamities of life. Not so. Hear Jesus as He prays for His disciples, and for us: "I pray not that thou shouldest take them out of the world, but that thou shouldest keep them from the evil [one] . . . . Sanctify [or mature] them through thy truth: thy word is truth" (John 17:15, 17).

These Bylaws of the Kingdom are His Word—His truth. Through the obeying of them, we shall be kept—not from the calamities, necessarily—but from the evil one who would delight to see our house tumble all around us when the winds of adversity begin to blow. Jesus told us we are to be the salt of the earth and the light of the world. (*See* Matthew 5:13, 14.) Those less fortunate than we may look to us for preservation and illumination when darkness and the storms of life descend.

What about financial reverses—epidemics—moral collapses— problems between husbands and wives in child rearing? These are all realities which must be faced, and the ensuing problems solved. Is the foundation of our lives strengthened to the point where we can overcome difficulties and move on into victory; or when the plug is pulled out, will we go down the drain with the majority which forms a broad spectrum of our society?

Remember our statement: It is not what happens to you in life, it is how you *react* to what happens. You may ask, "Where is God in all of this?" You may not see Him on stage, but He is standing in the wings—watching, waiting, directing. He is prompting through the Holy Spirit, reminding us of His presence—of His truths—of His interest in all that comes to us. He says, in effect, "These things that I permit to come your way are designed to bring us into a closer relationship. You are My child. I am your Father." He gives us the opportunity to stand in the testing—to bear witness of His Kingship.

How do we bear witness? By standing when the storms rage all around us. And how are we able to do this? Verse 25 says, ". . . and it fell not: for it was founded upon a rock." Jesus Christ is often referred to as the Rock, and rightly so. When our lives are founded upon Him, they stand. But there is much more to it than just saying, "Jesus is my Rock . . . on Him I stand." He, Himself, made a qualification: ". . . he that heareth . . . *and doeth.*" (*See* verse 26.) We have a responsibility.

In the matter of a Building Code, foundations are extremely important. The Building Inspector will carefully measure to the one-quarter inch the foundation before he will give permission to erect the above-ground structure. The same applies in the spiritual. God goes down in foundation in direct proportion to the size building He wants to build—all with your permission, of course. If you want a one-story cottage, that doesn't require much in the way of foundation —only shallow footers. But if you want God to do something great in your life, that is another story.

While in New York City, I was waiting for some friends and saw a fenced-in area nearby. Curiously, I went over to the fence and peered through a peephole. All I could see was down . . . down . . . down! *What a hole,* I thought. Then I heard a deafening noise that told me the story of that gaping opening in the earth. At the bottom of it was a giant pile driver, driving huge steel girders down into the rock upon which Manhattan is built.

About that time, the Lord spoke to me, "Do you see anything there that might apply to you?" Light dawned, and I began to weep. Every time that pile driver went *ka-loumpf . . . ka-loumpf,* I could feel it in my spirit. Then He added this word, "Son, I am going to drive steel into your soul. I am going to excavate—and clear—and clean." That was fifteen years ago.

Did you know that sometimes the foundation of a building goes

down as far as the superstructure rises above the ground? When God
starts building a life, He always begins with the foundation. He digs
it out—drives steel into the soul—and He may build four stories before you see the level ground. What happens in urban renewal? The
old wreckages must be cleared away—the trash and trappings of the
past must be completely demolished. Only then can the excavations
begin. It may seem an interminable length of time—but there is no
other way to build for endurance and acceptability according to the
Building Code.

Every life, character, and ministry will be tested. The storms *will*
come. Be prepared to meet them. Encircle them with the arms of
obedience. Every obedience makes the next storm easier to weather.
Jesus learned obedience by the things which He suffered. Why should
we expect preferred treatment? No use expecting it, for God plays
no favorites.

How many of you have been in a situation where God didn't do
what you *thought* He should? You were sure that He was going to do it
your way, and He didn't? Did your house fall under the onslaught?
Was "great the fall thereof" written across the nullified Building
Permit? It needn't have been. You must come to the realization that
there is a difference between what God *can* do and what He *will* do
in a given situation. We don't put God on the spot; we are the ones
who are under inspection. Perhaps we went out on a limb and sawed
off the limb—thinking He would be there to catch us—and He
wasn't. Does this give us grounds for doubt and turning back? No.
Let me explain a principle which may help us all to see how patiently
and perfectly God works with each of us.

In our Specifications given in the Law of the Building Code (*who-
soever,* as in verse 24), we see that God is the Author of equality.
In Him truly lies the equal opportunity the world is searching for.
We are not all born equal—but God knows all the circumstances—
background—inherited traits—environment—training that are ours.
All of these are taken into consideration in His dealings with us.
Once we come to Him and accept His Lordship, He goes to work on

us. We may say, "Jesus loves me just as I am." True, but that doesn't mean He is going to leave you as you are.

One of His basic principles of operation is what we call *Testing and Approval.* It works something like this: *If* we could take a long-range look, we might see a series of long, dark tunnels with our name on them. But God, in His goodness, permits us to only see one tunnel

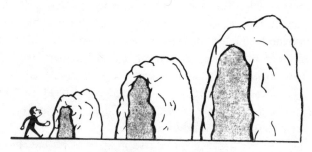

at a time! The tunnel looks confining—foreboding—constricting. And it is, once we get in. We are apt to turn away from it in hopes that it will go away—but it won't. We can turn back if we so desire, but the tunnel will not disappear and it stays right there blocking our progress into Kingdom territory.

We must trust our Guide and move into the particular situation which the tunnel represents. He has placed it in our pathway for our own good. Every Law of God is in our best interest. He gives us a choice of entering or turning back. Why does He do this? Why does God provide opportunity to turn us back at times? Because He loves us so much. He knows if we are ready to enter a given tunnel and emerge victorious on the other side—even when we may not know it.

Join Jesus and Peter in a discussion upon the occasion of an approaching tunnel in Peter's life. Read *Luke 22:31–34.* The setting is just prior to Jesus' arrest and trial.

JESUS   Simon, Simon, behold, Satan hath desired to have you, that he may sift you as wheat: But I have prayed for thee, that thy faith fail not; and when thou art converted, strengthen thy brethren.

PETER   Lord, I am ready to go with thee, both into prison, and to
death.

JESUS   I tell thee, Peter, the cock shall not crow this day before
thou shalt thrice deny that thou knowest me.

Did Jesus know what He was talking about? Yes, for Peter did
not make it through that particular tunnel of adversity. But because
of that one failure, he was able to go through many others—emerg-
ing triumphantly on the other side. He was also able to strengthen
his brothers as they came up against tunnels in their lives. That is
one of the purposes of tunnels. Once Kingdom living is established
in you, you can help bring in the Kingdom through sharing your
experiences and confidence in the King. Thus you learn to keep on
course regardless of the winds, rain, and fogs of life.

Let me illustrate keeping on course in spite of an enveloping fog.
Picture three destroyers headed out into open waters. The navigator
of each ship has been given the course and ordered to keep a steady
hand on the helm. Along comes an enemy destroyer and lays a heavy
smoke screen across the bow of each of the three ships.

Orders had been to proceed on course. But after receiving orders,
comes the testing. When in a fog, the natural tendency is to feel as if
the ship were veering to the left. The navigator can become confused
and disregard his compass, trusting in his own feelings. So, under
pressure of the fog and lack of definite direction, Destroyer Number
1 and Destroyer Number 2 lose their bearings, crashing into each
other. Both sink. Destroyer Number 3 manages to hold steady to the
course, not forgetful of the initial leading. The ship moves cautiously
but steadily and waits until the fog lifts—and when the battle clears,
she is still cruising—on course!

I have witnessed Satan lay a heavy smoke screen across many
lives. And I have seen many ships go down in defeat. Sex—money—
popularity—love for the spectacular—weak foundations—these all
take a toll. One of God's primary purposes in the tunnel principle
of testing and approval is to protect, not only you, but those who
may be led astray by your poor navigation, be it immaturity, dis-

obedience, or ignorance. If you are going to run aground and get into confusion, He would prefer you do it near the beginning of your journey, rather than after many people are looking to you for guidance and trust in you to help them find the way out of their own personal fog.

The Apostle Paul was brought to realize the importance of keeping on course—the necessity of proper foundations—and the Law of the Building Code instituted by the Master Teacher. He aimed always to build according to approved plans and specifications. Hear some advice he offered his pupils:

To the Colossians he said: As ye have therefore received Christ Jesus the Lord, so walk in him, Rooted and built up in him, and stablished in the faith, as ye have been taught . . . (2:6, 7).

To the Ephesians he adds this dimension: That we henceforth be no more children, tossed to and fro, and carried about with every wind of doctrine, by the sleight of men, and cunning craftiness, whereby they lie in wait to deceive; But speaking the truth in love, may grow up into him in all things . . . (4:14, 15).

To the Corinthians he gives this word about accepting his responsibility in this matter of building: According to the grace of God which is given unto me, as a wise masterbuilder, I have laid the foundation, and another buildeth thereon. But let every man take heed how he buildeth thereupon. For other foundation can no man lay than that is laid, which is Jesus Christ (1 Corinthians 3:10, 11).

We find him concluding his tunnel experiences with these words to a younger disciple: . . . the time of my departure is at hand. I have fought a good fight, I have finished my course, I have kept the faith (2 Timothy 4:6, 7).

We have *"heard these sayings"* (*see* verse 24 of the Law of the Building Code). Now what are we going to do about them? Upon our answer to that question hangs a tremendous issue: *The house stood . . . the house fell.* Who wants to see his investment go down the drain? Foolish question! Yet, Jesus says that is a very real possibility. We would do well to take seriously His words about impending "inspection."

Hearing and doing—hearing and doing not. This pinpoints the issue. The phrase, or its equivalent, "He who hath ears to hear, let him hear," is used more than fifteen times in the New Testament. What does this convey to you? How do we translate hearing into doing. Let's examine once again the basis Jesus presented for coming into our desired goal of freedom: John 8:31, 32:

> Then said Jesus to those Jews which believed on him, If ye continue in my word, then are ye my disciples indeed; And ye shall know the truth, and the truth shall make you free.

Do you see the progressive steps? Jesus spoke to believers and moved into a qualifying clause, "If ye continue in my word . . . ." Next He tells them what they may expect by continuing: *They will become disciples.* There follows a grasp of truth, as disciples: *And the truth would bring freedom.*

A determination to move from a believer to a continuer brings harassment from the Enemy. He will do everything within his power to keep you from "knowing the truth and becoming free."

Moving progressively, you have determined to step from believer to continuer. Jesus says this makes you His disciple. This has much to do with translating hearing into doing. Being a disciple involves discipline. It is a further commitment of your will and mental faculties —physical capabilities—emotional responses. All come into alignment. Further revelation of truth depends upon one's discipleship. *We might define discipleship as learning "to do."* One learns by doing —and that usually takes discipline. It also necessitates a constant attitude of teachableness.

A disciple familiarizes himself with the Building Code. He comes to know what is expected of him. Here is a quote from an article on *Discipleship* by Charles Simpson to bring some of these facts into focus:

THE LAW OF THE BUILDING CODE

Discipleship leads to *maturity*. Maturity makes one capable of *freedom*. To grant undue freedom to the immature is to destroy. Our baby is not free to play in the street. If he continues in our discipline, he will become mature and know the truth about the street. Then, upon maturing, he will be free to use it.

The more teachable one is, the more discipleship is possible and productive.

. . . The purpose of a true disciple is to carry out the will of Jesus Christ. . . . I believe He calls us into fellowship through discipline.

Discipline—maturity—freedom—continuers—discipleship—will of Jesus Christ—fellowship. These have all been familiar words in our study.

Yes, when the truth has made us free, we can face winds, floods, rains, and every element that may be hurled against us—and still stand. We can comply with every demand of the Law of the Building Code for our house is founded upon a rock—*the* Rock, King Jesus.

CONCLUSION

28   And it came to pass, when Jesus had ended these sayings, the people were astonished at his doctrine:

29   For he taught them as one having authority, and not as the scribes.

Matthew 7

The Teacher has completed the seaside session. The people were astonished at His doctrine. What is your response as you complete this book? Did you find occasions for astonishment, also?

We began our study together with a promise of freedom. Every segment of our society is straining to lay hold upon this commodity. However, society in general would be confounded to hear anyone say or teach that freedom can be obtained through *submission* and *obedience*. Yet, according to Kingdom principles, here lies the key to *complete* freedom. It is a paradox which can only be comprehended through experience.

Just as Jesus knew that freedom was something He could not communicate in one session, so I realize that it is not something you can *learn* from a book. Freedom is *created* in individuals by means of seeking His Kingdom, accepting its teachings, and putting them into operation in daily living. It has been my desire to lay before you, not only the reward of obedience, but how to put these principles into actual practice.

It has been said, "God didn't come to be seen, but to be obeyed." This capsulizes the message of *The King and You*. Hear the King say, "If ye love me, keep my commandments (John 14:15).

Speaking of love, I have always been impressed with the great transformation that occurred in the life of the Apostle John. Jesus once called him the "son of thunder" (Mark 3:17), which forms a short commentary on John's personality. And it was this same John who wanted to call fire from heaven to consume those who would not receive his Master. Soundly rebuked by Jesus, John began searching out the teachings of the Kingdom and putting them into practice in daily life. Eventually, he was called John, the Beloved. In his writings, he used the word *love* more than any other New Testament writer.

Tradition of the early church fathers has a story about the Apostle John that goes something like this:

"Master John, you have repeated 'my little children, love one another' so many times. Why do you always say that?"

To which John replied, "Because it is the Lord's command. Only if it is obeyed will He be satisfied."

In bringing to you these Kingdom Concepts and Kingdom Bylaws, I have sought to present the King in relation to the maturity and freedom available to the believer by becoming a continuer. Like the Apostle John, I should not be content with anything less than the King's satisfaction as He beholds your new life of obedience.

MINI-DISCIPLESHIP COURSE

THE KING AND YOU ON AUDIO TAPE

The word from God which seems to be uppermost in this nation and others is *discipleship!* A healthy cry to know and understand the disciplined life in the midst of our loose and decadent society fills me with hope.

Several months ago, a brother from Kentucky called me on the phone at the impulse of the Holy Spirit. In essence, he said that he just had to tell me that the teaching on *The Laws of the Kingdom* had made the difference in his life, between living in joy and victory and that of simply "existing" as a Christian. Originally, I had taught this series in 1963 at Princeton, New Jersey. Since then, I have retaught these lessons here in the Fort Lauderdale Thursday Night Bible Class. The fruit and effect of this teaching (actually an exposition of Matthew 5–7) is so strong that I have felt led to title it *A Mini-Discipleship Course.*

In the absence of someone to disciple you into the ways of the Spirit, may I suggest that these fifteen tapes may bring you light and life. It is needed preparation and foundation for embracing discipleship in some of its more advanced stages.

THE CONSTITUTION & BYLAWS OF
THE KINGDOM OF GOD SERIES
(15)

VOL. I CONCEPTS OF THE KING-
        DOM

7073 Concepts of the Kingdom
7074 Constitution of the Kingdom
7075 Bylaws of the Kingdom
7076 Character, Conduct, and Influence

VOL. II BYLAWS 1–5

7077 Law of Anger
7078 Law of Purity
7079 Law of Fidelity
7080 Laws of Flexibility and Imparti-
      ality
7081 Laws of Pure Motives and Liber-
      ality

VOL. III BYLAWS 6–11

7082 The Law of Reduced Interest
7083 The Law of Tolerance
7084 The Law of Spiritual Truth
7085 The Law of Father's Wisdom
7086 The Laws of Re-relating and Roots
      and Fruits
7087 The Laws of Obedience and the
      Building Code

15 CASSETTE TAPES
$59.95

Order from:
Bob Mumford
Box 22341
Fort Lauderdale, Fla.
33315